Pricing in the Age of AI

Pricing in the Age of AI

Maxime C. Cohen

The MIT Press
Cambridge, Massachusetts
London, England

The MIT Press
Massachusetts Institute of Technology
77 Massachusetts Avenue
Cambridge, MA 02139
mitpress.mit.edu

The MIT Press would like to thank the anonymous peer reviewers who provided comments on drafts of this book. The generous work of academic experts is essential for establishing the authority and quality of our publications. We acknowledge with gratitude the contributions of these otherwise uncredited readers.

This book was set in Stone Serif and Stone Sans by Westchester Publishing Services. Printed and bound in the United States of America.

Library of Congress Cataloging-in-Publication Data

Names: Cohen, Maxime C. author
Title: Pricing in the age of AI / Maxime C. Cohen.
Description: Cambridge, Massachusetts : The MIT Press, [2026] | Includes bibliographical references and index.
Identifiers: LCCN 2026012067 (print) | LCCN 2026012068 (ebook) | ISBN 9780262056779 paperback | ISBN 9780262056786 pdf | ISBN 9780262056793 epub
Subjects: LCSH: Pricing—Decision making—Data processing | Artificial intelligence—Marketing applications
Classification: LCC HF5416.5 .C64 2026 (print) | LCC HF5416.5 (ebook)
LC record available at https://lccn.loc.gov/2026012067
LC ebook record available at https://lccn.loc.gov/2026012068

10 9 8 7 6 5 4 3 2 1

EU Authorised Representative: Easy Access System Europe, Mustamäe tee 50, 10621 Tallinn, Estonia | Email: gpsr.requests@easproject.com

To my parents, whose love and guidance have shaped every step of my journey. To my father—no longer with us, but forever present—who sparked my earliest curiosity about the topic of pricing and taught me that behind every number lies a story of value, trade-offs, and human behavior.

To my wonderful children, Shai and Liam, who remind me every day of what truly matters: You fill my life with wonder, laughter, and purpose.

And to all the friends, colleagues, mentors, and collaborators I've had the joy and honor to work with and learn from: Thank you for your insights, your generosity, and the many conversations that challenged and enriched my thinking. This book may have my name on the cover, but your influence has shaped every chapter.

Contents

Foreword

Pricing has always been at the heart of economics. It is where supply meets demand, where markets balance, and where firms turn data and strategy into profits and growth. Yet as anyone who has ever had to make a pricing decision knows, this task is as much an art as it is a science. Today, with the rise of artificial intelligence (AI), real-time data, and algorithmic decision-making, pricing has entered a new era—one filled with opportunities for innovation but also with profound challenges for fairness, transparency, and regulation.

Maxime Cohen's *Pricing in the Age of AI* arrives at exactly the right moment. This is a book written for executives, policymakers, academics, and curious readers who want to understand not just where pricing has been but also where it is going. The book combines economic analysis and intuition, real-world case studies, and the latest advances in AI to provide a comprehensive guide for pricing in the modern era.

Few people are as well positioned as Maxime Cohen to write this book. As a leading scholar in pricing, operations, and AI, he has spent over a decade working at the intersection of academia and practice—advising companies, collaborating with regulators, and developing the analytical tools that now shape decision-making in retail, transportation, healthcare, and beyond. His ability to translate complex ideas into clear, actionable insights makes this book especially valuable to readers outside the academic world.

What is particularly impressive about this book is how it tackles the full spectrum of issues, including dynamic pricing and personalized recommendations, the use and ethics of algorithmic decision-making, and the risk of collusion in AI-driven markets. These issues are not abstract concerns but are the basis of real-world problems facing businesses and regulators today. As algorithms play a greater role in setting prices, understanding how they work, when they fail, and what principles should guide them is essential for anyone navigating the digital economy. The chapter on generative AI for pricing especially stands out as a unique and forward-thinking contribution.

Whether you are a business leader seeking to leverage data for competitive advantage, a policymaker grappling with pricing fairness and consumer protection, or simply a curious reader fascinated by the forces shaping modern markets, *Pricing in the Age of AI* will inform and inspire you. It is a thoughtful, rigorous, and highly readable guide to one of the most important topics in the economy today.

I strongly recommend this book. The future of pricing—and perhaps of markets—will be increasingly driven by AI. Thanks to this book, we now have a roadmap for understanding and shaping that future responsibly.

—Robert S. Pindyck

Bank of Tokyo Mitsubishi Professor of Economics and Finance,
MIT Sloan School of Management; research associate of the National
Bureau of Economic Research; and fellow of the Econometric Society

1 Introduction

> The single most important decision in evaluating a business is pricing power.
> —Warren Buffett

Pricing Is as Old as Civilizations

Pricing is a fundamental decision faced by all businesses in all verticals, for products and services alike, in both business-to-business (B2B) and business-to-consumer (B2C) settings, and in both online and physical environments. In fact, pricing goes as far back as the start of commerce. Ancient Sumerian clay tablets dating back to 2000 BC contain records of transactions that include prices for goods such as wool, meat, and barley. The Code of Hammurabi, a Babylonian law code from 1754 BC, contains provisions related to pricing, including laws that establish maximum prices for goods and services. In Ancient Greece, Aristotle wrote about the concept of "just price" in his book, arguing that prices should be based on a fair exchange of value between buyers and sellers. These are only a few examples that demonstrate that pricing has been an important part of commerce and economics for thousands of years and has been shaped by various cultural, political, and economic factors throughout history.

Interestingly, pricing and religion are also tightly connected. In his seminal work, Maimonides, the medieval Jewish philosopher, addresses ethical business practices, including fair pricing and market regulation. He advocated for honest pricing, warning against practices like overcharging and price gouging. One of the most notable principles Maimonides discussed is the prohibition of unfair pricing, which refers to the ethical obligation to avoid charging excessively above or below the fair market price. According to Jewish law, if a seller charges more than one-sixth above the market value, the buyer has the right to annul the transaction. This concept parallels modern consumer protection laws designed to prevent exploitative pricing. Jewish law also allows for market intervention and price regulation, advocating for oversight to prevent monopolistic practices and ensure that essential goods remain affordable. Such insights align with contemporary debates on price fairness, anticompetitive practices, and price transparency and are remarkably relevant today.

Other religious traditions have also addressed fair trade, pricing ethics, and market regulation. In Christian tradition, St. Thomas Aquinas (thirteenth century) expanded on Aristotle's concept of justice to develop the Just Price Theory, which argued that prices should reflect the true value of goods and be free from exploitation. Aquinas believed that charging excessively high prices, especially during times of scarcity, was unethical. This notion influenced later moral economics and laid the foundation for many modern price gouging regulations. In Islamic finance and trade, the principles of justice and fairness in pricing are also emphasized. The Qur'an and the Hadith (sayings of Prophet Muhammad) contain numerous references to honest trade. They also encourage price stability and warn against hoarding essential goods to artificially increase prices. In Hinduism, the concept of "dharma" (righteousness) extends to economic practices, including pricing. The Manusmriti (an ancient legal text) outlines guidelines for fair trade, condemning deceitful pricing. The text also calls for price regulation on essential goods to prevent exploitation, particularly during times of famine or crisis. Finally, Buddhism emphasizes ethical commerce as part of the Eightfold Path. This encourages fair pricing and condemns deceptive business practices. In some Buddhist economies, controlled pricing of essential goods was historically implemented to prevent exploitation. Interestingly, there is a common thread of promoting fairness, transparency, and ethical pricing across several religions. These principles have influenced modern regulations on price gouging, antitrust laws, and consumer protection, highlighting the enduring relevance of religious teachings in contemporary pricing ethics.

In the era of big data and artificial intelligence (AI), pricing strategies have been revolutionized. In e-commerce applications, pricing decisions can be updated every few seconds, are often personalized to different users, and are more accurate (in terms of identifying the price that shoppers are willing to pay) than ever. The ultimate goal is to charge the right price to the right user at the right time through the right channel. At the same time, such practices are raising several ethical, fairness, and privacy concerns.

It's natural for firms to rely on historical data when making pricing decisions, yet this immediately raises several questions. Which types of data are available, and which of these data fields are the most useful for setting prices? What happens when no relevant data exists at all? Consider the example of launching a new product in an unfamiliar market: How can we determine (or even guess) the right pricing strategy under such uncertainty? As we will see later in this book, a range of approaches have been developed to address precisely these situations.

Pricing Is Universal

I started working on pricing about fifteen years ago, and three elements immediately struck me. The first is that pricing is a truly universal decision, one that every business must confront regardless of size, industry, or structure. To illustrate, let's look at four different examples.

Consider first an independent professional such as a consultant, tutor, nanny, lawyer, business advisor, or tax accountant. In private practice, setting the right price for services isn't only unavoidable but also central to defining the value proposition and securing clients.

Now shift to a small or medium-sized enterprise (or even a micro-entrepreneur) selling products or services online. Here again, pricing becomes a critical decision point. The right price can determine whether the business thrives, barely survives, or fails to gain traction in competitive digital marketplaces.

The importance of pricing becomes even more pronounced in large corporations that manage extensive portfolios of products and services across diverse customer segments. For such firms, pricing sits at the heart of business strategy and is one of the most powerful levers for driving both revenue and profitability.

Finally, even outside the traditional realm of products and services, consider the act of hiring. When a company recruits a new employee or contracts with a freelancer, it must decide on the salary or wage to offer. This too is a form of pricing.

Similar pricing decisions arise in countless other contexts, whether it's buying or selling a house or a car, setting tuition and scholarships at colleges, or determining the prices charged by hairdressers, restaurants, dentists, medical clinics, or bakeries. The list could go on indefinitely. In this book, however, the discussion is focused specifically on monetary prices for products and services. It doesn't address nonmonetary costs that users may face when accessing an otherwise "free" service, such as the time and attention spent viewing or interacting with advertisements on a search engine or a social media platform.

The encouraging news is that pricing decisions can be informed by data, alongside experience and intuition. This leads to the second element that struck me in studying pricing: When available, data can be remarkably powerful in guiding decisions. Transactional records, cost structures, competitors' publicly available information, and survey results can all help determine the right price for a product or service. A key point is to clarify what we mean by the "best" price. The optimal price depends on the firm's objectives and the key performance indicators it seeks to prioritize. In some cases, companies may set lower prices to accelerate growth or capture market share, particularly in the early stages of a product launch or platform development. While this may reduce short-term margins, it can be a deliberate strategy to strengthen long-term profitability. Such approaches are especially common in digital platforms, where scale and network effects are essential. In other cases, higher prices may be more appropriate if the goal is to maximize immediate profitability or to signal a premium market position. In practice, every pricing decision reflects a balance among multiple competing objectives and different time horizons.

Pricing Is Both an Art and a Science

Finally, the third element that struck me about pricing is that it can be equally seen as an art and a science. On one side, it requires judgment, creativity, and intuition. On the other, it increasingly relies on data, algorithms, and advanced analytics. Large e-commerce companies such as Alibaba, Amazon, and Walmart have developed sophisticated systems that can adjust prices at massive scale, making millions of decisions in short time frames and re-optimizing every few minutes. Walmart alone collects 2.5 petabytes of data from one million customers every hour. To put this into perspective, a petabyte is a 1 followed by 15 zeros (yes, 15—and this is every hour). Such vast amounts of information create extraordinary opportunities to understand customer preferences and willingness to pay (WTP), but they also raise difficult technical and ethical questions. Importantly, e-commerce isn't the only industry deploying these state-of-the-art pricing algorithms. Airlines, hotels, ride-hailing services such as Uber, and online marketplaces such as Airbnb have all embraced data-driven pricing models. In short, access to large datasets combined with expertise in data science and statistics can enable the development of powerful pricing tools, increasingly powered by AI, that boost revenue and profitability by continuously learning, adapting, and refining pricing decisions.

At the same time, in many contexts pricing still remains very much an art. A customer's WTP is often shaped by emotional and psychological factors that defy strict rationality. Three examples illustrate this point. The first is the widespread practice of "charm pricing," which involves using prices that end in 0.99 or 0.95 instead of rounded numbers such as whole dollars. This tactic is common in gas stations, supermarkets, and fashion retailers and serves as a classic behavioral technique to nudge customers. We will return to this practice in greater detail later in the book. The second example concerns products that are unique and highly emotional in nature, such as luxury goods, limited editions, works of art, or exclusive real estate properties. Even with the vast amounts of data available from real estate transactions, predicting the price of one-of-a-kind properties remains challenging, especially when the asset carries symbolic value, as in the case of celebrity-owned homes. The third example involves discounts. Customers often react differently when a product is offered at a reduced listed price compared to when a discount is presented against the original price. The format of the discount also matters: A percentage reduction, an absolute dollar amount, or a buy-one-get-one-free promotion can each trigger different responses. Although these patterns highlight the psychological side of pricing, data and experimentation can help firms learn which tactics work best, for which products, and for which types of customers. This is precisely where art and science join forces to identify more effective pricing strategies.

Sometimes, setting the right price can feel like an impossible task, one that often ends in frustration. Consider the case of a skilled contractor determining her wage. She may be approached to assist with a wide range of projects, each requiring slightly different skills and levels of effort. A common approach is to set an hourly rate. In practice, however, this creates a delicate negotiation dynamic. Contractors often prefer to wait for the buyer to suggest a price, in order to gather more information, yet situations frequently arise where they must put forward the first offer. This creates a dilemma. If the buyer accepts the first offered rate, the contractor is left wondering whether she could have charged more (and how much more will never be known). If the buyer rejects the offer outright and refuses to negotiate, the opportunity may be lost altogether. The decision is further complicated by factors such as current workload, the potential for repeat business, and the opportunity cost of forgoing other projects that might arise in the future. This example illustrates how pricing decisions are rarely straightforward and why, in many cases, pricing remains as much an art as it is a science.

AI Is Transforming Pricing

In today's world, AI is rapidly transforming how businesses make decisions. A growing body of work has examined how AI is reshaping business practices (Agrawal et al. 2022a, 2022b), influencing strategy and leadership (Iansiti and Lakhani 2020), upgrading supply chain management (Cohen and Dai 2025), and even helping individuals adapt and thrive in a digital economy (Bapna and Ghose 2024). Pricing is no exception. The availability of big data combined with powerful AI tools has profoundly changed how prices are set. At a high level, AI has influenced pricing decisions in two ways. First, the rise of large historical datasets has enabled retailers to build machine learning models that prescribe profit-maximizing prices. These models constantly learn from vast amounts of data, allowing them to determine what price to offer different customers in varying contexts. With the ability to run experiments across millions of transactions, such algorithms can quickly distinguish effective price policies from ineffective ones. Second, the emergence of generative AI (GenAI) tools such as ChatGPT, Claude, Gemini, and Llama have given companies of all sizes direct access to powerful decision-support capabilities without requiring costly model development or proprietary data. In effect, GenAI has democratized access to powerful AI tools. Yet several questions remain. How accurate and reliable are the price recommendations from GenAI systems? How do they compare with human-set prices or traditional machine learning methods? What best practices should firms adopt, and what pitfalls must they avoid?

And finally, what happens if GenAI becomes the default tool for pricing? Could it drive more competitive markets and benefit consumers, or could it lead to new risks? These are questions we will explore later in this book.

AI has fundamentally transformed pricing decisions by enabling firms to move beyond static, rule-based approaches toward dynamic, data-driven, real-time adaptive strategies. By analyzing vast amounts of transaction data, customer behavior, and market signals often in real time, AI systems can optimize prices at a granular level, tailoring them to individual customers, contexts, and channels. This allows companies to capture more value through personalized pricing, improve demand forecasting, and rapidly adjust to changing market conditions. For example, many retailers, airlines, and ride-hailing platforms now use AI-powered models to continuously update prices, balancing revenue maximization with customer satisfaction and competitive pressures.

In this context, a common concern is price collusion, also known as price fixing. This occurs when competing firms conspire to fix prices, limit supply, or divide markets instead of competing freely and independently. Such practices are often illegal because they distort market forces, potentially resulting in higher prices and fewer choices for consumers. Price collusion can take various forms. Explicit collusion, such as formal agreements or secret meetings, is clearly prohibited under antitrust law. Modern economic thinking also recognizes a broader category of coordinated behavior known as tacit collusion. Tacit collusion involves unspoken coordination, often through signaling or parallel behavior. While it may raise serious competition concerns, it's not generally considered illegal unless there is evidence of an agreement or facilitating conduct. History provides many examples of collusion. The Airline Cargo Cartel case involved several major carriers, including Air France-KLM, British Airways, and Lufthansa, which were heavily fined for coordinating fuel surcharges. Another example is the European truck manufacturers scandal, where companies like Daimler, Renault, and Volvo were found guilty of colluding on prices and passing the cost of new emissions regulations to customers. With the rise of AI-driven pricing, a new worry has emerged: algorithmic collusion. Here, algorithms may, even without explicit communication, learn to align prices. This raises a pressing question: How can regulators and businesses determine whether competing firms using AI pricing systems are truly colluding or simply reacting rationally to the same market conditions?

This book will help readers grasp the fact that pricing is an intricate topic with many facets. In fact, each business may be facing different trade-offs, and the right pricing strategy can be highly dependent on the type of business, the maturity of the company, the types of customers, the competitive landscape, macroeconomics factors, and seasonal variation. Some businesses may have the luxury of changing prices as often as they wish, whereas others need to stick to a single constant price and face stringent restrictions. In addition, regulations and government interventions can also interfere with pricing decisions.

An important concept is "price gouging," which often refers to the practice of charging excessively high prices for goods or services that are in urgent demand or limited supply during emergencies. For instance, some retailers may raise the price of essentials such as bottled water, gasoline, or generators in the aftermath of a natural disaster, taking advantage of people's immediate needs. During the early days of the COVID-19 pandemic, online marketplaces saw striking examples of this behavior, with face masks and hand sanitizers being sold at astronomical prices as demand surged overnight. The difficult question is how to determine whether a price increase in such circumstances is legitimate. Much depends on context. Following a terrorist attack or other major security incidents, hotels and airlines may raise prices because travelers are willing to pay a premium to escape the affected area. Situations like these raise broader societal concerns, and regulators often intervene to prevent abuses or pursue legal action against companies deemed too opportunistic. The challenge lies in the ambiguity: The line between an unfair/abusive practice and a market-driven business decision is often thin and highly contested.

Another set of concerns arises around ethics, fairness, and privacy. Should businesses be allowed to charge different prices to different customers for the same product? The answer is far from straightforward. In fact, several companies have been doing exactly this for decades, and personalized pricing has become ubiquitous in the modern economy. Airline tickets provide a clear example. Two passengers sitting side by side on the same flight almost certainly paid different fares, with prices determined by factors such as the timing of the booking relative to departure. In that context, most people have come to accept differential pricing as standard practice. Contrast this with a restaurant that would charge two customers different amounts for the same meal on the same evening. Many people might view this as unfair, especially if the meals are identical and the price difference is unexplained. The key takeaway is that charging different prices to different customers can be considered acceptable in certain contexts but objectionable in others. This tension between economic efficiency and perceived fairness will be a recurring theme throughout this book.

This brings us to the challenge of setting prices that are both fair and respectful of users' privacy. Imagine a firm that found a way to offer different prices to different customers for the same product. In e-commerce, for example, retailers often customize discounts for shoppers based on attributes, such as the country in which they are located. The immediate question becomes, Which customer attributes should companies be allowed to use when setting prices? Due to privacy concerns, several attributes are protected. In our context, this means that firms are legally or ethically prohibited from using these attributes to support pricing decisions. Determining which attributes should be protected isn't straightforward since the issue is highly subjective and context dependent, and different people will often have differing opinions. If I tell you that race, gender, and national origin should be protected attributes, probably everybody would agree. By contrast, many would find it reasonable for geographical location not to be considered protected since it can be easily inferred from a shopper's IP address. Yet here lies a complication. Geographical location, such as postal codes, is often strongly correlated with race or other protected attributes. This means that pricing based on location can indirectly result in discriminatory outcomes, even if race isn't explicitly considered. As a result, it's not enough to define protected attributes narrowly; firms must also monitor correlations between protected and unprotected attributes to avoid unintended bias.

A second, equally difficult challenge is defining what constitutes a "fair" price. As we will discuss later in this book, there is no universally accepted definition, and fairness in pricing is often context dependent. Consider the question of whether male and female customers should ever pay different prices for the same product or service. Many readers might assume the answer is no, yet examples exist where such differences persist in practice. Exploring these cases, and examining how they might be mitigated, is essential to understanding how AI-driven pricing can be aligned with principles of fairness and equity.

In this book, we first discuss the different types of pricing decisions and strategies that firms must consider. We then present simple but powerful approaches that businesses can use to improve their pricing decisions and capture more value by leveraging data. From there, we turn to behavioral and psychological pricing tactics, where retailers rely on nudges and subtle cues to influence customer behavior and stimulate demand. The discussion then moves to the critical role of data in pricing, focusing on which types of information can be collected and how this data can be applied to make more effective decisions. Next, we consider the topic of price experimentation, or A/B testing, a widely used tool in e-commerce and online platforms that allows firms to test price points in real time and identify the strategies that work best. We briefly discuss some recent advances in algorithmic and AI-based pricing, which are already being deployed at scale by major corporations with large customer bases and strong technological capabilities. We then explore how GenAI tools like ChatGPT can be leveraged to guide pricing decisions in new and accessible ways. Finally, we elaborate on the ethical and privacy concerns that arise from modern pricing practices and emphasize the need for regulation to ensure that these powerful tools are applied responsibly.

Throughout this book, we will rely on many pricing applications I've worked on in different contexts, including retail (both online and brick-and-mortar), airlines, restaurants, ride-hailing, real estate, cars, hourly rates for contractors, gas stations, clinics and medical services, fashion, pharmaceuticals, delivery services, and software providers. In the past fifteen years, my work has centered on pricing and AI—two fields that are now more intertwined than ever. AI and big data have fundamentally reshaped how pricing decisions are made, affecting millions of people daily. Writing a book at this intersection is both an honor and a longtime aspiration. My hope is that this book will give readers some appreciation for the topic of pricing and in particular AI-driven pricing. The way that pricing decisions have been disrupted in recent years due to the proliferation of AI tools and algorithms is nothing short of a game changer. It thus raises new issues that need to be carefully addressed by both companies and regulators. While the topic of pricing is universal and paramount for business profitability, it's more involved than it looks and has several intricacies and challenges. Hopefully, you will find the content useful for your own pricing decisions, no matter whether you are selling products or services or if you are planning to put your house on the market. Finally, this book concludes by laying out eight predictions as well as strategic and policy recommendations.

While embarking on this project, I did so with a degree of hesitation. The field of AI, including its applications to pricing, evolves at a breathtaking pace. What feels cutting-edge today can quickly become yesterday's outdated practice, replaced by more advanced tools. This constant innovation cycle poses a challenge for anyone attempting to capture the state of the art in writing: the risk that by the time words are printed, the landscape will already have shifted. Yet this very dynamism makes the subject all the more important. While I fully recognize that AI technologies are advancing at an exponential rate, I believe that developing a deep understanding of how pricing strategies have been transformed in the past decade is essential to mastering the innovations that will shape the decades ahead. The past isn't merely prologue; it provides the conceptual foundation, the practical lessons, and the cautionary tales that will help us manage the future. In writing this book, I have sought to extract broad, durable insights that extend beyond the specific tools of the moment. My goal is to highlight principles and perspectives that will remain relevant even as algorithms improve, markets evolve, and new breakthroughs continue to emerge. If I have succeeded, this book should serve not only as a guide to understanding today's practices but also as a compass to navigate a future where pricing in the age of AI will only grow more complex.

2 Types of Pricing Decisions and Strategies

> Price is the only element in the marketing mix that produces revenue; all other elements produce costs.
>
> —Philip Kotler

What is the right price for my product or service? While seemingly straightforward, answering this question is harder than it seems. The first step is to define the word "pricing" and realize that in many settings, pricing isn't a single value but rather a multidimensional decision or strategy. If you sell several products (or services), you need to price each of them. Obviously, the price of one product may affect the demand for other products. These effects are often referred to as cross-item effects, and we distinguish between two types: cannibalization and complementarity. Cannibalization is when two products are competing, for example, Coke and Pepsi. If you decrease the price of Coke (by offering a promotion), it will likely increase Coke's sales but may also decrease (or cannibalize) Pepsi's sales because customers are switching between both brands. Complementarity is when two products are purchased together (e.g., shampoo and conditioner). If you decrease the price of the shampoo, it will likely increase shampoo sales and may also boost conditioner sales. So, the first conclusion is that you need to set the price of both products, and it's better to do so in a coordinated fashion (i.e., pricing them simultaneously by accounting for cross-item effects that can be estimated from data). Of course, if some of your products are totally unrelated, it may be safe to price them independently.

In addition to cross-item effects, a product's past prices or promotional history can also influence its future demand. These dynamics are commonly referred to as cross-time effects or the post-promotion dip. When a product is offered at a discounted promotional price, demand typically increases in the short run as consumers accelerate their purchases. However, this surge is often followed by a decline in future sales, as purchases that would have occurred later are pulled forward in time. Such effects are particularly pronounced for nonperishable goods, where consumers can strategically stockpile, as well as for discretionary or leisure-related products that are purchased infrequently and are often subject to temporary promotional offers.

A Multidimensional Decision

Interestingly, determining the price for a single product or service often involves more than selecting a single number. Instead, it involves a comprehensive strategy that includes several levers. Depending on the setting and industry, one can use price promotions, price markdowns, special incentives, discounts for subscribers, and so on. So, the first step is to decide on the strategy around pricing, including the marketing behind it and the communication plan. In fact, communication plays an essential role that is often neglected in the pricing process. Consider, for example, a service provider (e.g., a medical clinic) that decided to reduce its prices for several medical services. If customers (or in this case, patients) aren't aware of the price reduction, there will not be any impact or benefits. In short, I cannot say enough that communication is key in the context of price promotions. In the opposite example of increasing prices, direct communication with customers is also important. Price increases may naturally not be well perceived by customers, so having an effective communication campaign to ease the process can be helpful. For example, the messaging can be personal and explain rationally the justifications behind increasing prices (e.g., inflationary pressures, tariffs, cost of materials went up). Some ways that help customers better accept price increases involve being clear, upfront, and transparent about the rationale behind the increase, especially if these explanations are around improving the service quality for the customers (e.g., improved technology, new modern facility, faster processes) or providing them additional value (e.g., "your membership is more expensive, but it includes new features"). Another aspect can be more emotionally driven (e.g., we increased the salary of nurses, or we decided to donate 10 percent of our revenue to charity). In summary, communication should be transparent, ideally demonstrate additional value, explain that higher prices are associated with better quality, and potentially thank the customers for their understanding.

Figure 2.1 presents two such communication campaigns from Netflix (a) and Peloton (b). In both communication campaigns, a clear and transparent email was sent directly to customers and included a sentence about delivering additional value. Another important decision is how and when to communicate with customers. A straightforward approach is to send an email to all users for whom the company has contact information. This raises additional questions, such as when the email should be sent and whether it should be personalized for different users.

Once the communication plan is laid out, it's time to decide the actual pricing strategy. Several questions can guide such a decision:

- **Static versus dynamic pricing**: Will my price be static (i.e., a single price point that won't change for the entire product life cycle or selling season) or dynamic (i.e., I can change the price several times in the season)? If dynamic, how often do I want to change the price and based on what conditions? Should I aim to increase or decrease the prices over time?
- **Uniform versus personalized pricing**: Should I offer the same price to everyone or a different price to different customers? If personalized, how should I put such a strategy in place (e.g., having a uniform listed price and offering personalized targeted coupons)?
- **Pricing mechanisms**: Should I use additional mechanisms as part of my pricing strategy, such as a membership subscription, price promotions (uniform and targeted), coupons and loyalty rewards, or by bundling several products together?
- **Promotion vehicles**: Should I use additional promotion vehicles embedded as a pricing tool, such as buy-one-get-one-free offers and in-store discounts?
- **Pricing of ancillary products**: How should I price the ancillary products and services (e.g., breakfast or Wi-Fi connection for a hotel stay)? Correctly pricing the ancillary products often has a substantial impact on the total profits.
- **Deciding the terms of the offer**: How should I decide the terms of the offer (e.g., free returns, free delivery for purchases that exceed $99)? In e-commerce, for example, the terms related to delivery and returns often play a critical role in customers' buying decisions.

NETFLIX

We're bringing you new TV programmes & films

Hi

We're updating our prices to bring you more great entertainment. Your monthly price will increase by £2 to £13.99 on 28 February 2021.

This update will allow us to deliver even more value for your membership – with stories that lift you up, move you or simply make your day a bit better.

Figure 2.1
Two examples of communication regarding price increases: (a) an email from Netflix and (b) an email from Peloton.

This is a list of questions that one needs to reflect on. Of course, very often these decisions are driven by the competitive landscape and by the company's culture and strategy. For example, if all your competitors are offering free delivery, it's probably not a good idea to charge for delivery. In this context, it's important to understand the right price dynamics. For instance, for airlines, the price typically goes up as we get closer to the departure date. These dynamics are driven by the fact that leisure travelers (who are more price sensitive) often book their flight in advance, whereas business travelers (who are much less price sensitive) tend to book their flight at the last minute. Thus, airlines aiming to cater to both customer segments may start offering a low price for the first few tickets and increase the price closer to the departure date (while strategically keeping some tickets for the later part of the selling season). In contrast, the price dynamics for fashion apparel often follow the opposite pattern. A higher price is set at the beginning of the season, whereas lower price points (called markdowns) are used toward the end of the season to clear excess inventory. And in supermarkets, the price dynamics are also different, where they have a regular (nonpromotional) price most of the time with occasional price reductions (called promotions) and then go back to the regular price. In

PELOTON

Thank you for being a Peloton Member. Our Members and community are at the center of everything we do. We recently reached out about our All-Access Membership price change. We will be updating the monthly price from $39 to $44 starting with your first billing date on or after Wednesday, June 1, 2022.

With this update, we will continue to constantly add value to your Membership and deliver even more exciting content, new features, and new products you'll love.

Thank you for your continued support of Peloton.

Figure 2.1
(continued)

summary, different industries (and even different companies in the same industry) have different price dynamics: Airlines typically opt for a low-high price dynamic, fashion retailers for a high-low dynamic, and supermarkets for a high-low-high dynamic.

In addition to being industry dependent, the question of using static versus dynamic prices also depends on the context of the purchase. For example, prices for Uber rides are dynamic, whereas the prices for smartphones are mainly static. This decision depends on many factors including the perishability or obsolescence of the product, the frequency of purchases (one-time vs. recurring purchases), and seasonality. If a static pricing strategy is chosen, setting the right price point becomes even more critical. If a dynamic pricing strategy is chosen, the questions become how often to vary the price and by how much.

Here again, the answer depends on several factors. The first step is to determine the factors that would justify price adjustments. A common factor is an imbalance between supply and demand. Consider Uber rides as an example. Assume that in a given geographical location (e.g., LaGuardia Airport) at a specific time (a Tuesday morning between 8:00 a.m. and 8:30 a.m.), there are many more ride requests (demand) than available drivers (supply). Then, Uber may strategically decide to increase the prices for riders and offer higher rates to drivers (e.g., by using a surge multiplier). Such a price increase will lower the number of ride requests (some people will find it too expensive and opt for an alternative means of transportation) and increase the number of drivers (e.g., more drivers will be attracted to this geographical location because of the increased rate). Thus, a price increase (or surge pricing) will help regulate the market by balancing better supply and demand, often in real time. Conversely, if the number of ride requests (demand) is lower than the number of available drivers (supply), Uber may decide to decrease prices. The same principle can be applied to situations where inventory is limited, such as fashion apparel, hotel rooms, and concert tickets.

An alternative factor that can drive dynamic pricing is cost fluctuations and seasonal factors. If the cost of production (or transportation) varies, then the price can also vary reactively. A third factor could be perishability or obsolescence. Specifically, if the product becomes less valuable (or not valuable at all) at a given time, dynamic pricing can be used strategically. For example, if a large number of concert tickets remain unsold one week prior to the event, a discount may help drive last-minute sales. Similar dynamics apply to seasonal apparel (such as winter boots near the end of the season) or to technology products (when a next-generation device is about to be released). A final example arises in the pricing of entertainment events, where prices vary with seasonality, fluctuating between off-peak periods and high-demand times such as weekends, holidays, and summer months. For instance, Disney's pricing is a textbook example of modern revenue management applied to capacity-constrained experiences. In its theme parks, Disney has long used demand-based admission pricing, namely, charging different prices for different dates based on expected crowd levels to both monetize peak demand and smooth attendance across the calendar. What makes this especially sophisticated is the data foundation: Disney's ecosystem uses radio frequency identification (RFID)–enabled wristbands and the My Disney Experience app for park entry, purchases, hotel access, and attraction access—creating granular, time-stamped behavioral data on where guests go, what they do, and what they buy. That data (combined with booking curves, hotel occupancy, ticket sales, seasonality, school holiday calendars, and real-time operational constraints) can enhance demand forecasting and more precise segmentation, allowing Disney to potentially fine-tune prices, bundles, and availability across tickets, on-site hotels, and add-on products in ways that align WTP with scarce capacity. A similar playbook shows up in streaming: Disney+ has tiered plans and has repeatedly adjusted prices (including differentiated increases for ad-supported vs. ad-free tiers), reflecting ongoing experimentation with elasticity, bundling, and plan design. All these decisions can be guided by both data and experimentation, as discussed in chapter 5.

The second step in determining the factors that would justify price adjustments is to understand whether price changes will be acceptable to consumers from a cultural and societal perspective as well as in terms of not eroding their loyalty, trust, and satisfaction. This is a difficult question, and the answer may lie beyond the reach of standard economic theory. One needs to understand customers' preferences and determine whether they expect to pay a fixed price for the focal product or service. One option is to conduct market research to analyze whether competitors use dynamic pricing. Another option is to directly survey the potential customers, albeit the results from such surveys should always be taken with a grain of salt (due to the biases and potential unrepresentativeness of the surveyed population). Another great option to understand whether dynamic pricing is an appropriate strategy is by testing it. Price testing (or experimentation), if done properly, can be extremely valuable and allow one to identify the right pricing strategy with the right price points. More details on this topic will be discussed later in this book.

Another decision is the selling format. Should we offer a subscription membership, and if yes, which benefits should be included? It's quite interesting that close competitors sometimes opt for different strategies (e.g.,

Costco and Walmart, though now Walmart also offers a membership). Consider the example of a private medical clinic: Should you offer a yearly membership to retain patients and earn a constant revenue stream or simply provide services at higher prices without charging a membership fee? The answer to this question depends on various factors and differs on a case-by-case basis.

An interesting example worth discussing is GoDaddy, a leading domain registrar and web services provider, that employs a multifaceted pricing strategy designed to maximize customer acquisition, retention, and lifetime value. Its approach encompasses strategic pricing, targeted promotions, cross-selling, upselling, and innovative practices that have positioned it as a dominant player in the industry. First, GoDaddy strategically attracts new customers with low introductory prices for domain registrations, often offering discounted rates for the first year. These promotions are designed to reduce the upfront costs for individuals and small businesses seeking an online presence. However, renewal prices are typically higher, reflecting the company's strategy to capitalize on customer retention and the inertia associated with the aversion to switching providers.

Second, GoDaddy can be considered as a champion at cross-selling and upselling. Once a customer registers a domain, it strategically offers complementary services such as website hosting, email accounts, SSL certificates, and website builders. In addition, during the checkout process, customers are presented with options to add privacy protection or upgrade to a premium hosting plan. This approach not only increases the average transaction value but also enhances customer reliance on GoDaddy's ecosystem of services. Third, GoDaddy has leveraged customer segmentation and targeting by tailoring its marketing and pricing strategies to different customer segments, from individual entrepreneurs to large enterprises. By analyzing customer behavior and preferences (such as what keywords customers are searching for, their browsing history, and additional personal features), the company can offer personalized dynamic promotions and service bundles that meet the specific needs of each segment. In summary, GoDaddy's comprehensive pricing strategy leverages introductory offers, cross-selling, upselling, and customer segmentation with price personalization. Its ability to integrate all these elements into a cohesive strategy serves as a compelling case study on pricing.

Price Personalization

Up to this point, we have discussed the decision of static versus dynamic pricing, assuming all customers pay the same price if they purchase the product at the same time. Another lever is to offer different prices (or discounts) to different customers for the same product at the same time. This practice is often referred to as price personalization (or first-degree price discrimination). Price personalization can be defined as the art of tailoring prices to individual consumers based on their unique characteristics, behaviors, and WTP (Varian 1989). The concept of price personalization predates the emergence of AI by several decades. At the same time, AI is supercharging price personalization strategies by enabling firms to potentially tailor prices at the individual level, using real-time data on browsing history, purchase patterns, location, and even device type. Unlike traditional segmentation, AI can detect subtle behavioral signals and dynamically adjust offers, maximizing both conversion and margin. More precisely, AI is substantially upgrading both the granularity and automation of price personalization by combining many data points (your purchase history, geographical location, frequent flyer status, trip purpose inferred from browsing, houses you look up on Zillow, TV shows you watched, etc.) to set a truly (often real-time) personalized price. This allows companies to move from broad discounts to highly targeted incentives. As AI becomes more embedded in pricing decisions, firms must weigh short-term profit gains against long-term consumer trust.

Interestingly, personalized pricing can, in some scenarios, enhance efficiency (i.e., setting prices so that products are sold to the customers who value them most) and expand access by offering varying prices that enable more consumers to participate in the market. However, that efficiency comes with trade-offs: While some consumers benefit from lower prices, others may end up paying significantly more. It also raises questions of consumer trust: Overcharging or perceived unfairness can erode market goodwill. With richer data and powerful AI-driven tools, firms are increasingly capable of tailoring prices with precision. This ability raises ethical and economic questions: Who benefits? Who loses? And what does that mean for market fairness and consumer welfare?

Imagine two travelers booking the same flight: one, a budget-conscious student who searches multiple comparison sites, clears browser cookies, and finds a lower fare, while the other, a busy executive booking from a corporate IP address, sees a higher price. In this case, it would make sense for the airline to offer different prices to them, with the goal of maximizing revenue. More generally, airlines and online retailers leverage data—from browsing history to device type (as well as other available features as discussed later)—to adjust prices in real time. Similarly, several e-commerce platforms have been known to experiment with price changes based on user profiles and purchase history.

The concept is far from being new. Shopkeepers in old marketplaces and car dealers would instinctively assess a customer's wealth and desire to purchase a specific product and negotiate accordingly. But today's AI-driven personalization takes this old practice to another level. Consider a software company selling subscriptions: Casual users might be offered a discount after abandoning their cart, while frequent buyers see premium-tier recommendations.

That said, the practice of offering discounts following cart abandonments may be risky. Indeed, it may train shoppers to behave strategically by deliberately abandoning their carts to trigger lower prices. A good rule of thumb is to use price personalization strategies that aren't creating strategic incentives to game the system.

Even luxury brands quietly personalize pricing; for example, some high-end watchmakers quote different prices (or discount rates) based on a buyer's perceived affluence. When done ethically, price personalization enhances consumer satisfaction by offering better deals to price-sensitive shoppers while capturing higher margins from those less concerned about cost. However, the line between smart pricing and discrimination can often be thin. When Staples adjusted online prices based on zip codes, wealthier neighborhoods saw lower prices, sparking debates on fairness. The future of price personalization will likely balance business interests with transparency, ensuring customers feel empowered rather than exploited. We will revisit the important topics of ethics, fairness, and privacy in chapter 8.

When a company moves from a single uniform price to two distinct prices (such as student and regular tickets for museums), it may interestingly result in a win-win situation where both the company and consumers benefit. The company captures more revenue from those willing to pay more while still serving price-sensitive customers who would otherwise be priced out completely. This can increase the total consumer surplus, which is an important concept in economics that can be viewed as the difference between what consumers are willing to pay and what they actually pay. In other words, consumer surplus is the extra benefit you get when you pay less than what you were actually willing to pay and is often perceived as a metric of customer well-being in terms of the price charged.

However, as price differentiation becomes more personalized (i.e., using a large number of prices for different customers), the balance of power shifts. With perfect price personalization, where companies charge each individual exactly what they're willing to pay (think of having very large granular data to infer exactly how much each customer can pay), consumer surplus can diminish significantly and even approach zero. In this scenario, companies extract maximum value by charging each consumer their personal maximum price point, leaving little to no "deal" for the customers. Consider a concert venue: Under a single-price model, both dedicated fans and casual listeners pay \$50. With two-tier pricing (\$80 premium seats, \$30 standard seats), more people can attend while enthusiasts get better seats. But with complete personalization, the algorithm might charge the superfans \$150 and casual listeners \$28 to precisely hit what each would pay before walking away.

Consider a simple illustrative example with the demand curve (price as a function of quantity), as shown in figure 2.2. This graph shows two scenarios: one where the single optimal price is \$65 (red dashed line), and another with the same demand curve where the firm uses a two-price strategy (orange and green dashed lines). The shading (area of triangles) represents the consumer surplus. In the second scenario, adding a lower pricing tier would bring in additional customers, increasing both the seller's revenue and consumer surplus. In the uniform pricing scenario, the optimal price is \$65, and quantity equals 35 units. Thus, the seller's revenue amounts to \$2,275 (35 × \$65), and the consumer surplus equals \$612.50 (equivalent to the area between the demand curve and the price line). When we move to two prices, it's optimal to charge \$75 (premium price) for the first 25 units and \$25 (discounted price) for units 26–75. In this case, the seller's revenue equals \$3,125 (25 × \$75 + 50 × \$25), and the consumer surplus is \$1,562.50. This illustrates a situation in which moving from one price to two prices is beneficial for the seller and also for consumers (in aggregate). In other words, pricing segmentation may be a win-win!

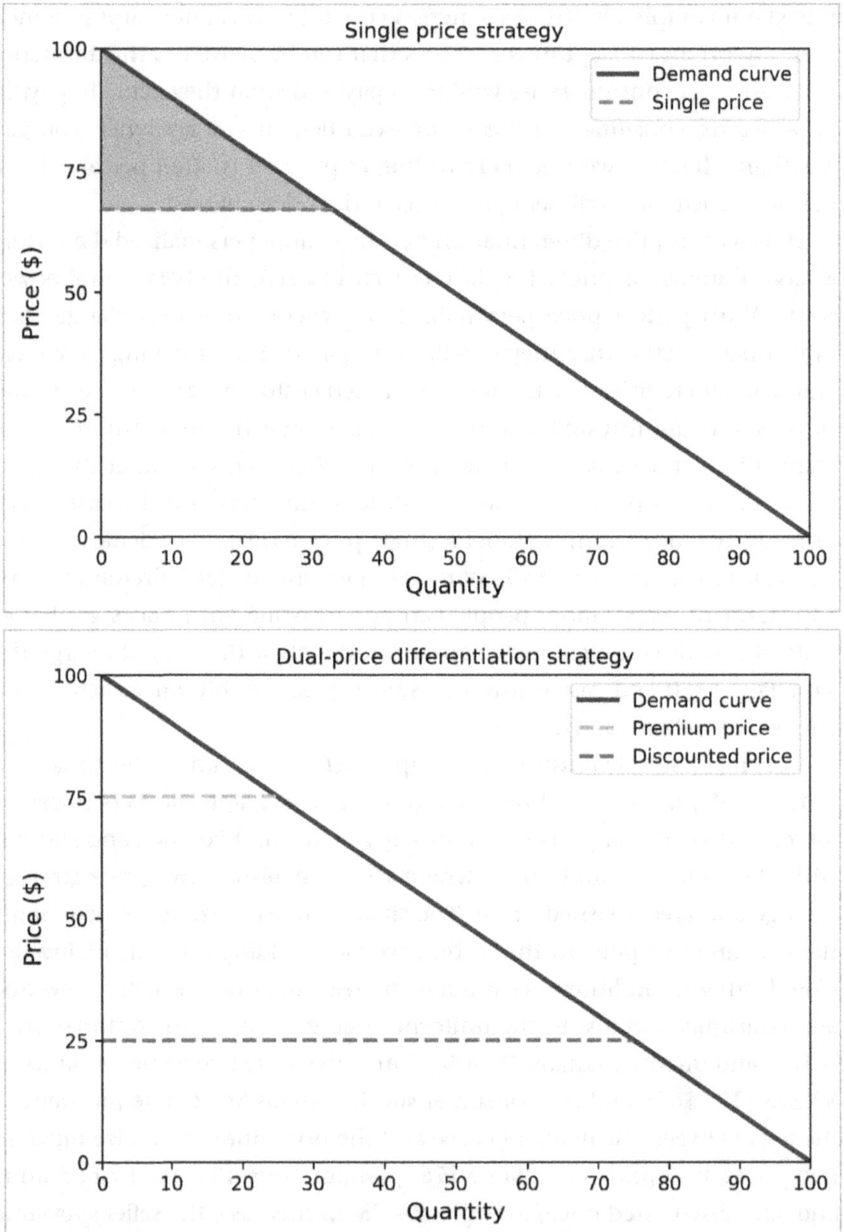

Figure 2.2
Illustration of demand curve and price differentiation. *Source:* Author.

The next natural question is whether consumers would continue to benefit from price discrimination as firms move beyond two prices. Specifically, what happens under full price personalization, where the seller could offer a different price to each customer? While this scenario may seem ideal from a revenue standpoint, the results are less favorable for consumers. As discussed above, under perfect personalization, the seller tailors each price to exactly match customers' WTP, thereby capturing the entire consumer surplus. In essence, the seller follows the demand curve precisely, extracting maximum revenue while leaving no value for consumers. Consumer advocates caution that extreme forms of price personalization risk "squeezing consumers for every penny," effectively shifting wealth from customers to firms. Beyond the financial impact, such practices raise fundamental fairness concerns: People resent discovering they paid more than others for the same product or service.

Although in practice it's unlikely that a firm would have the information or ability to charge each customer a price equal to their WTP, this dynamic illustrates an important insight: While moving from a single price to a handful of price points (e.g., two or three) can increase both seller revenue and consumer surplus, extreme personalization may tip the balance, disproportionately favoring the seller at the expense of consumers. Moreover, extreme personalization risks eroding trust, reducing perceived fairness, and ultimately backfiring if customers feel exploited. As with many pricing strategies, finding the right balance is key.

More generally, the seminal work by Varian (1985) provides an influential framework for understanding how price discrimination impacts social welfare, defined as the combined benefit to consumers and sellers. Varian investigates when and how third-degree price discrimination (charging different prices to different customer segments) improves or harms welfare. Using economic theory, he shows that a necessary condition for price discrimination to improve welfare is that it must increase total output. In simpler terms, if segmenting prices enables a business to serve more customers, then total welfare is likely to rise. However, if price discrimination simply enables the firm to charge more to some of its existing customers without expanding its consumer base, there is no welfare increase. In practice, price discrimination often does both: Some existing customers pay more, while the firm expands sales by reaching new consumers. This is reflected in the prior example. Some consumers who purchased when the firm charged a single price of $65 now pay the higher price of $75 under the two-price strategy and are thus worse off, while others who did not purchase at $65 now buy at $25 and benefit. In the same spirit, Bergemann et al. (2015) show that when a seller tailors prices to different customer segments, the overall gains are bounded: Firms will never earn less than with a uniform price, and the total benefits cannot exceed the fully efficient outcome (i.e., the situation where the product is sold to everyone whose WTP is above the marginal cost). In practice, this means that price segmentation reshuffles value between buyers and sellers.

Dubé and Misra (2023) examine the profit and consumer surplus effects of personalized pricing enabled by machine learning, using a large-scale randomized price experiment with ZipRecruiter, a B2B hiring platform. Their results are striking. First, by simply moving from its old flat rate of $99 to an optimized uniform price of $327, ZipRecruiter could have increased profits by 55 percent. Introducing personalized pricing generated an additional 19 percent profit on top of the optimized uniform price. The consumer side, however, is more nuanced. While consumer surplus declined under personalized pricing, confirming concerns that price personalization may shift more value to firms, over 60 percent of customers actually paid less than they would have under uniform pricing.

For executives, the takeaway is strategic: Price discrimination can be a powerful tool for expanding reach and boosting profits, but it only adds value to consumers when it leads to greater sales volume. If it merely extracts more revenue from existing buyers without expanding access, it risks harming customer satisfaction and triggering regulatory scrutiny. Understanding this distinction can help companies design pricing strategies that are both profitable and socially responsible.

Elmachtoub et al. (2021) offer a rigorous framework to help businesses decide whether personalized pricing is worth pursuing. As firms increasingly consider using data and AI to tailor prices to individual customers, this study focuses on a fundamental question: How much more profit can a company expect from personalized pricing compared to offering a single price? Instead of relying on complex simulations or full customer data (which are often unavailable), the authors develop clear formulas based on statistics, such as the average and variability of the WTP and the company's profit margin. They show that the potential value of personalized pricing is greatest in markets with high customer heterogeneity and limited margins and lowest when customers are relatively similar. The paper also extends to scenarios where prices are based on observable customer features (e.g., demographics or behavior) and quantifies how the quality of these features affects potential gains. The implications are concrete: Before investing in complex pricing technology or customer data infrastructure, firms can use this framework to estimate whether the expected return from personalized pricing justifies the cost. This study provides a valuable decision-support tool for product managers and pricing strategists evaluating the upside of personalization in their markets.

When personalizing prices, an important question is which data features or characteristics to rely on. At a high level, one can distinguish between three types of features or data attributes:

1. Customer features
2. Contextual information
3. Market characteristics

A smart and effective pricing strategy will aim to leverage these three feature types to identify the best strategy. Customer features refer to all the potential data that the company collects about its customers. This data can differ depending on the context (e.g., online vs. brick-and-mortar stores). In short, it includes several types of data, such as demographic data, behavioral data, psychographic data, technographic data, transactional data, social data, engagement and communication data, and mobility and location data. More details on these data types will be discussed in chapter 5.

Most companies will only have access to a small subset of this data and not for all their customers. While some companies have only access to a few features (e.g., age, device, IP address), others may have access to much richer information, sometimes up to hundreds of different features for every customer. In addition, these data features may be dynamic and evolve over time, thus making the data even richer.

The second type of features is contextual information and includes both temporal attributes and environmental data, such as weather conditions, local events, economic factors, and competitor interactions.

The third type of features is market characteristics and can include information such as market size, market maturity, number of competitors, market concentration, market share distribution, differentiation level, switching costs, economies of scale, supply chain and distribution complexity, regulatory, legal, and geopolitical factors, environmental factors, and market risks and uncertainties.

An additional type of data, which is less common and more sophisticated, involves new features created through predictive modeling. These features are sometimes referred to as predictive and AI-derived data and include likelihood to purchase, churn risk score, price sensitivity, customer lifetime value, and propensity for upsells/cross-sells.

It seems logical that as more data is available, the price personalization strategy will improve. At the same time, this is highly dependent on data quality and variation. If all customers have similar attributes, then the power of personalization will naturally be limited. If the data allows us to understand that different customers differ in their preferences and WTP, then price personalization may be powerful. The ultimate question is which data features can help best predict the WTP for each customer. Companies have developed proprietary algorithms to leverage available data and create price personalization strategies. They can deploy these strategies and assess their effectiveness by collecting new data. The new data can then be used to refine and improve algorithms iteratively, as discussed later in this book.

Combining all available data and developing pricing algorithms can enable companies to refine personalization strategies, optimize pricing, and enhance customer experiences. However, ethical considerations and data privacy laws like the General Data Protection Regulation (GDPR) and the California Consumer Privacy Act (CCPA) require careful handling to balance business benefits with consumer trust. Using specific data features for price personalization may be risky and even prohibited in some jurisdictions. Ultimately, the success of price personalization will depend not only on technological sophistication and economic gains but also on public acceptance. Achieving that acceptance will require thoughtful implementation, transparent communication, and a measure of restraint to ensure that customers don't feel as though they are being relentlessly nickel-and-dimed at every interaction. We will revisit this topic in chapter 8.

At one extreme, companies can offer the same price to all customers. At the other, they can offer a fully personalized pricing strategy, where each customer may be offered a different price. As discussed, the right strategy is likely somewhere in between. In this context, there are three types of price differentiation: first degree, second degree, and third degree. First-degree price differentiation, also known as perfect price discrimination, occurs when a seller aims to charge each customer a different price based on their WTP. For example, software companies offer custom enterprise pricing tailored to individual clients. Other examples include loans, insurance payments, and B2B contracts. Second-degree price differentiation involves offering different prices based on quantity or product format. Bulk pricing at Costco, tiered software and cloud computing subscriptions (basic, premium, enterprise), and API (application programming interface) calls all fall into this category. Finally, third-degree price differentiation segments customers into identifiable groups and charges them differently based on observable traits. In other words, it uses a specific signal about consumers (e.g., age, occupation) to differentiate prices. Common examples include student discounts at Apple or Spotify, older citizen fares on public transport, and location-based pricing where a McDonald's meal may cost more in New York City than in a small town.

Interestingly, price differentiation has been seriously disrupted with advances in machine learning. The idea is to leverage available data on customers and build "clusters" or groups of customers. These groups will be driven by data and aim to categorize customers based on their WTP. Then, the company can offer different prices to different customers based on the cluster they belong to. With this approach, the customer segmentation doesn't depend on simple rules (e.g., student vs. nonstudent) but instead relies on complex algorithms aimed at grouping different customers together based on their similarities across a high-dimensional array of data features. It allows companies to construct more sophisticated data-driven groups, sometimes at the expense of sacrificing explainability and transparency of understanding the different groups.

Ultimately, most companies opt for third-degree price differentiation over first degree, as the latter is often impractical. The process will proceed as follows: (1) decide the right number of clusters or price tiers; (2) group the different customers into the clusters by using historical customer data; (3) for each cluster, find the optimal price point; and (4) iterate on that process as more data becomes available. Of course, while this process is easy conceptually, the devil is clearly in the details. Fortunately, big data, machine learning methods, and experimentation can be successfully leveraged to perfect this process and find the best price differentiation strategy.

Other Types of Price Differentiation

When talking about price differentiation, one needs to clearly articulate what the rationale for offering different prices is. A typical answer would be based on a belief or intuition that a specific group of customers is willing to pay more (or less) than other customers. This intuition needs to be carefully validated before proceeding. A second answer could be that a specific group of customers could incur a different cost of service. More generally, a price differentiation strategy doesn't have to solely focus on separating customers into groups. It can also be based on alternative rationales, including time-based differentiation, volume-based pricing, channel-based pricing, product versioning, regional-based pricing, couponing, and bundling. In chapters 5 and 8, we will discuss several other types of price differentiation with a focus on controversial practices.

Time-based price differentiation (or dynamic pricing) adjusts prices based on when a purchase is made, leveraging fluctuations in demand and consumer behavior over time. For instance, as discussed before, airlines and hotels use dynamic pricing, where booking months in advance often results in lower fares, while last-minute travelers may pay a premium. Similarly, in the fashion industry, new collections launch at full price, but as the season ends, stores slash prices to clear inventory. And savvy shoppers know how to wait for these markdowns. Another example is peak versus off-peak pricing in electricity consumption, where homeowners can save money by running appliances at night when demand is lower. Even Uber's surge pricing that, for example, can charge more during high-demand periods like New Year's Eve illustrates how businesses leverage time as a pricing factor. While time-based pricing can reward early buyers and manage supply constraints, it can also frustrate customers who feel penalized for shopping at the wrong time.

Another effective and widely adopted time-based pricing strategy across industries is to offer discounts for longer-term commitments. This approach not only provides customers with cost savings but also ensures that businesses benefit from predictable revenue streams and enhanced customer retention. This approach is prevalent across industries, from Software as a Service (SaaS) and streaming platforms to gyms, telecom providers, and even educational services. For example, Amazon, Netflix, and Spotify offer discounted annual plans compared to their month-to-month subscriptions, encouraging users to commit upfront in exchange for lower effective rates.

Similarly, Adobe Creative Cloud charges significantly less for users who opt for a full-year subscription versus paying monthly, effectively improving revenue predictability. Mobile carriers like T-Mobile and Verizon also employ this tactic through discounted device pricing or bundled services tied to multiyear contracts. Even B2B companies such as Salesforce and Slack offer lower per-seat pricing for annual contracts versus monthly plans.

This pricing strategy isn't limited to digital services. Gym memberships and magazine subscriptions often employ similar strategies, incentivizing customers to commit for extended periods in exchange for lower rates. The rationale is clear: Customers enjoy reduced prices, while businesses benefit from cash flow stability and reduced churn rates (in addition to increased sales volume). However, it's crucial for companies to ensure transparency in their offerings. Ambiguities regarding cancellation policies or automatic renewals can erode trust and deter customers. When implemented thoughtfully, long-term commitment discounts can foster a symbiotic relationship between businesses and their customers, driving sustained growth and satisfaction.

A related practice is the Subscribe & Save program launched in 2007 by Amazon, which aims to foster customer loyalty and ensure predictable revenue streams. This program allows customers to schedule regular deliveries of essential items, such as household goods, personal care products, and pet supplies at various intervals (e.g., every two months). In return, subscribers receive discounts (typically from 5 to 15 percent) depending on the number of products subscribed to and the seller's participation.[1] The benefits of this model are multifaceted. For consumers, it offers convenience and cost savings on recurring purchases. For Amazon and participating sellers, it ensures steady demand, simplifies inventory management, and reduces customer acquisition costs. Recognizing the success of this model, other companies have implemented similar subscription-based strategies. For instance, Chewy's Autoship & Save program offers a 5 percent discount on recurring deliveries of pet supplies. Similarly, Target and Walmart have introduced subscription services for baby care and household essentials.[2] As consumer preferences continue to evolve toward hassle-free shopping experiences, such models are likely to play an increasingly important role in retail strategies. Importantly, programs such as Amazon's Subscribe & Save need to include a carefully designed communication plan when prices of specific products vary over time. In fact, to manage customer expectations and preserve trust, Amazon routinely notifies subscribers of upcoming price changes and give them the option to modify or cancel the subscriptions before the change takes effect.

Group-based pricing refers to the practice of tailoring prices to specific customer segments based on shared characteristics like age, profession, or affiliation. For example, universities often negotiate discounted software licenses for students and faculty, allowing students to purchase software licenses for a fraction of the regular price. Similarly, military personnel and veterans frequently receive exclusive discounts as a token of appreciation for their service. Another common example is membership-based pricing, where Costco shoppers pay an annual fee to access lower prices, while nonmembers pay more or miss out entirely. Even amusement parks, like Disneyland, offer resident discounts, where locals pay less than out-of-state tourists. A final common example is companies like Spotify that offer student-discounted rates. By recognizing distinct groups with different needs and price sensitivities, businesses can attract loyal customers while maximizing revenue. However, fairness concerns arise when eligibility is unclear. This is why it's critical to ensure that (1) there is a clear unambiguous group membership, (2) group membership correlates with price sensitivity, (3) there is no easy trading or exchanging among purchasers, and (4) the practice is legally and culturally acceptable.

Channel-based pricing involves setting different prices for the same product depending on the sales channel, such as in-store, a third-party retailer, or direct sales. For example, a shopper browsing Nike's website might notice that a pair of running shoes costs less than the same model in a physical Nike store, potentially reflecting lower overhead costs online. Conversely, a luxury skincare brand like La Mer may charge higher prices on its official website than through third-party retailers like Sephora, justifying the premium with exclusive packaging or loyalty perks. A common frustration occurs when travelers book a hotel room through an online travel agency like Expedia, only to discover that calling the hotel directly could have secured them a better rate with added perks like free breakfast. Another example is low-cost airlines like easyJet that used to offer different prices for customers in their online channel. By adjusting prices across channels, businesses optimize profitability, but inconsistencies can frustrate customers who expect uniform pricing. The rationale behind group-based pricing includes the fact that the service cost can be different on different channels and that different channels may have customers with different WTP.

Regional-based pricing adjusts prices based on a customer's geographic location and can reflect both cost- and demand-side differences across regions. On the cost side, prices may vary due to differences in rent, labor, or other input costs. For example, a Starbucks latte may be more expensive in New York City than in a small Midwestern town, reflecting higher rents and wages. On the demand side, prices may also reflect differences in consumers' WTP. Software companies often charge different subscription fees in emerging markets, making their products more affordable in countries like India compared to the United States. Even smartphone applications, online games, and streaming services like Netflix use regional pricing strategies. For example, a monthly Netflix subscription in Brazil might be half the cost of the same plan in Europe (as illustrated in figure 2.3), and

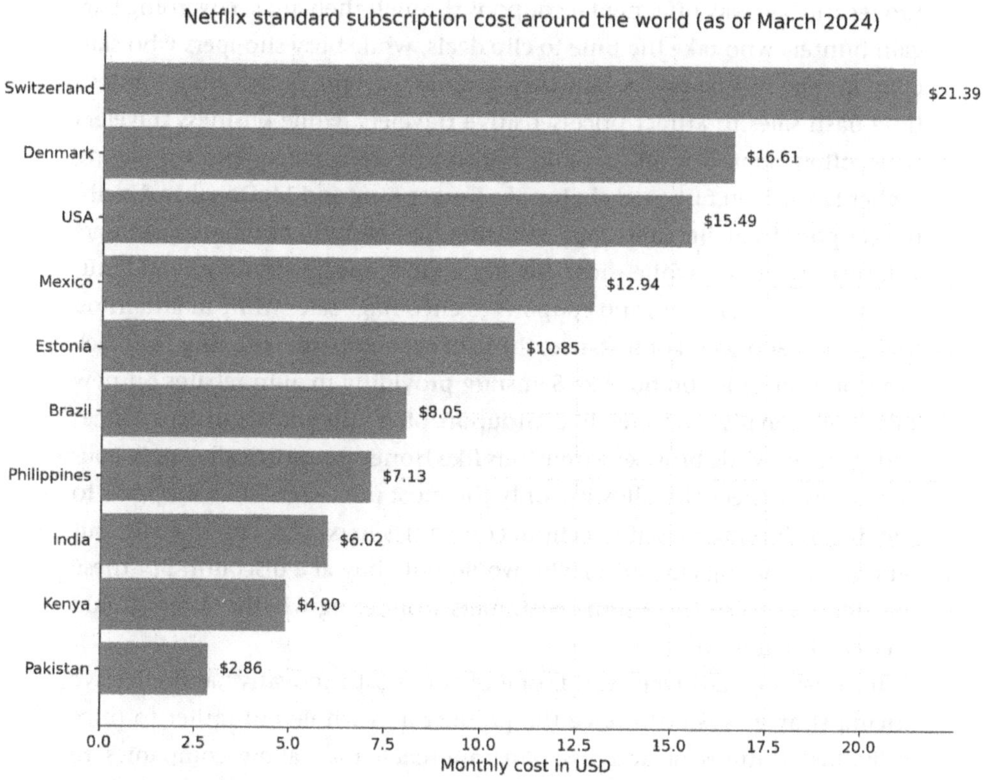

Figure 2.3
Prices of Netflix subscriptions in different countries. *Source:* Author.

content libraries and licensing agreements also vary by region. Some users exploit these pricing strategies by using VPNs to access lower rates in other countries. Other businesses, like McDonald's, combine both approaches: Menu prices reflect local input costs as well as consumer preferences and price sensitivity. A Big Mac in Switzerland is one of the most expensive in the world due to high wages and operating costs, while in India, McDonald's offers more affordable options like the McAloo Tikki burger to cater to price-sensitive consumers. While regional-based pricing helps firms optimize revenue and accessibility, it can also spark frustration when consumers perceive pricing differences as unfair or unjustified.

Couponing and self-selection in pricing allow businesses to segment customers based on their willingness to seek discounts, ensuring price-sensitive buyers pay less while others pay full price. For example, grocery stores like Kroger and Safeway offer digital coupons through their apps, rewarding bargain hunters who take the time to clip deals, while busy shoppers who skip coupons pay regular prices. Similarly, airlines use promo codes and limited-time flash sales to attract price-sensitive travelers, while business travelers (who often book last minute and prioritize convenience) end up paying higher fares. Even fast-food chains like Burger King and McDonald's distribute coupons in mailers and apps, knowing that budget-conscious customers will seek them out, while those craving a quick meal won't bother. Manufacturers also use rebates and coupons to encourage sales while maintaining higher sticker prices. For instance, think of car companies offering cashback deals or electronics brands like Samsung providing mail-in rebates on new TVs. Additionally, websites like Groupon offer discounts on experiences and services, while browser extensions like Honey automatically apply coupon codes at checkout, allowing only the most price-conscious shoppers to benefit. By leveraging self-selection, companies maximize revenue without outright alienating customers who would only buy at a discount. But these practices may also leave some customers wondering whether they should ever pay the full price.

In today's data-driven world, one of the most innovative and effective pricing strategies isn't to price the product as a whole but rather to price individual features or add-ons. This approach may allow companies to extract more value from different customer segments while offering customers greater choice and personalization. It reflects the broader evolution in pricing from traditional, flat-rate models toward more granular, flexible, and behavior-based frameworks. At the core of this shift is the concept of product versioning and tiered product lines, where companies strategically offer multiple variations of the same product, differentiated by feature sets, service levels, or access privileges.

Airlines have long been at the forefront of this strategy, offering a hierarchy of classes (economy, premium economy, business, and first class), each priced differently based on seating, flexibility, cancellation policy, baggage allowances, and perks like lounge access or early boarding. Rather than charging every customer the same price for identical seats, airlines monetize specific preferences and pain points, allowing them to generate significantly more revenue per flight. For example, while browsing the Air Canada website to book a flight from Montreal to Los Angeles, I encountered a rich and multilayered pricing structure. The initial results displayed a wide range of prices, reflecting variations across several dimensions. First, fares differed based on the departure day (e.g., Thursday vs. Friday). Second, prices varied depending on the time of day (e.g., early morning vs. afternoon departures). Third, there were distinct prices for each travel class: economy, premium economy, and business class, as illustrated in figure 2.4.

But the price differentiation strategy didn't stop there. When I selected the cheapest option displayed ($262, shown in the top left corner of figure 2.4), I was prompted to choose from five different economy fare types, each with different features such as carry-on inclusion, refundability, and seat selection (see figure 2.5). In other words, for the exact same flight (same origin, destination, airline, date, time) and same class, I was presented with five price options based solely on bundled features.

Figures 2.4 and 2.5 capture what has become the new normal in pricing: a proliferation of choices, with prices shaped by a wide array of variables and behavioral nudges like "1 seat left" to drive urgency and impulsive decisions. Upon selecting the standard economy option at $298, I was then prompted to upgrade, as shown in figure 2.6. The upgrade offer ("Upgrade to Flex") was prominently displayed in a darker color, with pricing now framed in terms of the differential (in this case, +$100). With the desire to proceed with my selected fare, I clicked the option on the left side expecting to finalize the transaction. But the journey didn't end here either. Instead of moving to the payment page, I was offered three additional upsell opportunities: (1) an upgrade to the Flex fare with free cancellation and no change fees, (2) third-party insurance allowing cancellation for any reason, and

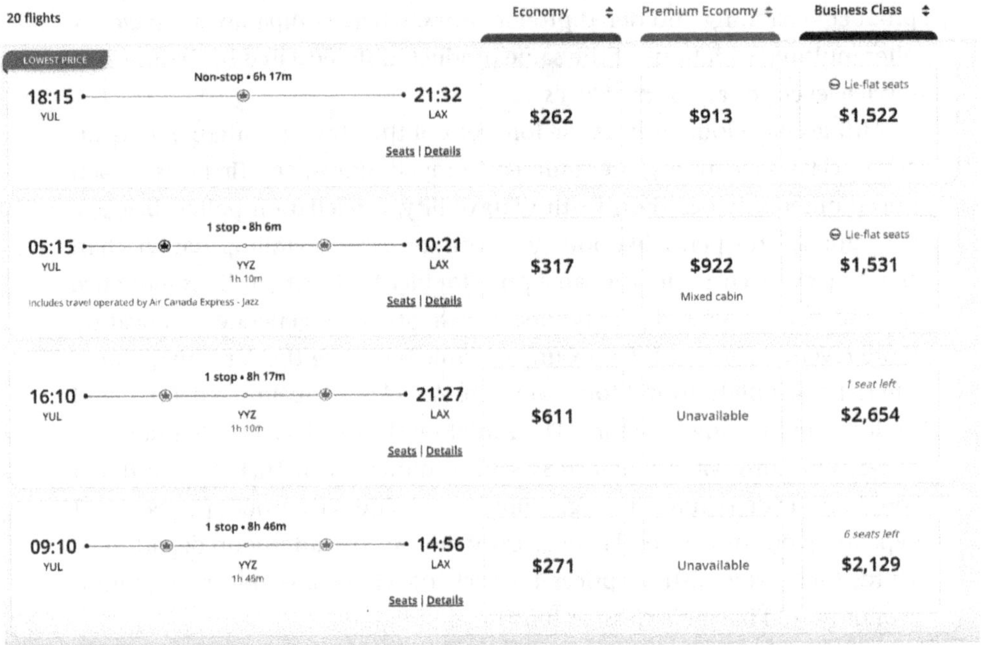

Figure 2.4
Illustration of different airline ticket prices for different classes. *Source:* Screenshot generated from AirCanada.com.

(3) a "limited-time offer" to apply for the airline's credit card, promising "up to a $200 statement credit and up to 40,000 points." This customer journey is a good example of how companies seek to upsell and increase the customer's basket value at every stage of the purchase funnel. It also highlights just how sophisticated and multidimensional modern pricing strategies have become: leveraging real-time data, behavioral economics, and digital design to shape not just what we pay but also how we experience the decision-making process itself.

A further innovation in the airline industry is when Delta Air Lines started rolling out AI-driven personalized ticket pricing, offering real-time fares tailored to individual customers. After small-scale tests in 2024, Delta's president explained that "we will have a price that's available on that flight, on that time, to you, the individual," envisioning a future with no fixed ticket prices.[3] The company reported "amazingly favorable" outcomes from the test and aims to scale this practice.

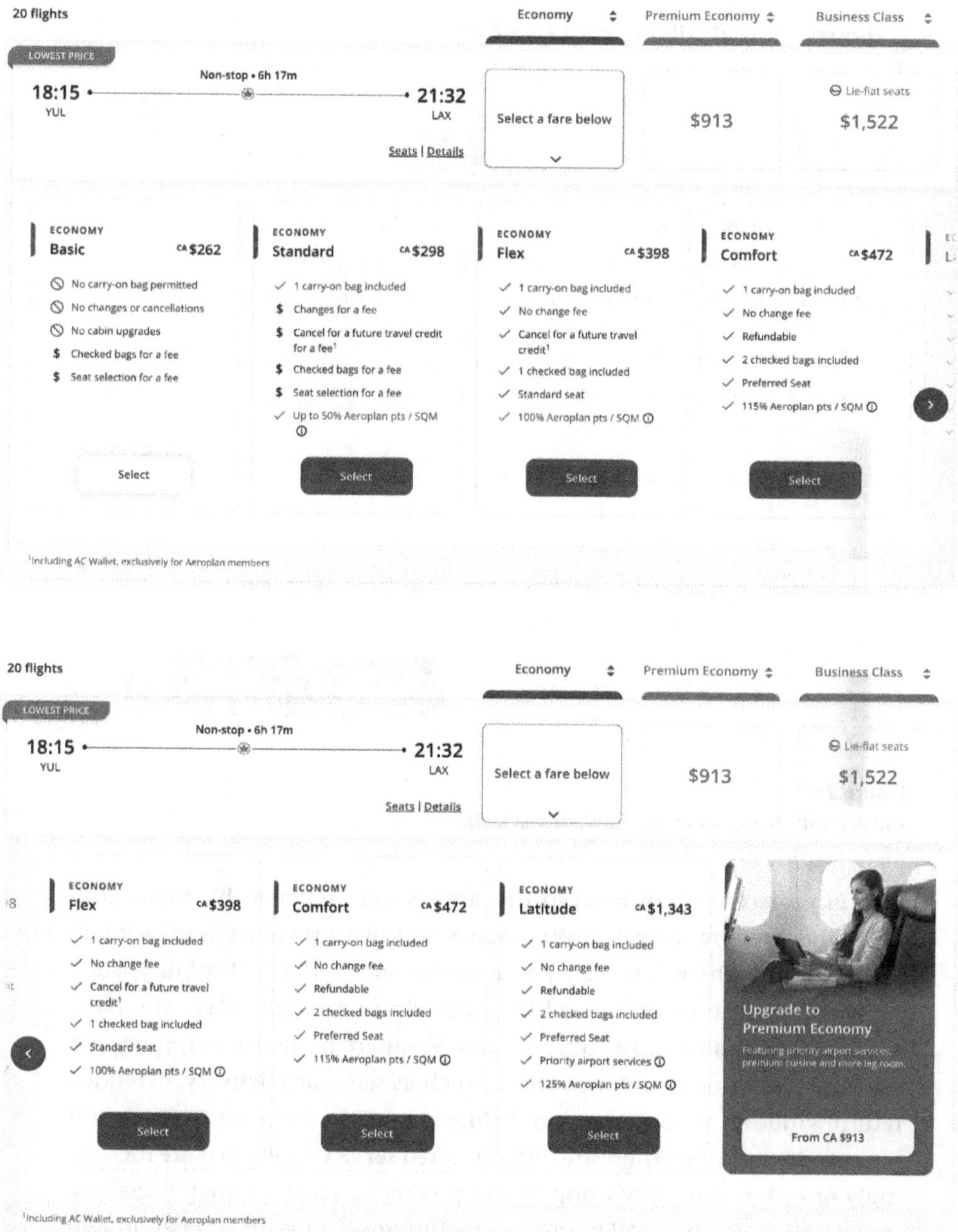

Figure 2.5
Illustration of price differentiation via features. *Source:* Screenshot generated from AirCanada.com.

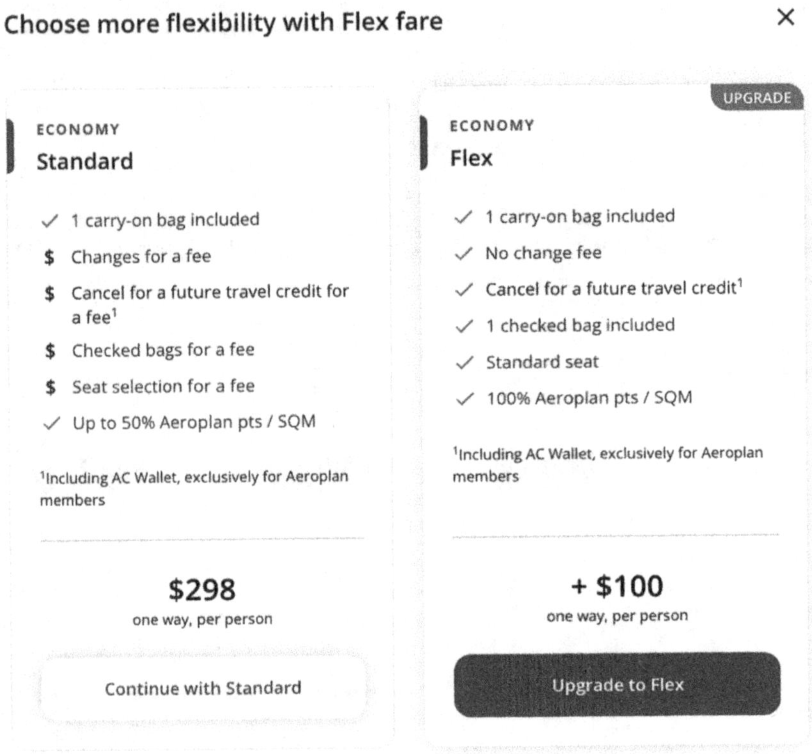

Figure 2.6
Illustration of an offer to upgrade my selection.

A more recent innovation in this area is the exchangeable ticket concept pioneered by several sports leagues and platforms like SeatGeek and Ticketmaster, where fans can pay a premium for ticket flexibility, such as swapping games or upgrading seats closer to game day. Similarly, e-commerce retailers like Amazon and Walmart monetize shipping and returns by offering premium options, such as same-day delivery, extended return windows, or carbon-neutral shipping for an extra fee. These aren't new products; rather, these are differentiated service layers that are increasingly priced dynamically using AI and predictive analytics that assess customer value, urgency, WTP, and even willingness to wait! In fashion and apparel, companies like Lululemon and Nike offer premium versions of the same products with slight feature tweaks (e.g., limited edition materials, exclusive colorways, or early access for loyalty members), effectively pricing the experience rather than just the item.

Product versioning in pricing involves offering multiple versions of a product at different price points to cater to varying customer preferences and WTP. A compelling example is Apple, which has mastered feature-based pricing across its product lines. Beginning in 2013, Apple began launching multiple models each year, marketing its iPhone 5C as a "budget" iPhone. In 2025, the company launched its iPhone 16 line, consisting of a base model (iPhone 16), the base model with a larger screen (iPhone 16 Plus), a lower-cost model (the iPhone 16e), and a higher-end model with additional premium features (iPhone 16 Pro, along with the larger-screen iPhone 16 Pro Max). Further, Apple continues to offer older models when launching new models, so earlier iPhone iterations present yet another example of Apple segmenting consumers based on preferences and WTP using product versioning. Beyond offering multiple device versions, Apple monetizes add-ons such as increased storage capacity, AppleCare+ protection plans, custom engraving, and accessories like the Apple Pencil or Magic Keyboard. Even services like iCloud storage, Apple Music, and Apple Fitness+ are layered on through subscription models, allowing Apple to potentially generate recurring revenue from differentiated digital offerings, thus turning feature pricing into a comprehensive ecosystem strategy.

The price difference between iPhones 16 and 16 Plus is a great example of market segmentation rather than a direct reflection of production costs. In the United States, as of April 2025, the iPhone 16 started at $799, while the 16 Plus began at $899, marking a $100 price gap. Both devices have 128GB storage and a Super Retina XDR display; however, the iPhone 16 has a 6.1-inch screen while the iPhone 16 Plus has a 6.7-inch screen. While the production cost differential between the 16 and 16 Plus is hard to estimate precisely, many experts believe that it's (drastically much) lower than $100. This indicates that the additional $100 charged to consumers isn't solely due to higher manufacturing expenses but is instead part of a deliberate pricing strategy.

Apple, and many other companies, employ this approach to cater to different customer segments by offering enhanced features in the more expensive models. These enhancements appeal to consumers willing to pay a premium for advanced functionalities, thereby maximizing revenue through value-based pricing. This strategy exemplifies how companies can effectively use product differentiation and strategic pricing to segment the market and extract greater value from different consumer groups.

A powerful advantage of feature-based pricing is that it allows companies to capture more consumer surplus by aligning offerings with each customer's preferences and WTP. Rather than offering a one-size-fits-all price, businesses can provide a ladder of options, encouraging upsell and self-selection. Advances in AI and big data analytics have made this strategy not only feasible but also scalable. Companies can now analyze customer behavior in real time to identify which features are most valued by which segments and adjust prices accordingly. For example, streaming services like Spotify offer a free, ad-supported version, a premium subscription without ads, a student subscription, and a family plan, each targeting different user segments. Similarly, Dropbox and other subscription-based platforms offer free tiers, basic plans, and premium plans with differentiated storage, or customer support, each priced to appeal to a specific segment. These approaches also help minimize churn by offering customers the ability to upgrade or downgrade instead of walking away entirely. Another example is in the book industry, where publishers often offer several formats (e.g., hardcover vs. paperback vs. audiobook), sometimes with staggered release dates. By strategically designing product variations, businesses capture a broader audience while encouraging customers to trade up for higher-margin options.

In this context, our study titled "Feature-Based Dynamic Pricing" in Cohen et al. (2020) addresses a common challenge in modern retail and online marketplaces: how to price highly differentiated products where each product has unique characteristics and no historical sales data. Examples include flash-sale sites, Airbnb listings, or online loan offers, where products typically arrive one by one and sellers must make pricing decisions on the fly. In such cases, instead of pricing the products, we propose to price the features that are embedded in the products. To solve this problem, we introduce a dynamic pricing algorithm that learns from past sales and product features (like location, size, or brand) to iteratively improve future pricing decisions. We develop an algorithm that can efficiently estimate the value of each feature while minimizing revenue loss over time. We then prove that this algorithm guarantees strong performance even when products are complex and varied. It balances exploration (learning feature values) with "exploitation" or optimization (setting revenue-maximizing prices) and remains effective even when features change over time. This is an interesting twist where feature-based pricing tools can significantly improve revenue without requiring large-scale experimentation or precise demand models.

Bundling in pricing refers to the practice of offering multiple products or services together at a single price, typically lower than the total cost of buying each item separately. This strategy encourages customers to purchase more by emphasizing value and convenience. In many cases, bundling can be beneficial and effective when the WTP for the products being bundled is negatively correlated across customer segments. For example, McDonald's "Value Meals" bundles a sandwich, fries, and a drink for a discounted price compared to purchasing each item individually, encouraging customers to spend a little more while feeling like they're getting a deal. Another classic example is Microsoft Office, where customers can buy Excel, PowerPoint, Word, and other software together at a discount rather than buying each program separately. Similarly, cable providers often bundle TV, internet, and phone services, offering a "better deal" than buying each service independently. Bundling can boost sales and clear out inventory, but it also risks undervaluing individual products and confusing customers who may not need everything in the bundle.

Bundling and discounting are among the most common promotion strategies, so which strategy is more effective is an important retail question. In Bandi et al. 2025, we attempt to answer this question by presenting a study on how bundling and discounting affect consumer behavior and financial performance in convenience retail. We collaborated with a major global convenience store chain across seven locations over eighteen weeks to implement six promotion strategies: bundling and discounting healthy snacks, unhealthy snacks, and both types of snacks (i.e., offering customer choice). The key findings are both surprising and actionable. For healthy snacks, bundling (e.g., adding a fruit box to a coffee purchase) proved more effective at increasing revenue and profit, while discounting was better at boosting sales volume. For unhealthy snacks, however, neither strategy had any effect on sales volume. In fact, promotions for unhealthy items reduced revenue and profit, suggesting deeply ingrained purchase behavior and weak price sensitivity. Additionally, the study uncovered notable cross-product effects: Healthy promotions triggered "moral licensing," increasing purchases of candies and cigarettes, while bundling coffee cannibalized beverage sales. The implications from this study are clear: tailor promotional tactics to product type, leverage bundling with high-margin anchors like coffee to boost profitability, and test regularly legacy promotions since some may be harming margins without driving incremental sales.

Limitations of Price Differentiation

While price differentiation may be a powerful strategy to maximize profits and cater to different customer segments (especially in the era of big data), it has several limitations, including imperfect segmentation, cannibalization, and arbitrage.

Imperfect segmentation arises when businesses fail to accurately classify customers based on their WTP. For instance, airlines attempt to distinguish between price-sensitive tourists and last-minute business travelers using available data. However, misclassifications are common, such as a high-paying business traveler securing a low fare or a budget-conscious tourist opting out due to high prices. These mismatches lead to inefficiencies and lost revenue, highlighting the challenges of imperfect segmentation. Similarly, streaming services like Netflix set regional prices based on economic factors, but this approach doesn't account for wealthy users in lower-income countries who benefit from lower fees.

In fact, imperfect segmentation is one of the biggest challenges (and realities) facing businesses that use price personalization. At its core, segmentation means grouping customers based on shared characteristics (like behavior, demographics, or preferences) to offer differentiated pricing tiers. But in practice, segmentation is rarely perfect. In many cases, businesses are working with partial, noisy, or outdated data, which can result in imprecise groupings. For example, a retailer might infer that a customer is highly price sensitive because they frequently shop during sales, but they may actually be a loyal, high-value customer who simply enjoys a bargain. One airline executive once shared how an algorithm mistakenly categorized business travelers as leisure travelers because they booked far in advance. This mistake led to lower fares being offered to passengers who would gladly pay more. The issue becomes even more acute with new users or anonymous visitors, for whom companies have little to no behavioral data.

Without a purchase history or a browsing profile, businesses must rely on proxy data—such as device type, location, or referral source—which naturally introduces bias and uncertainty. For instance, showing a discount to all mobile users might seem strategic, but it may unintentionally exclude desktop users who are equally price sensitive.

Yet imperfect data doesn't mean segmentation is useless. When done carefully, even rough signals can create meaningful value. Streaming platforms like Netflix and Spotify, for example, use early engagement patterns (e.g., the first few songs or shows a user interacts with) to make smart initial recommendations, which can later inform pricing offers such as free trials or upgrade nudges. Similarly, e-commerce websites often use geolocation data to offer region-based promotions, even when they lack individual purchase history. The key for executives is to treat segmentation as a fluid, evolving process rather than a fixed science. Strategies like progressive profiling (gradually collecting more data over time), using look-alike modeling, and setting guardrails to avoid overpersonalization mistakes can help mitigate the risks of imperfect segmentation. Ultimately, while data may be noisy or incomplete, with the right approach, even imperfect segmentation can drive meaningful impact, so long as businesses remain transparent, cautious, and adaptable in how they act on it.

Cannibalization happens when lower-priced versions of a product eat into sales of higher-margin offerings. For instance, when Apple introduced the iPhone SE at a lower price point, some customers who might have bought a premium model opted for the cheaper alternative, reducing overall revenue. Another example is Skiplagged.com, a website that finds "hidden city" flight deals, where travelers buy tickets with a layover at a destination they actually want to visit, which happen to be cheaper than direct flights. This disrupts the airline's pricing strategy by offering cheaper routes that may cannibalize demand for higher-priced direct flights. Figure 2.7 shows an example where the direct flight from Atlanta to Orlando is priced at $250, whereas the flight from Atlanta to Dallas with a layover in Orlando is priced at $130. Critically, the latter flight includes the former as its first leg, which creates an illogical situation and an incentive to game the system by booking the flight to Dallas while skipping the second flight. It's worth noting that airlines take active steps to discourage this kind of behavior. For example, they often cancel the return leg of a round-trip itinerary if a passenger skips a segment, and checked baggage must be routed to the final destination.

Figure 2.7
Example of Skiplagged.com.

Finally, arbitrage arises when customers find ways to exploit price differentiation, buying at lower prices and reselling or using the product where it's more expensive. For example, gamers often use VPNs to purchase digital games at lower regional prices and then play them in high-priced markets. Similarly, AbeBooks.com, a marketplace for used books, allows sellers to offer discounted books that can be resold at a premium in other markets, exploiting pricing differences between regions. These challenges show that while price differentiation can be highly effective, companies must carefully manage segmentation, product offerings, and pricing enforcement to prevent unintended revenue loss.

3 Common Approaches

> Your margin is my opportunity.
> —Jeff Bezos

Since pricing is such an important decision for businesses, it's natural that it has been studied for decades. Interestingly, it has been studied in several disciplines, including economics, marketing, operations management, and even psychology and computer science. Each discipline has developed a set of assumptions, models, and approaches. Some of these approaches are scientifically grounded, whereas others are more based on intuition and common sense. In this chapter, we discuss common approaches that have been widely adopted in a wide array of industries and applications.

Value Versus Price

When talking about pricing, it's important to first understand the fundamental difference between value and price. Value refers to the worth or usefulness of a product or service, as perceived by an individual or by society. Value is inherently subjective and can vary depending on factors such as personal preferences, needs, and beliefs. For example, a painting may have a high value to a collector because of its rarity, historical significance, or emotional resonance, while it may have little value to someone who doesn't appreciate art. It's important to highlight that value and WTP aren't the same. Value refers to the perceived benefit a customer derives from a product or service, while WTP is the maximum amount the customer is prepared to spend. For instance, customers may highly value a product but still have a low WTP due to budget constraints, competing options, or purchase context.

Price, on the other hand, is the amount of money that a buyer pays for a product or service. Price is objective and set by the firm selling the product or service based on several factors, such as supply and demand, production costs, and market competition. The relationship between value and price is that the price of a product or service is often influenced by its perceived value. If a product is perceived as having high value, its price may be higher than that of a similar product with lower perceived value. Still, the price of a product may be higher or lower than its perceived value due to various market factors.

In summary, value and price are related but distinct concepts. Value is subjective and determined by personal preferences and societal beliefs, while price is objective and determined by market forces. The price of a product may be influenced by its perceived value, but it's not always the same as its value. In general, prices reflect the intersection of supply and demand, while value reflects the subjective perceptions and preferences of individuals. However, the two concepts can influence each other. For example, if demand for a product increases, its price may rise as well, which can affect how much people value it. Additionally, if a product is priced too high (relative to its perceived benefits or compared to competing options), consumers may assign it less value, assuming it's overpriced or not worth the cost. For instance, a no-name smartphone priced higher than a comparable iPhone or Samsung model may be perceived as offering poor value, even if its technical specs are similar, simply because the brand lacks credibility. In an ideal world, companies would find a price point that is as close as possible to the value attributed to the product or service by each customer.

Three Simple Approaches

In my experience, more often than not, simple approaches to pricing are doing the job very well. Simple approaches have the important advantage of being interpretable and logical and can be easily implemented. They can be used as a starting point to reflect on the pricing strategy in place. At a high level, there are three simple approaches to pricing that businesses can use (e.g., Philipps 2021):

1. **Cost-plus pricing**: This approach relies on adding a certain markup to the cost of producing a product (or providing a service). For example, if it costs $10 to produce a product and the targeted markup is 50 percent, then the price would be $15.
2. **Competition-based pricing**: This approach aims to set the price based on the amounts that competitors are charging for similar products or services. For example, if a competitor is charging $15 for a similar product, a business may choose to charge $14 or $15 to be competitive.
3. **Value-based pricing**: This approach involves setting the price based on the perceived value of the product (or service) by the customer. For example, if a product saves the customer time or money, the price can be set higher.

In addition to these three simple common approaches, it's worth mentioning two important practices in the world of pricing: dynamic pricing and behavioral or psychological pricing. As discussed before, dynamic pricing refers to the practice of varying prices over time and typically involves setting prices based on market demand and supply (and their imbalances). For example, airlines and hotels may charge higher prices during peak travel seasons and lower prices during off-peak seasons. We will revisit the topic of dynamic pricing later in this chapter. Behavioral or psychological pricing intends to set prices based on the psychological impact on customers. For example, pricing a product at $9.99 instead of $10 can make it seem more affordable. This topic will be further discussed later in this book.

Now the question reduces to which approach is more suitable. The answer, of course, depends on the products, industry, and customers. Cost-plus pricing has the advantage that profit margins are fully set upfront so that cash flow and financial forecasts become easy and stress-free. From a finance or accounting perspective, this approach offers simplicity and predictability by allowing firms to ensure all costs are covered while securing a target return. The challenge, however, lies in determining the appropriate markup.

While this approach is standard, it's generally not optimal. In particular, it totally ignores competition and customers' behaviors and hence may not be effective in several settings. For example, if you set prices purely based on your cost without considering how much your competitors are charging and how much your customers are willing to pay, you may end up with a very suboptimal price point.

In practice, cost-plus pricing often emerges under constrained conditions: When firms face uncertainty about demand, lack reliable market data, or operate in environments where price experimentation is difficult. For instance, manufacturers in government contracting, utilities, or construction frequently rely on cost-plus formulas because of regulation, transparency requirements, or negotiated procurement processes. Similarly, small businesses or firms producing highly customized products may use cost-plus pricing simply because they lack detailed insights into customer WTP or competitors' prices.

Importantly, the "right" markup varies across industries depending on the level of competition, cost structure, and perceived risk. In highly competitive sectors such as retail or airlines, margins are typically thin (e.g., 2–10 percent) because prices are disciplined by market forces. In contrast, industries with limited competition, differentiated products, or high switching costs, such as pharmaceuticals, defense, or luxury goods, often have substantially higher markups. Thus, while cost-plus pricing provides internal consistency and ease of implementation, its effectiveness depends on external market dynamics: Ignoring competitive benchmarks or customer sensitivity can quickly lead to suboptimal or even unviable price points.

Competition-based pricing has the advantage of being market-driven and takes a more global view of the competitive landscape. Under this approach, one must first collect competitors' data on prices. There are several ways to do so. In some industries (like airlines and gas stations), firms can purchase comprehensive, granular datasets on prices, while in other industries firms need to find ways to collect the data themselves. For example, in e-commerce it became common to scrape competitors' websites and routinely collect pricing information (as well as reviews, product features, and web page layouts). Several start-ups even offer such services, collecting the desired data at the requested frequency (e.g., daily or hourly).

Today, many companies routinely collect competitor data, either directly or through specialized third-party providers, as part of their pricing, assortment, and marketing strategy. This practice has become a standard component of competitive intelligence, particularly in industries like retail, travel, and consumer goods, where prices and promotions change frequently. For instance, e-commerce giants track competitor pricing nearly in real time across thousands of products and locations to adjust their own pricing dynamically, a strategy that can help build and sustain a strong market position. Major retailers like Best Buy, Walmart, and Zara may use competitor insights to optimize markdowns, assortment, and pricing tiers.

On the data provider side, firms such as DataWeave, Price2Spy, Profitero, and Wiser offer comprehensive scraping and analytics services that deliver stock keeping unit (SKU)–level pricing, stock availability, promotional activity, and customer reviews across competitors' websites. These companies typically operate on a subscription-based SaaS model, with pricing that ranges from $500 per month for small brands to tens of thousands of dollars per month for enterprise clients, depending on the number of SKUs, competitors tracked, and regions covered. For example, DataWeave provides detailed dashboards and APIs that can update multiple times per day and can cover thousands of online stores globally. In the travel and hospitality sector, companies like OTA Insight and RateGain offer competitor rate monitoring for hotels and airlines, helping revenue managers adjust fares dynamically based on real-time local market conditions. Ultimately, these services provide business managers with granular, timely, and actionable intelligence, enabling smarter pricing, better positioning, and faster responses to market shifts.

In some cases, collecting competitors' data isn't easy. Consider, for example, the case of a ride-hailing platform that wants to obtain data about its competitors. One hypothetical way is to ask employees (or contractors) to take rides with competitors and record the data (prices, waiting times, etc.). Then, such data can be used to create benchmarking practices and find out if their prices are competitive. In this context, the first step is to determine who your main competitors are (it's possible that you have a different set of competitors for each of your products). The second step is to understand the key differentiating features between your products and those of your competitors. Then, the ultimate step is to assign a monetary value to these differentiating features. For example, if you offer a faster delivery time, can you charge a price 10 percent higher than your competitors? Such questions aren't easy to answer, but data can help.

An interesting, although somewhat extreme, example arises when a firm faces no direct competitors, such as a new drug or a unique medical procedure offered by the only provider in a particular city. In this situation, the logic might suggest setting a high price, but two important considerations must be kept in mind. First, antitrust laws are designed to prevent firms from obtaining and exploiting monopoly power, and excessive pricing may attract regulatory scrutiny. Second, setting prices too high can invite new entrants to develop similar products and capture market share by offering them at lower prices.

In most cases, you will have competitors, and a major risk with undercutting competitor prices is entering a "price race to the bottom." To illustrate this concept, consider the case where two competitors offer a similar version of the same product. If the products are exactly the same, then consumers will have no preference and will be likely to always select the cheaper one. It's then tempting to say that if your competitor offers a specific price (say, $9.95), you could cut this price by a small amount (say at $9.90) and steal all the customers. But then the competitor can hit back by further decreasing the price (say $9.85). Then, the spiral continues until both get to the minimal price at which profits are still made, that is, the marginal production cost. This phenomenon was introduced in 1883 by the French mathematician Joseph Bertrand as the Bertrand paradox (Bertrand 1889). It's important to note that the Bertrand paradox applies only under stringent conditions, namely, homogeneous products, no capacity constraints, and one-shot competition (as opposed to repeated interactions). While price competition can benefit consumers who will tend to enjoy lower prices, it can also lead to a reduction in both quality and innovation as companies prioritize cutting costs over improving their products or services.

Finally, value-based pricing can be a great approach, under which the firm sets the price based on what consumers are willing to pay for the product or service. It sounds nice, but it's far from easy to do in practice. How can we know how much consumers are willing to pay? One way is to conduct market research studies (e.g., focus groups) and ask customers directly. Another way is by running surveys (several companies specialize in designing and running surveys and market studies). However, the information obtained from surveys may not always be accurate. Indeed, expressing opinions in a survey isn't the same as opening our wallet to spend money.

Another way to accomplish value-based pricing is through experimentation, which can be highly successful in certain applications. By properly and efficiently testing different price points, firms can develop an accurate understanding of how much customers are willing to pay and how they shift their purchasing decisions in response to price changes. In economics, customer responsiveness to price changes is referred to as the price elasticity of demand. Formally, the price elasticity of demand is defined as the ratio of the percentage change in quantity demanded of a product to the percentage change in price. At a high level, it measures the sensitivity of demand variation to price changes. We will revisit the concepts of price elasticity and price experimentation in chapter 5.

Each approach discussed in this chapter has both virtues and drawbacks. One potential option is to combine several of these approaches. For example, we can set a price that accounts simultaneously for cost, competitors' prices, and consumers' WTP. We then need to give different weights (i.e., relative importance) to each of these factors. Another argument can be that value-based pricing, if possible, is the golden standard since customers are speaking to you directly, and their WTP implicitly includes information about your competitors' prices. But sometimes value-based pricing isn't an option (especially if price experimentation isn't possible).

To make the above approaches successful, it's important to be guided by data. In fact, each of these approaches relies on different categories of data (e.g., cost data, competitors' data, price elasticity data via experimentation). The idea is to spend time collecting the most accurate and comprehensive data before making pricing decisions. As the saying goes, "Garbage in, garbage out." This expression highlights the importance of ensuring that data is accurate and reliable to make informed decisions. When the data used for decision-making is flawed or of poor quality, then the resulting decisions are likely to also be flawed. The recommendation is to collect reliable data sources as much as possible by putting in place a concrete plan. For cost data, it's important to have a rigorous method to compute the total cost and to track cost values in a timely fashion. For competitors' data, it's crucial to come up with an extensive set of relevant competitors along with the key differentiating factors. The set of competitors needs to be refreshed periodically, and their prices need to be tracked ideally in nearly real time. For data on customers' WTP, this is the most exciting part in which price experimentation (when possible) brings a magic touch, as we will discuss later.

As noted earlier, pricing is also an art. Having a good dataset is helpful, but sometimes the right price also involves some human touch, for example, by leveraging psychological tools to entice customers, as discussed in the next chapter.

Dynamic Pricing

Dynamic pricing is a strategy where businesses adjust prices based on factors like demand, competition, customer behavior, and external conditions. This approach allows companies to maximize revenue but also carries drawbacks and risks. Among successful examples are Alibaba and Amazon, which have the ability to update prices millions of times per day using sophisticated algorithms. A shopper searching for a laptop on Monday might see one price, only to return on Friday and find it's changed. Similarly, Uber's surge pricing ensures that more drivers are available when demand spikes, such as after popular concerts or during bad weather, by charging higher fares when ride requests exceed supply. This strategy helps balance demand and supply but can also spark customer frustration.

While dynamic pricing algorithms long predate the AI era, they have become far more sophisticated with the integration of machine learning and access to large, granular datasets. Modern systems continuously learn from user behavior and market conditions, enabling pricing decisions that are highly adaptive and optimized at a fine-grained level.

Importantly, dynamic pricing isn't without its pitfalls. One infamous failure occurred on Black Friday 2014, when a flaw in Amazon's pricing algorithm slashed prices on expensive products, such as camera lenses and electronics to just a few dollars, causing chaos as savvy shoppers rushed to buy before the mistake was corrected. Another bizarre case occurred in 2011 when Amazon's automated pricing algorithms caused the price of a biology book, *The Making of a Fly: The Genetics of Animal Design*, to skyrocket to close to $24 million (as discussed below).[1] Another case arose at Staples, which used location-based dynamic pricing to offer lower prices to customers near competitor stores while charging higher prices to those without alternatives. When the practice was exposed, it raised ethical concerns about fairness. Additionally, in 1999, Coca-Cola tested vending machines that increased prices in hot weather, assuming customers would be willing to pay more.[2] The backlash was so strong that the idea was scrapped, as people felt they were being unfairly penalized for needing a drink in the heat.

So, how did a biology book end up priced at nearly $24 million on Amazon? Let's unpack what happened in this example. This book typically sold for around $70. As shown in figure 3.1, it was offered by two sellers, "profnath" and "bordeebook," on Amazon. The two competitors likely

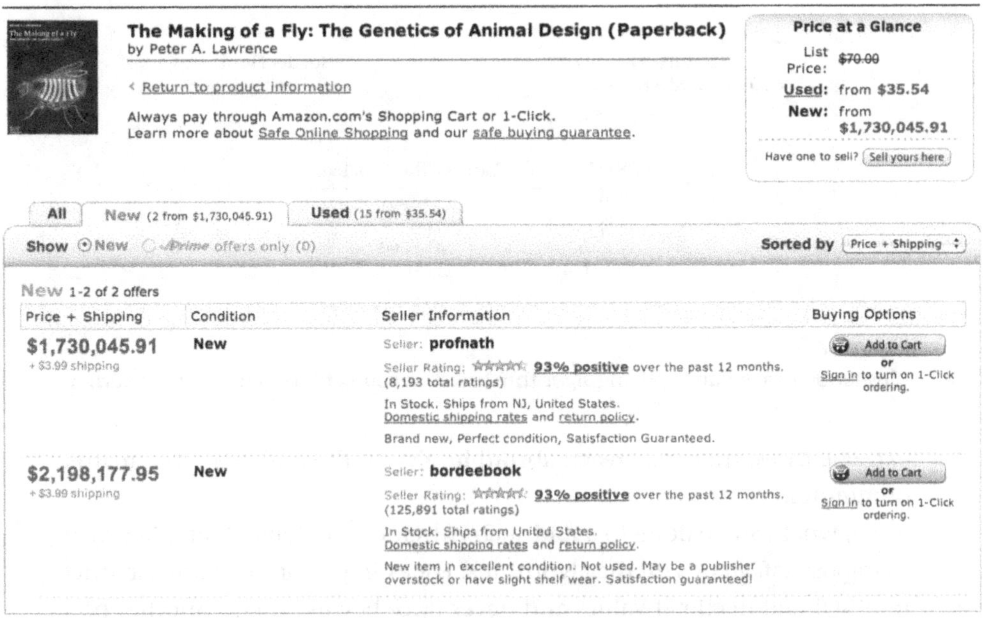

Figure 3.1
Example of dynamic pricing gone wrong.

monitored each other's prices and set their own price solely based on the other's price.

Consider, for instance, the simple iterative dynamic pricing algorithm summarized in figure 3.2. In this case, the first seller (profnath) adopts a straightforward undercutting strategy, consistently pricing its product 0.2 percent below its competitor. This strategy might be intended to secure top placement in search results, especially when shoppers sort listings by price. A seller might also offer its product at a discount to compensate for a weaker reputation (such as fewer reviews or lower ratings) in an effort to boost visibility and generate positive reviews. The second seller (bordeebook) adopts a premium pricing strategy, maintaining a 27 percent markup over its competitor's price. This could reflect a desire to position the product as a more premium option with, say, a faster delivery and a free-return policy.

When these pricing strategies are implemented simultaneously, and especially when they are automated without guardrails, the result can be a feedback loop where the prices spiral upward. With each seller reacting to the other in successive iterations, prices can rise dramatically. In

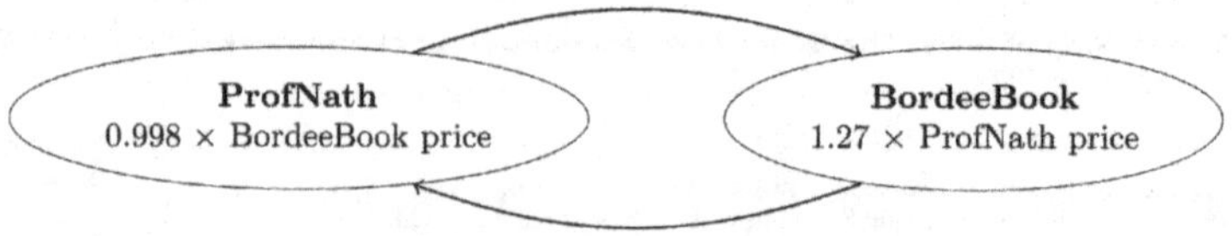

ProfNath price	BordeeBook price
$70.00	$88.90
$88.75	$112.71
$112.52	$142.90
$142.66	$181.17
...	...

Figure 3.2
Illustration of a dynamic pricing algorithm based on competitors' prices. *Source:* Author.

extreme cases, they may reach absurd levels—in the millions—in a matter of minutes.

So, what can be done to avoid such extreme situations? A simple way is to impose safeguards on the algorithms. For example, one can impose strict minimal and maximal values and never price beyond them. Another possibility is to request human validation before deploying a price that seems too high or too low. The algorithm can recommend a price but then send an email to the manager to validate the price before implementing it. Such simple safeguards can help avoid unwanted situations, which can sometimes have long-term consequences on customer perception and loyalty.

Despite its challenges, dynamic pricing remains a powerful tool when used wisely. Airlines, hotels, and e-commerce retailers successfully leverage it to optimize revenue and fill inventory efficiently. However, companies must carefully balance profit maximization with consumer trust. Indeed, if customers feel they're being exploited, they may take their business elsewhere.

A common and widespread type of dynamic pricing is the practice of adjusting prices in real time based on supply and demand imbalances. In recent years, this has become a cornerstone strategy in several industries. Companies like Airbnb and Uber have long used this approach: Uber's surge pricing increases fares during peak demand to incentivize more drivers to operate, while Airbnb hosts adjust nightly rates based on local events and seasonal trends. As discussed, retail giants such as Amazon and Walmart also use dynamic pricing, frequently updating product prices in response to competitor pricing, inventory levels, and consumer behavior.

In the restaurant and bars sector, pubs like O'Neill's in London have implemented time-based pricing, charging higher prices for drinks during late-night hours. Specifically, the London pub is charging customers an extra £2 a pint after 10:00 p.m.[3]

As mentioned, dynamic pricing isn't without controversy. Consumers often perceive sudden price hikes as unfair, especially when they occur during emergencies or peak demand periods. For instance, during natural disasters, ride-hailing services have faced backlash for implementing surge pricing, leading to allegations of price gouging. Similarly, fast-food chains like Wendy's have encountered criticism for plans to introduce dynamic pricing, with customers expressing concerns about the perceived unfairness of fluctuating meal prices. In smaller settings, such as a bakery contemplating a higher price for the last sandwich of the day, the decision becomes delicate (and sometimes even political). If a shop has their last available sandwich by 11:00 a.m. and knows for a fact it will sell, why not strategically adjust the price to be higher? While increasing the price could capitalize on scarcity, it risks alienating loyal customers who may feel exploited.

The key takeaway for business leaders is that while dynamic pricing can optimize revenue and manage demand, it must be implemented thoughtfully. Transparency is crucial: Clearly communicating the reasons for price changes can help maintain customer trust. Moreover, businesses should be aware of regulatory frameworks governing pricing practices to avoid legal repercussions. Later in this book, we will discuss the important dangers and pitfalls, such as price gouging and price collusion. Ultimately, the success of dynamic pricing hinges on balancing profitability with fairness, ensuring that pricing strategies enhance customer relationships rather than undermine them. Interestingly, dynamic pricing practices (with frequent price changes) have become well accepted in specific contexts and situations (e.g., airlines, ride-hailing) but less acceptable in others. It's puzzling that most consumers are fine with paying different prices for the same airline ticket (in the same airplane, on the same date) depending on the booking date (e.g., booking two vs. twenty weeks before departure) but would be upset to see different prices charged for the same dish at a restaurant. For what products and services can dynamic pricing be applied? The answer is far from easy and depends on many dimensions, including cultural factors, perceptions of fairness, types of products (e.g., necessity vs. luxury), and regulations.

An interesting approach is to rely on competition-based dynamic pricing. This approach will vary prices dynamically while also carefully and strategically benchmarking price levels relative to competitors. A simple approach in that regard would be to set a predefined strategy, such as always matching the lowest competitor's price (within some reasonable bounds), always marking up (or marking down) the competitors' prices by 10 percent, or always setting a price equal to the median of competitors. A more sophisticated approach would be to constantly learn and refine what could be the best dynamic pricing strategy while monitoring competitors' activities. While a myriad of academic studies and real-world approaches have been tested, we next discuss three examples: one in the airline industry, one in online retail, and one in ride-hailing.

The first example is Cohen et al. (2023), where we challenged a longstanding industry norm in airline pricing: the widespread practice of matching competitors' base (or "lead-in") fares across nearly all markets. We examined whether this strategy—which ignores differences in service quality such as nonstop flights, layover durations, or departure times—results in revenue inefficiencies. Partnering with a major global airline, we conducted a large-scale field experiment across nearly five thousand high-quality itineraries in twenty-two markets, marking up the lead-in fares by about 5 percent while holding all other pricing mechanisms constant. The results were clear and actionable: Compared to the standard fare-matching strategy, quality-based fare management (i.e., proactively charging more for better itineraries) led to a smoother price path and boosted revenue, without reducing ticket sales or market share. These improvements resulted in shifting booking patterns, where the airline sold fewer discounted tickets early in the season and more higher-priced tickets later, which increased profits. We also showed that this strategy works best in competitive, high-demand markets and for longer trips. The takeaway is that airlines (and other industries with tiered offerings) can unlock substantial value by incorporating quality differentiation into their initial pricing architecture rather than relying solely on dynamically matching competitors' prices.

The second example is in online retail, where Fisher et al. (2018) presented a rigorously validated approach for implementing competition-based dynamic pricing. The study was conducted in partnership with a leading Chinese e-commerce firm and focused on how retailers should react to competitor price changes. Instead of blindly matching competitors, the authors developed a sophisticated pricing model that incorporates consumer behavior, product substitution patterns, and competitor availability (such as stockouts). Using data from over fifteen top-selling products and a large-scale randomized field experiment, they showed that traditional models based on historical sales or basic heuristics (like "always match the lowest price") fail to capture true customer price sensitivity and competitive dynamics. Their methodology used randomized pricing to accurately measure price elasticity and leveraged stockouts to infer competitor importance. The results were compelling: The optimized algorithm increased revenues by 11 percent. A follow-up field test across different customer segments and regions confirmed these results. For business leaders, the key takeaway is that thoughtful, data-driven competitive pricing strategies, which are grounded in consumer choice modeling and regularly updated through experimentation, can significantly boost revenue and protect margins. Moreover, success requires not just tracking competitors but also understanding how consumers perceive value and make choices across retailers.

The third example is based on a study that my coauthors and I conducted to better understand customers' multihoming behavior in ride-hailing. In Chitla et al. 2023, we explored whether ride-hailing customers treat platforms like Lyft and Uber as interchangeable commodities or as differentiated services. Using an extensive dataset of over 1.4 million rides from 162,000 riders in New York City, we built a structural model that accounts for both operational factors (e.g., price, wait time) and behavioral dynamics (e.g., brand affinity, search costs, and platform "stickiness"). Our findings challenge the assumption that ride-hailing is purely price-driven: Most customers (83.4 percent) use only one platform, and even among multihomers (16.6 percent), only 43.4 percent consider both apps before booking a ride. This behavior is shaped not only by price and wait time but also by cognitive frictions and habits. Our model shows that customers learn and evolve their beliefs over time, thus making early customer experiences particularly influential. Based on this, we ran counterfactual simulations and found two actionable pricing strategies: (1) front-loading promotions (offering discounts early in the customer life cycle) increases market share by up to 77 percent more than typical promotions, and (2) targeting low-search-cost users (who are more likely to compare platforms) boosts market share by 25 percent relative to high-search-cost users. The key takeaway is that optimizing promotions requires understanding not just pricing but also customer psychology and behavior, especially when it relates to how customers substitute between competing firms. By tailoring incentives to customer types and timing them effectively, platforms can drive sustained market share gains without increasing their marketing budgets.

There are decades of research on the field of dynamic pricing. Various methodologies were developed and tested in real-world applications. The academic world has produced a vast body of related studies across several disciplines, including textbooks and handbooks (e.g., Talluri and Van Ryzin 2004; Rao 2009; Gallego and Topaloglu 2019; Phillips 2021). At a high level, many of the recently developed methods combine demand modeling, statistical analysis, and optimization. While the specific mathematical and statistical foundations behind these methods are beyond the scope of this book, common methods for dynamic pricing include parametric methods, optimization-based approaches, and global gradient-free approaches.

Interestingly, several studies have found that simple, static pricing policies can often beat complex dynamic pricing strategies. For example, Besbes et al. (2020) presented a cutting-edge pricing solution for a highly specialized but critical market: rotable spare parts in the aviation industry. These are high-value components (often costing hundreds of thousands of dollars) that can be repeatedly repaired and reused and thus pose several pricing challenges, such as limited demand data, long product life cycles, uncertain repair times, and fixed inventory pools. Working with a major aircraft manufacturer, the authors developed and implemented a data-driven pricing analytics tool that considers market competition, repair logistics, and inventory constraints. Rather than using dynamic pricing, they found that a static but optimized price could achieve nearly the same profit outcomes and therefore simplify implementation. Through a large-scale controlled experiment involving 1,700 parts, their system increased profits by 3.9 percent over ten months. Just as importantly, it changed the firm's internal practices and sparked broader initiatives in pricing analytics. Thus, the takeaway is clear: even in data-scarce and slow-moving B2B markets, structured pricing strategies supported by smart analytics can drive meaningful financial results, build organizational capabilities, and offer scalable tools to improve decision-making across the value chain.

Several other studies have developed economic models to show that static pricing often outperforms dynamic pricing. Cachon and Feldman (2010) showed that when customers behave strategically (i.e., consider how prices may change in the future when deciding whether to purchase now), static pricing can surpass dynamic pricing. Using an analytical model, the authors showed that strategic consumers prefer the predictability of a static price because it removes the risk of last-minute price increases. In contrast, dynamic pricing may create uncertainty, which will deter some customers from even considering a purchase, especially when they must incur effort or cost (e.g., travel or time) to engage. This reduced engagement can ultimately hurt revenue. The results of this study suggest that when demand is uncertain and customer effort is required, firms should consider committing to transparent, stable pricing rather than pursuing full flexibility.

Nasiry and Popescu (2011) explored how customer memory and behavioral biases affect the effectiveness of dynamic pricing strategies. The authors built a model grounded in psychology where consumers form price expectations based on the lowest and most recent prices they have encountered. Combined with loss aversion (where customers react more strongly to price increases than to discounts), this memory model shows that consumers are highly sensitive to price volatility. Their study showed that when customers anchor on low past prices, dynamic pricing can hurt long-term profits. Instead, the optimal strategy in many scenarios is to maintain stable, constant prices, especially when initial customer expectations are low. In summary, behavioral pricing dynamics can render frequent price changes counterproductive. Maintaining consistent prices, however, can help preserve perceived fairness and long-term profits, particularly in markets with frequent repeat purchases (like food, fashion, music, or apps). This study provides a strong case for favoring everyday low pricing in certain contexts.

Schlereth et al. (2018) explored why many consumers strongly prefer static pricing plans over dynamic ones. This study is set in the context of electricity markets, where dynamic pricing (e.g., real-time pricing) is promoted to balance supply and demand. Using survey and billing data from nearly eight hundred German households and a choice-based modeling technique, the authors investigated what drives consumers' reluctance to adopt time-variant pricing. They found that economic considerations such as price consciousness, perceived effort, and perceived risk have a stronger impact on consumer preferences than price fairness concerns. Specifically, consumers are most likely to adopt simple, predictable "time-of-use" pricing plans and largely reject complex dynamic models like real-time or critical peak pricing, even if those could save them money. The implication is clear: While dynamic pricing may offer operational benefits, success requires managing perceived risk, reducing complexity, and building trust. Static pricing, when well structured, may still be a great customer-friendly and commercially viable option in many contexts.

Finally, Chen and Gallego (2019) tackled a common concern among executives and regulators: Does dynamic pricing hurt consumers and reduce overall social welfare? The authors found that dynamic pricing can increase both firm profits and consumer welfare, especially in industries with limited capacity (like airlines, hotels, or events). The study compared revenue-maximizing dynamic pricing strategies to static pricing and showed that under many common demand conditions, dynamic pricing leads to a win-win: Firms earn more revenue, and consumers benefit from more efficient inventory allocation, which can increase access to the product. The paper debunks the "zero-sum" myth that firms' gains must come at consumers' expense. Thus, the takeaway is twofold: (1) dynamic pricing can potentially be designed to benefit both the firm and the customers, and (2) communicating this alignment clearly to stakeholders can help overcome reputational concerns and build trust in pricing transparency. We further discuss the topic of algorithmic dynamic pricing in chapter 6.

How Can I Beat Dynamic Pricing?

This section is specifically addressed to consumers like you and me. As a pricing expert, I often get asked, "When is the best time to book a flight?" While there's no one-size-fits-all answer, decades of airline pricing data and consumer behavior analysis offer some guidelines. On average, the sweet spot for booking domestic flights is often one to three months in advance, while international flights are typically best booked two to six months ahead. Airlines use sophisticated dynamic pricing algorithms that adjust fares based on demand, historical trends, and even the day of the week. A 2023 study by Hopper found that Tuesday and Wednesday bookings tend to be cheaper than weekend ones, largely because airlines often release fare discounts early in the week and competitors quickly match them.[4] Anecdotally, I recall a friend who monitored prices for a Thanksgiving flight from New York to Los Angeles. She saw it hover around $300 in September, jump to $450 in October, and then shoot past $600 by early November. The reason? Airlines know that demand spikes for traveling during holidays and are likely to raise prices accordingly. Booking too early, however, can also be risky as airlines often hold back cheaper seats until they have a better sense of demand. Another pro tip: set fare alerts and browse in incognito mode to avoid personalized pricing based on your search history. And remember that Tuesdays and Wednesdays may often be cheaper days to fly, too, not just to book. In short, book early, be flexible, and stay alert. The best fares don't always last, but with little planning, you can outsmart the algorithm.

As a pricing expert, I can tell you that avoiding overpaying online, especially in categories like fashion, electronics, and vacation deals, requires a smart mix of timing, tools, and psychological awareness of how dynamic pricing works. Unlike flights, which often follow rigid fare buckets and yield management systems, other categories are more varied but may still use algorithmic pricing that adapts to browsing behavior, demand, stock levels, and competitor pricing. We next discuss seven major categories of products (mainly in the online world).

Let's start with fashion. Retailers like ASOS, Nike, and Zara frequently adjust prices based on seasonal demand and inventory cycles. For example, winter coats are typically most expensive in November when demand peaks, but prices start dropping right after the holidays, such as Boxing Day and end-of-season sales. A friend once paid full price for a $160 jacket in early December, only to find it discounted to $89 by mid-January. Fashion deals tend to improve at the end of each season, so unless you're shopping for a one-off event, waiting would typically pay off. Newsletter sign-ups, loyalty programs, and browser extensions like Honey and Rakuten can also surface hidden coupon codes or price histories. Price personalization is common here, and browsing behavior can sometimes influence future prices shown to you. Another common trick could be to leave items in your cart since several retailers are likely to send discounts via email within twenty-four to forty-eight hours.

With electronics, prices fluctuate wildly due to release cycles and flash sales. These fluctuations can also be based on competitor activity and stock levels. Apple rarely discounts, but stores like Amazon and Best Buy use real-time repricing engines that adjust prices, sometimes multiple times a day. For example, TV prices in North America are often lower in late January and early February, ahead of the Super Bowl, while laptops and tech gear dip around Black Friday and back-to-school sales. These promotions are often used to drive customers to the store with the goal of encouraging additional purchases. One friend I advised tracked a gaming laptop on Amazon for weeks; the price hovered around $1,199 and then dropped to $949 for just six hours. My friend luckily set a price alert via tools like CamelCamelCamel and Keepa and scored the deal before it bounced back. The key here is a combination of patience and timing and not to buy electronics impulsively unless it's a launch product. Quick tips include avoiding buying just before major tech events and shopping around big events like Cyber Monday, Prime Day, or Super Bowl weekend.

For vacation deals, especially package trips and hotel bookings, timing is everything. Booking too early often means paying a premium, while booking too late risks limited availability. A sweet spot is typically six to eight weeks in advance for domestic trips and three to four months for international vacation packages. Also, hotels tend to offer better rates on Sundays, especially for business destinations that empty out on weekends. Be cautious, though, as repeated searches can sometimes trigger price hikes, a practice often called "search-based dynamic pricing." Compare your prices to the ones offered when using incognito mode, clearing cookies, or using a different device or IP address (e.g., via a VPN) to check for better rates. A final suggestion could be to use tools like Hopper, Skyscanner, and Travelzoo for trend-based deal forecasts.

For furniture and home goods, retailers like Home Depot, IKEA, and Wayfair may use demand-driven algorithms and promotional calendars to adjust prices on furniture and appliances. Prices often drop around long weekends (especially Labor Day, Memorial Day, and Presidents' Day in the United States) and seasonal clearance events. A friend I advised saved 30 percent by holding off on a sofa purchase until mid-February. The best strategy? Add items to your cart and wait! You may receive a coupon code via email or see a price drop within a few days. Also, furniture prices tend to dip at the end of each season, as retailers make room for new styles. And of course, always compare prices across platforms.

For groceries and everyday consumables, the story is a bit different. And yes, even online groceries are subject to dynamic pricing. Platforms like Amazon Fresh, Instacart, and Walmart may adjust prices based on local demand, real-time stock levels, and even weather conditions. As mentioned before, subscribing to a recurring order (e.g., Subscribe & Save on Amazon) can often lock in better pricing, and shopping early in the week (Monday–Tuesday) generally tends to yield better prices than weekends.

For event tickets (concerts, sports, theater), dynamic pricing is also widely used. Ticketing platforms like SeatGeek, StubHub, and Ticketmaster potentially use real-time demand and competitor behavior to adjust prices. Such platforms are also known for using surge pricing algorithms based on real-time interest (e.g., news popularity, social media trends). For popular events, prices may start low during presale but spike dramatically once demand builds (e.g., when an artist announces on social media that it's their "final tour"). Ironically, prices often drop again a few days before the event as sellers offload unsold inventory. For less-popular events, waiting may often pay off. The recent emergence of price alert bots on resale platforms can also be informative in timing purchases.

For airline tickets and ride-hailing, there are anecdotal claims that repeatedly checking prices in a short time frame can lead to higher fares. While this behavior has not been formally verified, it may be wise to avoid excessive price checks. For instance, when using a smartphone app to check the fare for a ride, it's often better to make a decision on the first attempt rather than returning multiple times. One argument is that repeated checking signals urgency and strong purchase intent, which platforms may interpret as a higher WTP.

Finally, for digital products and software subscriptions, such as antivirus software, cloud storage, and video editing tools, pricing is often highly personalized and time sensitive. Companies like Adobe, Dropbox, and Microsoft offer discounts based on your browsing history, location, or whether you're a student or a business entity. In many cases, starting a free trial and then canceling just before it ends triggers a retention discount. For example, I once downgraded a productivity app and received a "50% off if you stay" email within forty-eight hours.

In summary, there are several strategies to outsmart dynamic pricing algorithms:

- Use incognito mode or VPNs to avoid personalized price increases.
- Set price alerts and wait for deal notifications.
- Clear cookies or switch devices when revisiting a product.
- Compare carefully across platforms, not just prices but also total value and benefits (warranty, return policy, shipping fees).
- Avoid repeatedly checking prices in a short time frame.

- Be skeptical of urgency and scarcity tactics ("Only 2 left in stock!"), which may aim to trigger impulsive purchases and not be real scarcity events.
- Avoid buying in high-demand windows (holidays, payday weekends, or just before product launches) unless it's a clear promotional event.
- Use price tracking tools like CamelCamelCamel, Honey, Keepa, and Google Shopping price history.

In short, today's online shopping world is powered by algorithms that know more about your behavior than you might expect. Smart buyers treat it like a game: knowing the rules, staying patient, using the right tools, and letting the data do the work. That's how you beat the algorithm and save hundreds of dollars along the way. Later in this book, we discuss the recent emergence of AI-powered shopping assistants that can partially or fully automate the purchasing process, continuously scanning a multitude of websites to identify the best available prices.

Promotions and Markdowns

In various retail settings, the pricing strategy is composed of two components: a base price (also called a regular price or listed price) and promotional levers. The former simply refers to the price under regular conditions. This price doesn't vary often and may be revised only based on macroeconomic factors, such as inflation, supply chain considerations, and competitive strategy. The latter allows businesses to offer temporary discounts to boost sales and clear inventory. In the world of fashion, these are often called markdowns (or clearance discounts), whereas in supermarkets (and many other retail environments), they are called promotions. The key difference is that markdowns are typically successive price reductions over the course of the selling season, whereas promotions are temporary price reductions after which the price goes back to its regular level. As discussed earlier, prices in fashion often follow a high-low trajectory, prices in supermarkets follow a high-low-high trajectory, and in airlines, prices often behave according to a low-high dynamic, as shown in figure 3.3.

Retail promotions—such as discounts, coupons, or buy-one-get-one-free offers—are critical tools used across virtually all retail sectors. The topic of retail promotions has been extensively studied in marketing and

Figure 3.3
Price trajectories in three different industries. *Source:* Author.

management (e.g., Blattberg and Neslin 1990). Supermarkets, drugstores, and online retailers routinely implement hundreds or thousands of promotions:

- To boost short-term sales and store traffic
- To introduce new products and clear old inventory
- To increase customer loyalty and competitive positioning
- To engage in subtle price discrimination (e.g., targeting price-sensitive customers)

Despite their importance, many retailers still rely on manual, intuition-driven processes to decide which items to promote, at what price, and when. The rise of big data and analytics has offered a major opportunity to enhance this decision-making process with systematic, data-driven tools.

Promotions vary in form, and understanding their types is key to optimizing strategy:

- **Manufacturer versus retailer promotions**: Sometimes manufacturers fund promotions (e.g., Coke directly offering discounts or coupons), while other times the retailer alone bears the cost. These arrangements can involve complex negotiations and contractual terms.
- **Markdowns versus temporary discounts**: Markdowns clear inventory at the end of a season (e.g., summer clothes in September), while temporary price discounts are short term and used for all-year-long products like toothpaste or cereal.
- **Mass versus targeted campaigns**: Mass promotions reduce the price for everyone, whereas targeted promotions use data (e.g., loyalty cards, browsing history) to selectively offer discounts.

- **Price cuts versus nonprice incentives:** Price isn't the only lever. Retailers use coupons, in-store signage, displays, and advertising (TV, radio, flyers) as promotional tools. Optimizing the strategic use of nonprice promotional levers is often referred to as promotion vehicles optimization (Baardman et al. 2019).

Retailers face several practical hurdles, including three that are especially common. First, it's important to account for cross-item effects. Indeed, promoting one product (e.g., Coke) can affect demand for others (e.g., Pepsi). These cross-item effects must be considered when planning promotions in a holistic fashion. Second, the post-promotion dip (or cross-time) effect is also important and captures the fact that customers may stockpile during a promotion, reducing future sales (especially for nonperishable items). For example, a detergent promotion could cause a temporary spike in sales, followed by a decline. Third, it's crucial to ensure that all the relevant business rules are satisfied as constraints. More specifically, retail promotions often must adhere to rules, such as fixed price points (e.g., 10 percent off, 20 percent off, prices ending by 9 cents), limits on how often an item can be promoted, time gaps between successive promotions to avoid customer fatigue, and requirements for simultaneous promotions of certain product bundles (e.g., shampoo and conditioner).

A Scientific Framework to Decide Promotions

One of the reasons that deciding promotions is challenging is due to the scale and complexity of the problem. A typical supermarket has tens of thousands of different products, so deciding which products to promote each week while capturing all cross-item effects is a complex challenge. I spent significant time in the last decade helping retailers optimize pricing and promotion decisions (Cohen et al. 2017; Cohen, Kalas, et al. 2021). One strategy we found effective is to use a structured, data-driven approach. The core components include two building blocks: demand modeling and optimization.

Demand Modeling

Each product's demand is modeled as a mathematical function of its own current price (to capture price elasticity), its own past prices (to capture post-promotion effects), potentially the prices of certain other products in the same category (to capture cross-item effects), seasonal factors, holidays, and store-specific effects. It's naturally possible to add several other factors as features in the model (e.g., marketing activities, product location, product features). The goal is to build accurate, predictive demand models using historical sales data. Tools like regression, time-series models, and machine learning can be applied. For more details on the topic of demand prediction, see Cohen, Gras, et al. 2022. As we will discuss in chapter 7, recent attempts were made to automate this step by using GenAI.

Optimization

Once demand is modeled and can be accurately predicted, the next step is to find the prices that maximize profit (or any other desired KPI), subject to the relevant business constraints. More specifically, one needs to decide (1) which products to promote, (2) the appropriate discount level, and (3) the timing of the promotions. Because this type of problem is highly complex, exact solutions are often infeasible. Instead, it's common to solve the optimization problem via efficient approximation methods that can produce solutions in seconds, even for thousands of products across dozens of stores. This step is more technical and requires scientific expertise.

While decomposing this approach into two building blocks (modeling demand and optimization) is a common (and often successful) approach, several studies have challenged this practice by aiming to smartly intertwine both steps (e.g., Elmachtoub and Grigas 2022).

Based on my experience working on this problem with several retailers, a concrete recommendation could be to follow a high-level five-step process:

Step 1: Data collection

Gather point-of-sale data, including prices, units sold, promotional vehicles used, product attributes, and store features. Clean and aggregate the data at the right level (e.g., weekly sales per store).

Step 2: Clustering

Group similar products or stores to increase prediction accuracy and reduce complexity. For example, combine sales data from geographically close stores or similar product variants.

Step 3: Demand estimation

Use historical data to build predictive models that estimate how sales respond to prices and promotions. Models can leverage several data sources and include various modeling features to capture consumer behavior (e.g., cannibalization). Validate models through out-of-sample prediction accuracy measures.

Step 4: Optimization (and sensitivity analysis)

Apply the optimization model to determine the best promotion schedule. Run "what-if" scenarios to test the plan's robustness under different assumptions (e.g., cost changes, demand variability).

Step 5: Impact assessment

Compare the optimized promotion strategy to historical practices. In tested cases, we found improved retailer profits by 2–7 percent, which is a significant boost given retailers' thin margins.

In addition to boosting profits, using this analytics framework has helped uncover various key strategic insights, including the following:

- **Cross-item strategy**: Avoid promoting highly substitutable products simultaneously. Instead, schedule them in alternating weeks to reduce cannibalization.
- **Post-promotion dip management**: Avoid frequent promotions on the same product. Instead, space them out to reduce fatigue and stockpiling effects.
- **Loss leader identification**: Use data to detect products that, when discounted, drive profits via complementary product sales.
- **Vendor negotiation**: Quantify the value of vendor-funded promotions and assess whether exclusivity clauses or simultaneous promotions make sense financially.
- **Business rule trade-offs**: Explore the cost of business rules (e.g., limited promotions per period, not allowing concurrent promotions). Relaxing some rules may yield significant profit gains.

Ultimately, promotion decisions often seem simple but are deceptively complex. Relying on gut feelings or past habits can leave substantial money on the table. By leveraging data analytics and modern AI methods, one can intelligently combine historical data, predictive modeling, and advanced optimization to decide promotions via a more scientific approach. For managers, this translates into a better return on promotional investment, reduced inventory waste and improved planning, and a competitive advantage in an increasingly data-driven retail landscape.

Personalized and Innovative Promotions

While many promotions are optimized at the aggregate level and will be offered to all customers, the presence of big data has allowed retailers to design personalized promotions that can be different for different customers. In fact, the practice of personalized promotions and coupons has rapidly become one of the most dynamic and creative areas of modern pricing, with companies across industries using data-driven insights to tailor offers that feel relevant, timely, and often surprisingly personal. Unlike traditional, broad-based discounting, personalized promotions are targeted to individual customers or microsegments based on their behaviors, preferences, purchase history, and contextual signals. For example, retailers like Sephora use loyalty program data to send birthday or anniversary discounts, customized based on a customer's favorite product categories. Starbucks has become a benchmark case, offering hyperpersonalized rewards via its mobile app, such as bonus stars for visiting at a specific time, trying a new drink, or returning after a period of inactivity. These offers are often generated algorithmically, using behavioral clustering and predictive analytics to determine not only who should receive a promotion but also what kind, when, and through which channel (e.g., app, email, or in-store). In the grocery space, Kroger has used its rich shopper card data to deliver personalized coupons based on purchase frequency, basket composition, and even dietary preferences.

The innovation doesn't stop at just "you bought this, so we'll discount that." Companies are now experimenting with context-based and emotion-triggered promotions. For instance, Nike has sent customers discount codes on the anniversary of their first online purchase or after completing a fitness milestone in the Nike Run Club app, thus blending loyalty, health data, and emotional engagement. Several other companies have used anniversary promotions, especially on online platforms and e-commerce. Figure 3.4 shows two examples of such anniversary-driven promotions: Wayfair has offered a 10 percent promotion on the next order, and the email promotion from Lyft provides a badge (nonmonetary incentive) aimed at activating via some sort of gamification, namely, by rewarding users with symbolic achievements similar to those found in games.

More generally, companies constantly strive to be creative in the way they design new promotions. For example, they aim to leverage specific

Figure 3.4
Examples of anniversary promotions. *Source:* Author's email for both.

contexts and events (e.g., birthdays, national holidays) and feelings (e.g., empathy, charity). It has also become common to leverage gamification combined with promotions. The key is to leverage available data about customers in innovative and appealing ways.

The world of promotions has evolved dramatically in recent years, moving far beyond simple percentage discounts and coupon codes. Thanks to advances in data analytics, mobile technologies, and AI, retailers and service providers are now offering highly creative, socially engaging, and emotionally resonant promotions designed to drive not only sales but also brand loyalty, community engagement, and sometimes even social impact. For example, several scooter and bike-sharing companies such as Bird, Lime, and Voi have experimented with repositioning-based promotions, offering

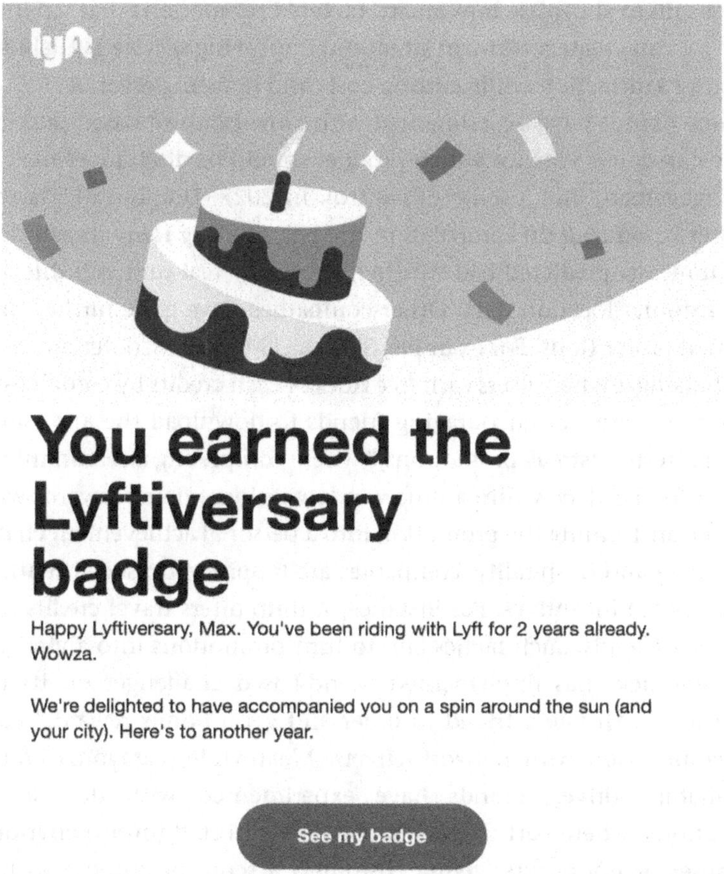

Figure 3.4
(continued)

ride discounts to users who help rebalance fleets by parking scooters in designated "hot zones." This strategy not only reduces operational costs but also turns users into micro-collaborators in the supply chain.

In this context, several studies have investigated how electric scooter- or bike-sharing platforms can use repositioning-based promotions to tackle a key operational problem: scooters (or bikes) being parked in inconvenient or low-demand areas, which leads to long idle times and lost revenue. For example, platforms have tested a promotional strategy where users could ride for free if they parked the scooter in specific designated locations. Such studies aim to showcase how smart, targeted promotions that tap into user behavior can create a win-win situation: improving service availability and customer satisfaction while cutting costs and boosting revenue.

Some brands have experimented with crowdsourced-based promotions, where customers vote for which product should be discounted next, creating engagement and a sense of control. In 2022, Domino's Pizza tested a weather-based coupon campaign in the UK, offering rainy day deals when local forecasts predicted bad weather, driven by real-time API integrations and customer location data. Other companies have gone further, creating gamified promotions. For example, Spin, a US-based e-scooter operator, has run challenges where users earn free rides or cash credits by completing eco-friendly activities or encouraging friends to download the app. Similarly, Uber has tested "streak promotions," where completing a certain number of rides or food orders within a time window unlocks tiered rewards with the goal of transforming the promotion into a personal achievement challenge.

In retail and hospitality, companies are tapping into social sharing and referral-based incentives. For instance, Airbnb offers travel credits to users who refer friends. Such tactics aim to turn promotions into a viral growth tool. Starbucks has implemented friend-based challenges on its mobile app, such as "Invite a friend to order and get a bonus reward," combining gamification with network effects. Meanwhile, Patagonia and other sustainability-driven brands have experimented with donation-based promotions, where part of the discount is redirected toward environmental causes or nonprofits, giving customers a sense of purpose with every purchase. These values-aligned promotions help reinforce brand identity and drive customer retention. Some companies have added an element of chance, such as lottery-style promotions. For example, the Dutch company Picnic, an online grocer, entered customers into a weekly lottery for free groceries, turning the promotion into a recurring engagement hook.

The advantages of these modern promotional strategies are significant: They foster deeper emotional connections, leverage network effects, and often require less financial outlay than traditional discounts. They also allow companies to segment offers more precisely using AI-driven insights by targeting specific behaviors, preferences, or even values. However, there are downsides. Creative promotions must be clearly communicated to avoid confusion, and they can backfire by seeming invasive if they rely too heavily on user participation or data collection. Moreover, regulatory compliance and ethical considerations are essential, especially when personal data is involved in gamified or crowdsourced schemes. Still, for business executives looking to differentiate their brand and enhance customer engagement, these innovative, data-driven promotions represent a powerful shift in how value is created and shared in the customer journey. Companies that embrace this evolution by aligning promotions with personalization, purpose, and play are well positioned to win the hearts and wallets of modern consumers.

In Cohen, Fiszer, et al. 2022, we collaborated with the ride-hailing platform Via to explore how companies should respond when customers experience a poor service experience, which we call a "frustration," such as long waiting times or unexpectedly long rides. We designed and executed three field experiments involving thousands of riders across major US cities to test whether proactively offering compensation (proactive in the sense that customers did not complain about the poor quality of service) could restore engagement and increase future usage. We tested various compensation strategies, including doing nothing, sending an apology without a monetary compensation (which I like to call a "cheap apology"), waiving the fare (i.e., reimbursing the charges), offering credit for a future ride, and providing a discount. The findings were clear and actionable: Offering a small credit (e.g., $5) significantly increased customer engagement and spending, outperforming both apologies and refunds. This strategy proved especially effective for frequent users and in cases of long wait times.

The key takeaway is that proactive, data-driven targeted compensation, especially in the form of future-use credits, is a cost-effective strategy to turn service failures into customer loyalty opportunities, particularly in competitive, high-frequency service industries like ride-hailing, food delivery, or e-commerce. Similarly, airlines like Delta and United have started offering frustrated travelers special upgrade offers or lounge access proactively after delays or cancellations, turning a negative experience into a recovery moment, a practice called frustration-based promotion.

The advantages of these strategies are significant: Personalized promotions tend to drive higher conversion rates, deeper loyalty, and better margin control since discounts are given only when necessary to trigger a purchase. However, the approach isn't without drawbacks. If not executed transparently, these promotions can feel manipulative or discriminatory, especially if customers learn that others received better deals for the same product.

Overpersonalization can also backfire if customers feel surveilled or if promotions rely on sensitive personal data (e.g., inferring that someone may be pregnant or going through financial hardship). There's also a fairness challenge: Long-time loyal customers may become resentful if new or inactive customers are consistently offered better incentives. The takeaway is clear: Personalized promotions are powerful but must be grounded in empathy, ethics, and transparency. When done well, they shift the focus from "cutting price" to "creating relevance," thus a far more sustainable strategy for both customer satisfaction and long-term profitability. We will revisit the potential concerns in terms of ethics, privacy, and fairness in chapter 8.

An alternative creative and increasingly relevant pricing strategy for businesses is selling "opaque products." These are items where a specific product feature, such as color, brand, or destination, is hidden from the customer until after purchase. Common in e-commerce and travel (e.g., Amazon's "color may vary" items or Eurowings' mystery destinations), opaque products let firms offer price discounts while maintaining control over inventory and customer segmentation. Elmachtoub and Hamilton (2021) studied this topic and strived to answer whether opaque selling can outperform traditional pricing approaches, such as charging a single price for all variants or using differentiated pricing for each version. The authors showed that opaque selling can yield significantly higher revenue, especially in markets where consumers either distrust the seller or perceive some variants as undesirable. Remarkably, even a single opaque product option can achieve over 70 percent of the revenue of full-fledged differentiated pricing.

The authors also designed practical algorithms and showed that firms can implement this strategy effectively, even with limited knowledge about customer preferences. The key insight is that opaque products offer a smart, customer-friendly, and often legally safer alternative to traditional price discrimination, especially when customers value different product attributes differently and where explicit segmentation could trigger fairness or regulatory concerns. Adopting opaque selling can improve profitability, smooth inventory imbalances, and enhance perceived fairness.

Markdowns

Markdown optimization has become a critical and strategic component of pricing in the fashion industry, especially as brands face increasing pressure to clear seasonal inventory quickly while preserving margins. Traditionally, markdown decisions for fashion items—namely, when to reduce prices, for which products, in which stores, and by how much—were largely intuitive, made by merchandisers and store managers based on intuition, experience, and anecdotal trends. A well-known intuition-based approach is the "run-out rate heuristic," which seeks to deplete inventory exactly by the final week (or day) of the season. The goal is to implement the (ideal) markdown strategy that avoids both stockouts during the season and excess inventory at the end of the season. Indeed, running out of stock midseason is clearly suboptimal, as it suggests that markdowns were too steep and margins could have been higher. Conversely, ending the season with unsold inventory is also undesirable, as those units will likely need to be salvaged at a low price.

But today, leading fashion retailers rely on advanced data analytics, machine learning, optimization software, and even AI agents to automate and constantly refine this process, transforming markdown planning into a data-driven science. These tools analyze vast volumes of data (e.g., sales velocity, inventory levels, style popularity, color preferences, weather patterns, regional differences, online browsing behavior) to determine the optimal timing and depth of markdowns for each product, often at the SKU and store level, allowing retailers to strategically clear inventories while boosting revenue.

Companies like Zara have been pioneers in data-driven inventory and pricing strategies, using real-time sales feedback and store-level demand to optimize markdown decisions that minimize unsold inventory without prematurely sacrificing profits (Caro and Gallien 2012). Aldo Group, a global footwear brand, implemented advanced markdown optimization software to better manage end-of-season clearance and leftover inventory. By integrating machine learning models, Aldo strived to increase sell-through rates and reduce unnecessary deep discounts to preserve profit margins. Other retailers, such as H&M, Macy's, and Nordstrom, have adopted similar tools that allow for dynamic markdown planning, where prices can be automatically adjusted based on updated demand forecasts and competitive pressures. In one notable case, a US department store chain reported that its AI-guided markdown system led to a double-digit percentage improvement in gross margin during end-of-season sales, simply by optimizing when to apply the first markdown and by how much to discount different products.

The advantages of this shift are significant. Retailers can now react faster to slow-moving inventory, personalize markdowns by store or region, and mitigate both stockouts and overdiscounting. The automation reduces human error, ensures consistency across locations, and frees merchandising teams to focus on strategic planning. However, the approach isn't without challenges. These systems rely heavily on accurate and timely data, and if forecasts are off, or if unexpected events like a pandemic or a supply chain disruption occur, then the recommendations can be seriously off. There's also a brand perception risk: Frequent or aggressive markdowns can condition customers to wait for sales, potentially weakening the perceived value of premium products. Still, the message is clear: In a world of short product life cycles, fast fashion, and fickle trends, markdown optimization is no longer a tactical afterthought. Instead, it became a strategic lever that can make or break seasonal performance. Retailers who invest in intelligent data-driven, reactive markdown systems aren't just clearing racks more efficiently; they're protecting their margins, strengthening their brand, and staying ahead in a competitive marketplace.

While markdown optimization offers powerful tools to enhance profits and inventory efficiency, it also raises important questions about the broader impact of fast fashion, particularly when it comes to environmental sustainability. The rise of data-driven pricing and rapid markdown cycles has helped fast fashion brands like H&M, Shein, and Zara move products quickly, minimize waste, and adapt swiftly to shifting consumer preferences. But this agility has potentially come at a cost: overproduction and overconsumption. The same systems that optimize inventory clearance and drive down prices can also incentivize disposable shopping habits, where garments are purchased cheaply, worn briefly, and discarded quickly, often ending up in landfills. According to the Ellen MacArthur Foundation, the average person today buys 60 percent more clothing than they did fifteen years ago but keeps each item for half as long.[5] This overconsumption is unfortunately straining natural resources, increasing carbon emissions, and creating massive textile waste.

As businesses embrace technology to enhance pricing and inventory decisions, there's an emerging responsibility to balance commercial performance with environmental impact. Some retailers are starting to respond. For example, H&M has introduced AI-driven markdowns alongside sustainability efforts like in-store garment recycling and its "Conscious" clothing line.[6] Zalando, the European online retailer, has pledged to generate 25 percent of its gross merchandise volume from more sustainable products by 2023, using data to improve sourcing and end-of-season sell-through.[7] These efforts signal a growing awareness that while markdown and merchandizing optimization is essential for operational success, it should also be aligned with more responsible production cycles and longer-term value. The future of fashion pricing may hinge not just on how efficiently products are marked down but also on how intelligently companies can integrate sustainability goals into their pricing and merchandising strategies. In doing so, brands can align economic value with environmental priorities to win over both price-conscious and purpose-driven consumers.

B2B Pricing

So far, our focus has been on B2C pricing. Let's now discuss B2B pricing. Pricing B2B products, especially dematerialized offerings such as SaaS, data platforms, and APIs, differs significantly from B2C pricing. In B2B, pricing is typically less dynamic than in consumer-facing industries like airlines or retail, where real-time price changes are common. This is because businesses require greater predictability and stability to plan budgets and justify procurement decisions. However, B2B pricing requires deeper strategic thinking on how to monetize value, not just how much to charge. Companies must decide how to package, meter, and scale their pricing models to align with customer needs and expectations. At its core, successful B2B pricing must balance four pillars:

1. Simplicity: Easy to understand and sell, enabling deal velocity
2. Scalability: Works from start-ups to large enterprises
3. Flexibility: Allows for practical adjustments as needed (to accommodate diverse customers and evolving needs)
4. Accuracy: Supports growth and margin targets

Simplicity in B2B pricing isn't a weakness. Rather, it's often a key competitive advantage. Pricing models succeed when they are intuitive for buyers and sellers alike. For instance, Slack and Zoom scaled rapidly in part because of transparent per-user pricing models that made costs predictable as organizations expanded. In contrast, pricing models tied to less predictable metrics (e.g., charging for CPU usage in marketing software) often fail because they are misaligned with customer value drivers (e.g., monthly active users or campaign volume for marketing software).

Best practices include defining a primary usage meter (e.g., per user, per API call) with minimal secondary restrictions and offering clear "good–better–best" packaging. Companies like Atlassian, HubSpot, and Salesforce have successfully used such tiered structures, where each level adds distinct features while preserving clarity and upsell opportunities.

B2B markets span orders of magnitude in scale: One client may require thousands of API calls per month, while another may need billions. To handle this, firms often rely on volume discounting strategies such as

- volume pricing (discount applied to all units after a certain threshold),
- tiered pricing (discount applies only to incremental units),
- block pricing (flat fee within a usage band), and
- rolling discounts (future rates drop based on past purchases).

Without automation, managing these schemes is complex and prone to errors. Firms like Amazon Web Services and Snowflake use sophisticated "price curves" that dynamically adjust based on consumption. This approach provides scalability and precision while allowing quick adjustments to discount strategies.

Another dimension is customer segmentation. Enterprise software vendors often tailor pricing to verticals (e.g., healthcare vs. retail) or regions, sometimes with discretionary adjustments during negotiations. Historically, such flexibility has been hard to manage without introducing substantial complexity; today, AI-enabled pricing platforms (e.g., PROS, Vendavo, Zilliant) help orchestrate rules and monitor consistency across deals.

While airlines and retailers have long invested in advanced pricing analytics, many B2B firms still rely heavily on manual processes within CPQ (Configure-Price-Quote) and Q2C (Quote-to-Cash) systems. Dedicated pricing optimization layers are often missing, making list price and discretionary adjustments slow and costly. Machine learning has already improved B2B pricing through segmentation and elasticity estimation, but it requires skilled teams and can suffer from "black box" opacity. GenAI tools now have the potential to transform the field by (1) proposing entirely new pricing rules (not just fine-tuning parameters); (2) simulating customer reactions across different markets and segments; and (3) explaining recommendations in natural language, making them digestible for executives and sales teams. For example, several companies are experimenting with AI-driven scenario modeling to design tailored pricing offers, whereas others are embedding AI copilots in their pricing and quoting workflows to streamline sales conversations. Recent innovations allow companies to adopt flexible, AI-powered usage-based pricing approaches to experiment with models like per-seat, per-transaction, or hybrid structures.

B2B pricing decisions have outsized financial impact. Unlike consumer markets where millions of small transactions diffuse the effect, a single enterprise contract in B2B can be worth millions or lost entirely due to misaligned pricing. Research from McKinsey shows that even a 1 percent improvement in B2B pricing can potentially boost operating profits by 8 percent.[8] In competitive industries such as cloud services, cybersecurity, and enterprise SaaS, getting the right pricing strategy is often as critical as product innovation. In the age of AI, B2B firms that master pricing simplicity, scalability, flexibility, and accuracy, while harnessing AI to generate and test new models, will likely hold a clear competitive advantage.

4 Behavioral and Psychological Pricing

> Outcomes are coded as gains or losses relative to a reference point.
> —Daniel Kahneman and Amos Tversky

This chapter examines how retailers employ psychological pricing tactics to influence consumers and how these methods have evolved in recent years. In other words, it explores the interplay between consumer behavior and pricing strategies in the age of AI and algorithms.

Introduction

Behavioral pricing is a strategy that draws on insights from psychology and behavioral economics to account for how consumers perceive and respond to prices not just in terms of objective cost but also through the lens of psychology. It recognizes that consumer decisions are influenced by emotional reactions, social cues, and mental shortcuts, which can cause them to respond to prices in ways that deviate from traditional assumptions of stable, context-independent preferences. In this view, price plays a broader role not just as a cost to be weighed against benefits but also as a signal, a reference point, or even a source of emotional response. For example, a company might offer a product at a seemingly low price but then add extra fees at checkout to increase the final price. This strategy, often referred to as drip pricing, leverages consumers' tendency to focus on the initial low price and overlook the additional charges. Behavioral pricing is often used in e-commerce, where companies have access to vast amounts of data on consumer behavior and can experiment with different pricing strategies to find the most effective ones.

Psychological pricing is a strategy that leverages psychological principles to influence consumer behavior and increase sales and profits. It's based on the idea that consumers can be influenced by subtle psychological cues in the pricing of a product. As mentioned, a common tactic is to set prices just below a round number, such as $9.99 instead of $10.00. This is known as "charm pricing" and is designed to make the price appear more affordable to consumers. Another tactic is to use "prestige pricing," where a product is priced higher than its competitors to create the perception of higher quality and exclusivity. Psychological pricing can also involve creating pricing tiers that encourage customers to buy in bulk or upgrade to a more expensive option, and hence it can sometimes be combined with price differentiation. By understanding how consumers think and make decisions, businesses can use psychological pricing to boost profits.

As discussed, the past decade has led to a fundamental transformation in pricing practices, fueled by advances in machine learning and AI. While behavioral and psychological pricing tactics predate the AI era, recent AI advances allow such tactics to be taken to the next level and at a larger and faster scale. Firms are increasingly capable of implementing dynamic, real-time pricing strategies tailored to individual customers based on detailed behavioral data, contextual information, and competitive signals. From algorithmic surge pricing in ride-hailing services to personalized promotions on e-commerce platforms, AI is redefining how prices are set, adjusted, and perceived.

Traditional economic theory often models price as a straightforward variable that consumers respond to in predictable ways. However, extensive research over the past decades has revealed a more nuanced reality. Scholars have shown that consumer responses to price can be heavily influenced by how prices are framed or presented, suggesting that psychological and contextual factors play an important role in shaping behavior. This insight gave rise to the field of behavioral pricing (e.g., Liu and Soman 2018), which examines how firms design pricing tactics and how consumers perceive and respond. Research in consumer behavior has further illuminated a wide range of cognitive, emotional, social, cultural, and even biological mechanisms that shape consumer price perceptions and reactions. These behavioral responses, in turn, have profound implications for firm profitability, branding, consumer welfare, and public policy aimed at protecting consumers. Table 4.1 summarizes the differences between traditional and behavioral pricing approaches, especially in the age of AI.

Table 4.1
Traditional versus behavioral pricing in the age of AI

Aspect	Traditional pricing	Behavioral pricing with AI
Consumer perspective	Consumer with stable preferences and consistent trade-offs	Behaviorally driven decision-maker
Role of price	Objective signal of value and cost	Subjective perception influenced by context and framing
Pricing objective	Profit maximization with limited consideration for psychological and social factors	Profit maximization with long-term trust and fairness considerations
Pricing mechanism	Static or periodically updated, homogeneous	Dynamic, in real time, and personalized
Data inputs	Historical sales, market averages	Behavioral patterns, emotional responses, social signals
Misalignment risk	Underpricing or overpricing relative to value	Erosion of trust, perceived unfairness, exploitation concerns

While traditional economic models often assume that individuals respond to prices consistently and predictably based on stable preferences, behavioral pricing acknowledges that real-world decision-making is also shaped by cognitive biases, emotional responses, and heuristic shortcuts. Prices aren't simply numbers; they are perceived and interpreted through the lens of personal experience, social context, and internal narratives.

Behavioral pricing draws from decades of research in economics, psychology, and decision theory. For a more comprehensive discussion on behavioral retail tactics, see Bandi et al. 2024. We next explore common behavioral pricing tactics and how AI can be leveraged in this context.

Common Behavioral Pricing Tactics

Behavioral pricing starts with the understanding of how consumers psychologically interpret prices. Executing these insights at scale, across regions, segments, products, and even moments, used to be logistically impossible. This is where AI becomes transformative. AI enables firms to move from intuition-driven behavioral tactics to data-driven, continuously learning pricing systems that can personalize and optimize contextual differences in real time and at a large scale.

Whereas traditional pricing tactics relied on fixed heuristics and static promotions, AI now allows for a dynamic and adaptive implementation of behavioral pricing. Machine learning algorithms process vast streams of behavioral signals such as clickstream data, purchase frequency, dwell time, and in-store interactions to not only detect pricing sensitivities but also constantly experiment and learn. Tools like contextual bandits, reinforcement learning (RL), and sentiment analysis now make it possible to automate, evaluate, and constantly refine behavioral pricing tactics far beyond what humans can do.

We next highlight several widely used pricing tactics that shape customer decisions. Backed by research and commonly applied across industries, these approaches are increasingly refined and customized through continuous experimentation.

Reference Price and Anchoring

Human judgments about price are rarely made in isolation. Instead, consumers evaluate prices relative to reference points, which may be explicit (e.g., a previous discounted price) or internalized (e.g., a belief about what something "should" cost). This phenomenon, known as reference dependence, implies that a price is only "good" or "bad" relative to some mental anchor (Kalyanaram and Winer 1995). In short, a reference price is the mental benchmark that consumers use to judge a new price. Retailers can establish this anchor using original prices, strike-through discounts, or competitor comparisons. For example, a tag stating "Was $100, Now $70" not only signals a discount but also creates a value perception. The presence of a salient reference point fundamentally shifts the perceived value. This isn't about deception; it's about perception. Even arbitrary anchors can influence judgments, a well-documented psychological effect.

Retailers often use tiered price labels to highlight savings. Brands have long leveraged reference pricing. E-commerce platforms frequently implement dynamic pricing strategies that include crossed-out prices derived from historical averages or third-party benchmarks. These visual cues are designed to emphasize perceived savings and influence consumer perception. Research has increasingly focused on personalizing these displays by learning from consumer context, including prior searches, purchase history, and product characteristics (Shah et al. 2019). Figure 4.1 illustrates a common retail strategy where an original anchor price of $999.99 is presented, followed by a $200 discount. This example effectively demonstrates how retailers often blend multiple behavioral pricing tactics: in this case, combining a reference price with charm pricing to influence consumer perception and decision-making.

In restaurant pricing, a well-known behavioral pattern is that many consumers tend to select the second-cheapest wine on the menu. Psychologically, diners want to avoid appearing cheap by ordering the lowest-priced option, yet they remain price sensitive and hesitant to splurge. This leads them to choose what feels like a socially acceptable compromise: the second least expensive bottle. From a behavioral economics perspective, this is a classic example of relativity and anchoring. Customers often lack deep knowledge of wine, so they use price as a proxy for quality, anchoring their decision on the lowest price and trading one level to maintain face while managing cost. Savvy restaurateurs may thus be tempted to exploit this behavior by ensuring that the wine in this second-cheapest slot has the highest margin. This tactic highlights how consumer choices are shaped

Figure 4.1
Example of reference pricing combined with charm pricing.

not purely by intrinsic preferences but by perceived social norms and contextual cues embedded in the pricing structure.

Another increasingly popular strategy involves the use of automated A/B testing, a topic we will discuss in the next chapter. This method is applied to optimize reference pricing by experimenting with various anchoring formats across customer segments. Over time, firms can learn which presentation styles, such as percentage discounts or strike-through pricing, result in higher conversion rates and better customer engagement (Shah et al. 2019).

Decoy Effect

The decoy effect is a common pricing tactic in which an additional, asymmetrically dominated option is introduced solely to influence consumer choice. This option isn't intended to be selected but rather to make one of the existing alternatives appear more attractive by comparison. This strategy exploits a cognitive bias that is frequently used to guide consumers toward higher-margin products.

A classic example comes from *The Economist*'s subscription pricing where customers were offered online access for $59, a print-only subscription for $125, or a combined print and online option also priced at $125. As shown in figure 4.2, the print-only option serves as a decoy, making the combined package appear to offer significantly better value by comparison. Although the decoy was rarely chosen, its presence dramatically increased the selection of the higher-value bundle (Ariely 2008).

This mechanism also functions as a form of reference pricing, where the decoy option sets a comparison point that enhances the perceived value of the target offer. However, recent findings suggest that the effect can vary depending on personalization. Mousavi et al. (2023) found that introducing a decoy decreases demand for the target product when personalized recommendations are used, a reversal of the conventional decoy effect. In contrast, under nonpersonalized conditions, the decoy tends to increase demand, consistent with the classic pattern.

Drip Pricing and Junk Fees

Drip pricing refers to the practice where a company advertises a low initial price but reveals additional fees progressively throughout the purchasing process, often at checkout. These extra charges, sometimes called junk fees (or hidden fees), can include service fees, resort fees, administrative

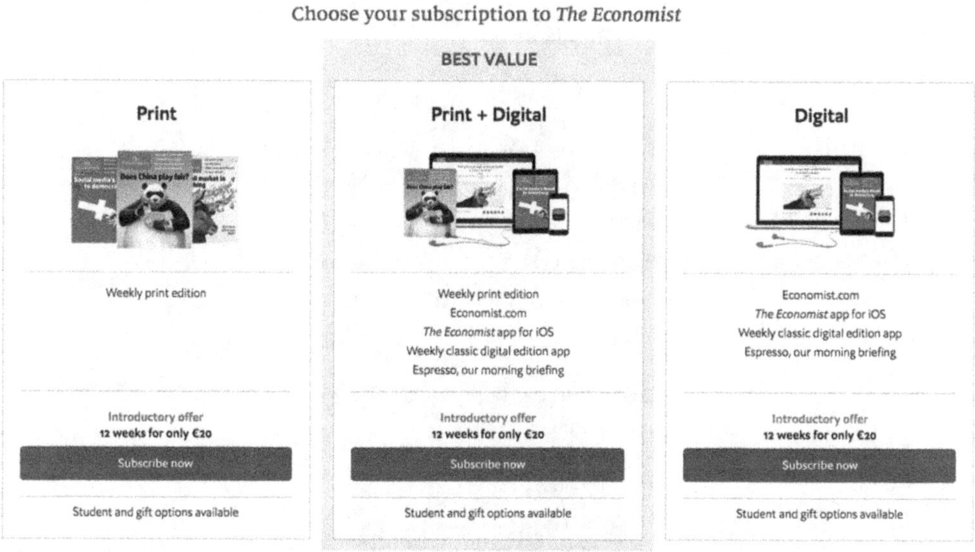

Figure 4.2
Example of the decoy effect. *Source:* Ariely 2008.

surcharges, or processing costs that were potentially not clearly and explicitly disclosed upfront. This is in contrast to displaying a clear, upfront, all-inclusive price. More precisely, all-inclusive pricing consists of presenting a single, comprehensive price that includes all mandatory fees and charges from the outset, allowing consumers to immediately assess the full cost of a product or service, hence potentially facilitating more accurate comparisons across sellers. For example, in some food and grocery delivery apps, an order that initially appears to cost $48.68 can end up totaling nearly $70 after additional fees, such as service, delivery, and order charges, are revealed at checkout, as illustrated in figure 4.3. Similarly, vacation or short-term rentals often display a low nightly rate, but the final price surges after disclosing cleaning, service, and occupancy fees late in the booking process.

The drip pricing tactic leverages framing effects, often leading consumers to underestimate the final price or commit to a purchase before fully evaluating the total expense. A related phenomenon is partitioned pricing, in which a seller decomposes the total price of a product or service into multiple components, such as a base price plus shipping, handling, or service fees (Morwitz et al. 1998). Unlike drip pricing, these components may be

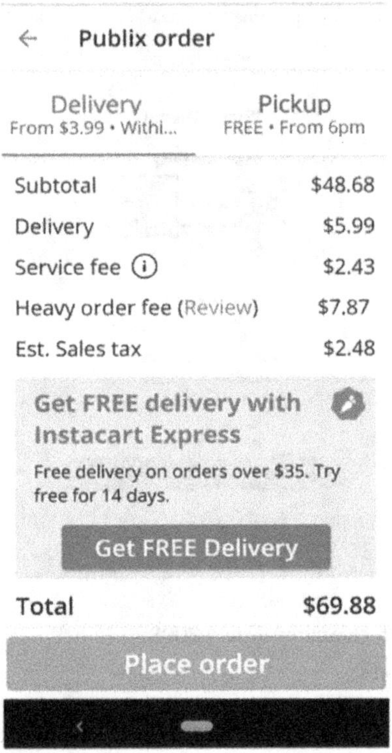

Figure 4.3
Example of junk fees in a delivery app.

disclosed simultaneously. However, the act of partitioning can still sometimes shift consumers' attention disproportionately toward the base price, potentially making the full cost less salient at the time of evaluation and comparison. Studies show that drip pricing, and other related tactics such as partitioned pricing, can sometimes increase purchase rates and profitability, particularly in competitive digital markets such as travel booking, ticket sales, and e-commerce (Greenleaf et al. 2016; Santana et al. 2020). Gümüş et al. (2013) compared two online pricing strategies: partitioned pricing (low product price plus separate shipping fee) and non-partitioned pricing with free shipping. The authors found that retailers choosing a partitioned pricing strategy often had a lower product price, but it tended to result in a higher total price.

While such practices may increase conversion (the likelihood that a consumer completes the purchase) in some contexts by attracting customers with a lower headline price, they may often result in consumer frustration and loss of trust. However, in some contexts and specific situations, firms may still find drip pricing profitable in the short term, especially in low-frequency or one-time purchase markets where reputational consequences are limited. As such, regulators in several jurisdictions are cracking down on hidden fees to promote transparency and fair competition. For instance, drip pricing is explicitly banned in Canada under the Competition Act (apart from government-imposed taxes). Similarly, a 2019 policy change in the EU requires cleaning and service fees to be shown upfront in search results. Nevertheless, determining whether a pricing practice constitutes drip pricing or partitioned pricing is not always straightforward, and understanding its impact on consumers is often even more nuanced and context dependent, requiring careful analysis. Tran et al. (2024) examined the 2019 EU policy change in the context of Airbnb, focusing on its impact on cleaning fees. Transparency reduced cleaning fees slightly (by 2–4 percent) but led some hosts, especially those appearing cheaper under the new rules, to raise nightly rates by 5–6 percent. The authors concluded that transparency shifted pricing strategies in ways that may increase total costs for consumers.

As another example, in 2023, US President Biden spoke about "junk fees" in his State of the Union address, stating, "Junk fees may not matter to the very wealthy, but they matter to most folks in homes like the one I grew up in. They add up to hundreds of dollars a month. I know how unfair it feels when a company overcharges you and gets away with it." He proposed a junk fee prevention act to reduce inconvenient "convenience" fees. Finally, California's SB 478 (Honest Pricing Law), effective July 1, 2024, bans junk fees by requiring businesses to advertise the full, all-in price of goods and services up front. Mandatory add-on charges must be included in the displayed price, with limited exceptions for taxes and shipping. The law applies broadly across industries, from travel and hospitality to online platforms, though restaurants and some sectors have carve-outs. In closing, businesses should be cautious: While strategies like drip pricing can sometimes boost short-term revenues, it may harm long-term brand equity and invite legal scrutiny. We will revisit this topic in the context of regulations such as the Federal Trade Commission (FTC) Junk Fee Act in chapter 9.

Framing Effects

Framing refers to how information is presented and structured. In the context of pricing, framing can significantly impact how consumers interpret value. This sensitivity to presentation opens the door to a wide range of pricing tactics. Whether in physical stores or digital interfaces, firms may use various framing techniques to increase perceived affordability, nudge purchase behavior, and reduce the psychological friction associated with spending.

A common framing technique involves spreading a price over time, known as temporal price framing. Instead of presenting a product as a single lump sum, firms often express prices in smaller daily or monthly installments. For instance, a yearly gym membership of $365 might be described as "just $1 a day," shifting attention from the total cost to a smaller, recurring amount. This approach makes the purchase feel more accessible and easier to justify.

In a related spirit, "buy now, pay later" (BNPL) is a modern application of framing that focuses not on the price itself but on how and when it's paid. Instead of presenting the full price at the time of purchase, retailers offer payment plans such as "$50 per month for four months" in place of a single $200 payment. This strategy changes the psychological experience of the transaction and the emotional experience of spending, making purchases feel more manageable even when they may not be. This subtle reframing has become a powerful tool for retailers, which increasingly partner with fintech companies like Affirm, Afterpay, and Klarna to offer BNPL solutions at checkout. These programs have proven effective for discretionary and midrange products that may otherwise trigger hesitation. Figure 4.4 shows an example of BNPL being offered in a relatively low-transaction scenario.

But behind ease and convenience lies a potential concern. Klarna, one of the largest BNPL providers, reported a 17 percent increase in credit losses in Q1 2025, amounting to $136 million.[1] As delinquency rates rise, financial institutions are taking notice. In the United States, FICO announced that BNPL activity will be factored into credit scoring starting from the fall of 2025, meaning that missed installment payments could soon have lasting consequences on consumers' creditworthiness. Some banks have already begun monitoring BNPL usage or imposing limits on credit card payments to BNPL providers, citing concerns about overextension. The appeal of BNPL lies in its simplicity. But as it grows in popularity, so too does the evidence that its psychological advantages may come at a real financial cost.

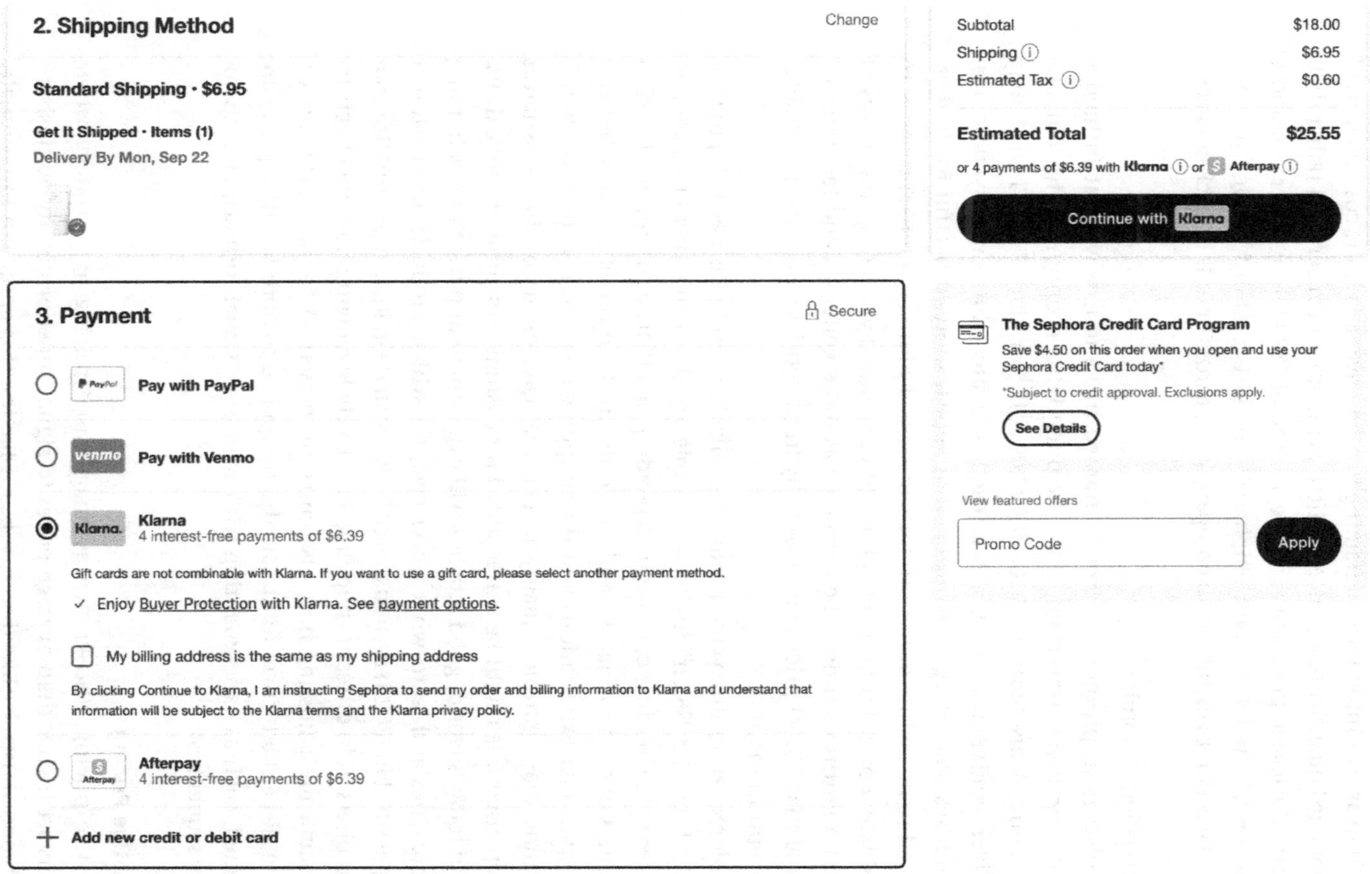

Figure 4.4
Example of BNPL.

Another common form of framing involves displaying the cost in terms of a standard quantity (e.g., price per liter, per gram, or per serving) rather than the total package price. For example, instead of "$24.99 for 1 liter of laundry detergent," the label might emphasize "$0.33 per wash," making it sometimes easier for consumers to compare value across brands or package sizes.

Promotional Framing

As discussed, promotions can be framed in various ways that influence consumer perception even when the underlying economic value remains the same. A discount of "$10 off," "20% off," or "Buy 2, get 1 free" may deliver equivalent savings, but each activates different psychological responses. Percentage discounts often appear more impactful for higher-priced items, while dollar-off deals often feel more concrete and easier to evaluate. Bonus framing, which highlights added value (e.g., free items or extra quantity), tends to be perceived as more generous and less transactional than direct price cuts, especially in categories where trust or quality perception matters.

Moreover, multilayered promotions like "25% off plus free shipping" or "Buy 1, get 1 50% off" introduce complexity that can either enhance perceived value or cause confusion, depending on clarity and timing. The effectiveness of each format depends not only on the product category but also on consumer expectations and the shopping context. For instance, bonus framing may reinforce quality in personal care or luxury items, whereas steep discounts might be better suited for clearance or time-sensitive deals.

In today's world, good retailers will experiment and test various framing approaches and learn what works best, for which products and customer segments. Liu (2023) demonstrated how batch deep RL can personalize coupon offers in livestream shopping, effectively leveraging framing effects by dynamically adjusting how discounts are presented to maximize conversions. Recent advances in RL can also be applied to optimize how prices are framed, such as experimenting with wordings, visual formats, and disclosure sequences.

Prestige Pricing

Prestige pricing, also known as image-based pricing, is a strategy where firms set higher-than-average prices to signal superior quality, exclusivity, or brand status. Unlike discount-based tactics, this approach intentionally avoids price reductions, relying instead on the psychological association between price and perceived value. Consumers often infer that a more expensive product reflects better craftsmanship, performance, or social distinction.

Brands like Apple, Chanel, and Rolex have long relied on prestige pricing, maintaining high price points even in the face of competitors offering similar functionality cheaper. This tactic is especially effective in categories where quality is hard to judge or where ownership carries symbolic or aspirational meaning. On the other hand, companies like L'Oréal have opted for a customer differentiation strategy via its multibrand portfolio, which spans from mass market to luxury segments. Each brand under L'Oréal is differentiated by its identity, target audience, and price point. For instance, L'Oréal Paris serves the mass market with accessible, affordable products, while Lancôme (L'Oréal's premium skincare and cosmetics brand) targets a more affluent consumer base with high-end offerings. This segmentation allows L'Oréal to maximize reach and profitability by aligning price with perceived value.

Behaviorally, prestige pricing works by activating signaling and self-identity mechanisms. Consumers may choose premium-priced products not only for their utility but also for what they represent: status, taste, or membership in a desirable group. As shown in Lichtenstein et al. (1993), consumers are often willing to pay more for products simply because others cannot, thus reinforcing exclusivity.

Scarcity and Urgency Cues

Scarcity and urgency cues are widely used psychological marketing tactics to trigger impulsive decisions and increase purchase intent. For instance, messages like "Only 2 left in stock" or "Sale ends in 3 hours" signal limited availability or time, thereby enhancing perceived value and urgency (Inman et al. 1997; Cialdini 2009). Figure 4.5 shows an e-commerce example featuring a utensil set with a price marked as discounted "Last day $21.04," creating a sense of urgency (the deal is also combined with BNPL and anchoring with a higher original price).

A key distinction exists between quantity scarcity (limited stock) and time scarcity (limited-time offers), each influencing consumer psychology differently. Quantity scarcity often increases competition and desirability, while time scarcity creates pressure to act quickly, particularly on online

Figure 4.5
Example of a limited-time discount, highlighting urgency.

platforms (Tan and Chua 2004; Hmurovic et al. 2023). These cues aim to activate the fear of missing out (FOMO) and increase the perceived value, even if the actual utility remains the same. They may hinder consumers' ability to thoroughly search for the best deals and potentially reduce consumer welfare. By pressuring consumers to make decisions with insufficient information and in limited time, these offers potentially expose consumers to decision-making errors. Furthermore, overuse or manipulation of scarcity signals can lead to consumer skepticism, undermining trust and long-term loyalty.

Cui et al. (2019) examined how real-time inventory information influences consumer purchasing behavior. Using data from over twenty-three thousand lightning deals on Amazon, the authors showed that when customers see inventory levels dropping quickly, they interpret it as a signal of popularity or scarcity, which accelerates future sales. The study also found that customer reviews amplify this effect, while deep discounts weaken it, suggesting that buyers combine multiple signals when making decisions. The key takeaway is that showing inventory information can be a powerful demand lever, but it must be carefully aligned with pricing and product signals.

Social Media Influence

In the age of constant connectivity, social media has become a powerful behavioral amplifier. It actively shapes consumer preferences, price perceptions, and the urgency to buy. A prominent example of this has been the widespread impact of the "TikTok made me buy it" trend.

The hashtag #TikTokMadeMeBuyIt has surpassed eighty billion views as of 2025. It has driven massive spikes in demand for a wide variety of products, including everyday household items, cosmetics, and niche lifestyle goods. These viral moments often result in temporary demand surges that are triggered by emotional reactions to relatable or aspirational content. For instance, a single TikTok video featuring a $15 milk frother led to product shortages and secondary market price increases of up to three times the original price. Consumers continued to purchase the item despite price hikes, influenced by FOMO and a sense of communal endorsement.

From a behavioral perspective, this reflects the influence of social proof and behavioral contagion. These are phenomena where people look at the actions of others, especially peers or influencers, for cues on what to do or purchase (Cialdini 2009). In the context of pricing, such social validation can significantly reduce price sensitivity. When a product becomes trendy or widely endorsed, consumers tend to focus less on the price and more on the perceived popularity or scarcity of the item.

AI is critical in identifying and responding to social media–driven behaviors. Using tools such as natural language processing, hashtag tracking, and sentiment analysis, AI systems can monitor platforms like Instagram, TikTok, and YouTube to detect emerging product trends in real time. Some firms now integrate social media signals directly into their demand forecasting models, allowing them to anticipate when a product may go viral and adjust both pricing strategies and inventory planning.

Behavioral Price Fairness and Trust

While we will thoroughly discuss the topic of fairness in chapter 8, perceptions of fairness also play a critical role in how consumers respond to pricing, often outweighing the actual price level in shaping satisfaction and loyalty. Behavioral price fairness refers to the psychological judgment consumers make about whether a price, and the process behind setting it, are fair and reasonable or exploitative. These judgments are influenced not only by the price but also by contextual cues, reference points, and the seller's perceived intent. Ultimately, these judgments affect how consumers view the firm, affecting their loyalty.

Price Increases and Fairness

Consumers tend to find price increases unfair when they are attributed to firm-driven motives (e.g., opportunistic profit taking) rather than external factors like inflation or supply shocks. Campbell (1999) showed that identical price changes are judged differently depending on how the firm frames its rationale and consumers' existing trust in the brand. For example, during the COVID-19 pandemic or global supply chain disruptions, consumers were generally more accepting of price increases on essential products when retailers explained the rise because of limited supply or increased logistics costs. In contrast, when egg prices surged sharply in 2025 in the United States without clearly communicated explanations, despite stable production in some regions, many consumers viewed the increase as unfair, leading to backlash and negative sentiment.

Trust and Transparency

Trust plays a vital role in how consumers respond to behavioral pricing strategies, such as framing, dynamic offers, and personalized discounts. While such strategies can enhance perceived value and increase conversions, they risk backfiring if consumers perceive them as manipulative, confusing, or unfair.

Transparency helps shape that perception. When companies clearly explain how prices are determined, such as time of purchase, location, inventory, or user behavior, consumers are more likely to view the pricing strategies as legitimate. For instance, Uber introduced upfront pricing and in-app explanations for surge pricing after early criticism and regulatory pressure, which helped mitigate negative reactions to dynamic fare adjustments (Chen and Sheldon 2016). In contrast, opaque pricing practices often trigger distrust. Several companies have faced scrutiny for using urgency cues and incomplete pricing disclosures that reveal added service charges only near the end of the booking process. These drip pricing tactics can reduce purchase satisfaction and damage trust even when the price is competitive (Santana et al. 2020). Overall, algorithmic price changes not accompanied by clear explanations can lead consumers to feel manipulated if they suspect unfair treatment or inconsistencies.

Studies suggest that consumers are more tolerant of personalized or fluctuating prices when they understand the underlying logic and feel that it aligns with external conditions rather than seller opportunism (Xia et al. 2004). Transparency not only improves fairness perception but also acts as a buffer in long-term customer relationships. Brands that proactively communicate the basis of their pricing decisions are more likely to maintain credibility in competitive markets.

Ultimately, companies that prioritize transparency in their pricing strategies, clearly articulate value, and avoid deceptive tactics are more likely to earn consumer trust, improve satisfaction, and foster loyalty. Research indicates that trusted brands are more inclined to receive the benefit of the doubt when using aggressive tactics such as scarcity cues, surge pricing, or drip pricing (Haws and Bearden 2006). Over time, consistent and fair pricing practices contribute to stronger customer relationships and higher retention.

Ethical Considerations

As pricing becomes increasingly personalized through AI and behavioral data, the ethical boundary between serving consumers and exploiting them becomes blurry. On the one hand, personalization can improve pertinence and satisfaction, such as offering targeted discounts to price-sensitive shoppers based on their browsing history and past purchases. This type of customized pricing can clearly enhance perceived value and accessibility.

On the other hand, when personalization is opaque or based on psychological triggers, for example, by deploying urgency cues more aggressively for impulsive users, it risks venturing into manipulation. Consumers may feel deceived if they discover that they paid more than others for the same product or were nudged using tactics designed to exploit cognitive biases rather than empower informed choices. Once again, transparency, consistency, and explainability are essential to building and preserving trust.

A controversial example of behavioral pricing is the so-called pink tax, where products marketed to women (e.g., razors, deodorants) are priced higher than nearly identical products marketed to men. These price differences often cannot be justified by cost or quality but instead reflect perceived WTP, brand positioning, and subtle behavioral cues. A 2015 report by the New York City Department of Consumer Affairs found that, on average, women's products cost 7 percent more than men's across several categories.[2]

Despite increasing awareness, algorithmic pricing systems risk reinforcing such biases when trained on historical data without fairness considerations. The pink tax not only raises ethical concerns but can also erode brand trust and loyalty. When consumers detect unfair or biased pricing, intentional or not, it may be viewed as exploitative. To maintain consumer trust and regulatory compliance, firms must evaluate their pricing algorithms for implicit bias, ensure transparent communication, and implement corrective measures as needed. Ethical personalization should prioritize user privacy and equity, focusing on long-term relationships rather than short-term extraction. Much more on this topic in chapter 8.

5 Data Is King and Price Experimentation

> Without data, you're just another person with an opinion.
> —W. Edwards Deming

This chapter explores how the availability of rich, granular data has disrupted pricing practices. It discusses the types of data that can be collected and leveraged for effective pricing decisions. Data is like fuel for AI, so it can be seen as the necessary foundation to develop AI models. This chapter also covers the concept of price experimentation and how companies are now using data and continuous experimentation to estimate price elasticities across customer segments and market contexts.

Big Data Is a Game Changer

Access to rich, granular data is a game changer for optimizing pricing decisions, as it allows businesses to move beyond broad assumptions and make precise, data-driven adjustments. Instead of setting a single price for all customers, companies can analyze detailed data points, such as browsing behavior, purchase history, demographics, and even real-time demand, to personalize prices and maximize revenue. Imagine an online electronics retailer that previously priced its products based on general market trends. With granular data, the retailer can now see that tech-savvy shoppers tend to buy high-end gaming laptops in the evening, while budget-conscious students make purchases when discounts are offered in the morning. By dynamically adjusting prices, such as offering a small discount to price-sensitive users while maintaining premium pricing for those willing to pay more, the retailer can capture more sales without unnecessarily lowering prices across the board. Similarly, ride-hailing apps like Lyft and Uber can use real-time data on traffic, demand, and weather conditions to implement surge pricing, ensuring cars are available when demand spikes. Without granular data, businesses rely on guesswork, potentially leaving money on the table or deterring customers with poorly optimized pricing. Without access to data, the best you can do is guess. With access to data, you can determine what works, what doesn't work, and constantly refine your pricing strategy.

As discussed before, when personalizing prices, an important question relates to which data features or characteristics to rely on. Equivalently, this translates into which types of data can be collected and leveraged to optimize future pricing decisions. We next elaborate on the three main types of features or data attributes mentioned before:

1. Customer features
2. Contextual information
3. Market characteristics

A smart and effective pricing strategy will aim to leverage these three types of features to identify the best pricing policy. Customer features refer to all the potential data that the company has about customers. This data can be different depending on the context (e.g., online vs. brick-and-mortar stores). It encompasses various types of data, including the following:

1. **Demographic data**: Features such as age (e.g., young adults vs. retirees), gender (e.g., male, female, nonbinary), marital status (e.g., single, married, divorced), household size (e.g., number of dependents), education level (e.g., high school, bachelor's, graduate degree), occupation (e.g., job title, industry, employment status), income level (estimated based on spending patterns or surveys), and geographic location (e.g., city, country, postal code).
2. **Behavioral data**: Features like purchase history (e.g., frequency, recency, amount spent), browsing behavior (e.g., pages visited, session duration), cart abandonment patterns (e.g., leaving items without purchasing), click-through rates (e.g., engagement with emails or ads), preferred shopping channels (e.g., online vs. in-store), loyalty program participation (e.g., points earned, rewards redeemed), return history (e.g., frequency

of returns, reasons), and customer support interactions (e.g., complaints, reviews, feedback).

3. **Psychographic data**: Features such as personality traits (e.g., risk-taker vs. cautious buyer), values and beliefs (e.g., sustainability-conscious shoppers), lifestyle preferences (e.g., fitness enthusiasts, gamers), brand affinity (e.g., preference for premium vs. budget brands), hobbies and interests (e.g., travel, music, sports), and emotional sentiment (e.g., tone in reviews and feedback).
4. **Technographic data**: Features like device type (e.g., mobile, tablet, desktop), operating system (e.g., Android, iOS, Windows), browser type (e.g., Chrome, Firefox, Safari), app usage (e.g., frequency, session length), internet speed (e.g., high-speed fiber vs. mobile data), and IP address and location (e.g., home vs. work, VPN use).
5. **Transactional data**: Features such as payment method (e.g., credit card, PayPal, cryptocurrency), average order value (e.g., spending per transaction), subscription status (e.g., active, inactive, free vs. premium), discount usage (e.g., frequent-coupon redeemer vs. full-price buyer), billing history (e.g., late payments, auto-renewals), and fraud risk indicators (e.g., unusual purchasing patterns).
6. **Social data**: Features like social media activity (e.g., brand mentions, engagement), friends and followers (e.g., influence level, network size), referral behavior (e.g., inviting friends to use a service), and user-generated content (e.g., reviews, forum participation).
7. **Engagement and communication data**: Features such as email open rates (e.g., frequency of interaction with campaigns), chatbot and live chat interactions (e.g., FAQs, issue resolution), call center logs (e.g., frequency, tone, complaint history), and SMS and push notification engagement (e.g., click rates).
8. **Mobility and location data**: Features like geofencing interactions (e.g., entering a store triggers a discount), commute patterns (e.g., daily routes, frequent travel destinations), transit usage (e.g., Uber, public transport), and dwell time in physical stores (e.g., time spent in different sections).

Of course, most companies will only have access to a small subset of this data for a subset of customers. While some companies only have access to a few features (e.g., age, device, IP address), others may have access to much richer information, sometimes up to hundreds of different features for each customer. In addition, these data features may be dynamic and evolve over time, thus making the data even richer.

The second type of features is related to contextual information and includes both temporal attributes (e.g., day of the week, time of the day, product life cycle length) and environmental data such as weather conditions (e.g., demand for winter gear in cold areas), local events (e.g., concerts, sports games affecting spending), economic factors (e.g., recession vs. economic boom, inflation rate, unemployment rate), and competitor interactions (e.g., comparing prices elsewhere).

The third type of features relates to market characteristics and can include various types of information, such as market size, market maturity, number of competitors, market concentration, market share distribution, differentiation level (i.e., how unique products/services are in the market), switching costs, economies of scale, supply chain and distribution complexity, regulatory, legal, and geopolitical factors (e.g., taxation and tariffs, consumer protection laws), environmental factors, and market risks and uncertainties.

Finally, as an additional type of data, which is less common and more sophisticated, involves new features created through predictive modeling. These features are sometimes referred to as predictive and AI-derived data and include the following: likelihood to purchase (e.g., scoring models predicting conversion), churn risk score (e.g., probability of customer leaving), price sensitivity (e.g., WTP at different price points), customer lifetime value (e.g., projected total revenue per user), and propensity for upsells/cross-sells (e.g., likelihood to upgrade).

Controversial Data Features

While data-driven price personalization can enhance efficiency and even sometimes unlock value for both consumers and businesses, certain features used in personalization models may be controversial and raise concerns around fairness, privacy, transparency, and discrimination. One such controversial feature is zip code or geographic location. Although it may reflect cost of living or regional competition, using it to charge higher prices to customers in areas with fewer competitors can backfire. For instance, Staples came under fire when it was revealed that customers in lower-income neighborhoods were shown higher online prices simply because there were no nearby competitors, igniting debates around economic redlining.[1] A 2012 investigation by *The Wall Street Journal* revealed that Staples.com displayed different prices to customers based on their geographic location. Specifically, the website offered lower prices to users whose IP addresses indicated they were within twenty miles of a competitor's physical store, such as Office Depot or OfficeMax, while customers located farther from these competitors often saw higher prices for the same products. This pricing strategy disproportionately affected consumers in rural and less affluent areas, where competitor stores were scarce, leading to concerns about economic redlining.

Another controversial feature is device and browser type. Some travel websites have been caught showing higher prices to Mac users, assuming they have greater purchasing power than Windows users. This tactic may feel like digital profiling. Similarly, purchase history and browsing behavior can be risky, especially when used to infer a customer's desperation or urgency. Imagine a parent frantically searching for children's flu medication late at night, only to be quoted a higher price by an algorithm that detects emotional urgency; while profitable in the short term, such practices can severely erode trust. Even demographic features like age or marital status can lead to controversy. Charging newlyweds more for honeymoon packages may seem like smart segmentation but can easily be perceived as opportunistic exploitation and tarnish the seller's long-term reputation. Perhaps among the most controversial features are inferred features like income or psychological traits derived from online activity or social media. These features are opaque, often hard to verify, and risk crossing ethical lines when used to set prices. In short, many features may boost profits while also carrying reputational and regulatory risks. Using them without careful governance and transparency can make price personalization a controversial practice, as we will elaborate in chapter 8.

A notorious example worth mentioning is the use of device battery levels as a feature in price personalization, which has sparked significant controversy due to ethical and privacy concerns. Investigations have suggested that ride-hailing apps monitor users' smartphone battery levels and may adjust pricing accordingly. For instance, a study by the Belgian newspaper *Dernière Heure* indicated that users with low battery percentages were quoted higher fares compared to those with fully charged devices, implying that the urgency induced by a low battery could lead users to accept higher prices.[2] Similarly, in January 2025, a Delhi-based entrepreneur observed that Uber's fares were higher when his phone's battery was low, sparking debates over potential fare manipulation.[3] While Uber has denied exploiting battery information for pricing, the mere possibility has raised alarms. At a high level, this practice seems potentially problematic because it capitalizes on a user's vulnerable state of having a low battery, which may limit their ability to seek alternative transportation options, thereby coercing them into accepting inflated prices. Such tactics not only breach consumer trust but also tread into ethically dubious territory by exploiting personal device data without explicit, clearly communicated consent. To maintain integrity and customer trust, companies must ensure transparency in their data usage policies and avoid leveraging sensitive personal information in ways that could be perceived as manipulative or unfair.

In addition to battery level, companies have used (or been accused of using) other subtle, situational, or device-related data features for price personalization, which raise similar ethical and privacy concerns. As discussed, a notable example is the device type, whereby some companies opted to charge higher prices for Apple users. One of the most widely cited cases involves travel booking websites such as Orbitz. In 2012, *The Wall Street Journal* reported that Orbitz showed more expensive hotel options to Mac users compared to PC users.[4] Their reasoning? Data showed that Mac users tended to book higher-end hotels and spend more per night. While the site didn't change the prices directly, it adjusted the ordering and availability of options by subtly nudging Mac users toward more expensive choices. This sparked a backlash and raised questions about the fairness of using device type as a proxy for income or preferences. A second example relates to the time of day and repeated searches. More specifically, some online retailers and travel sites have been adjusting prices based on time of day and search frequency.[5] For instance, users who repeatedly search for a flight or hotel over a short period may see the price increase over time, possibly creating urgency and pressure the customer into buying. While companies like Expedia and Priceline have denied this, many users have reported price jumps that disappear when switching browsers or using incognito mode, suggesting that cookies and session tracking play a role.

This leads to a common consumer story: A traveler searches for a flight to Paris, sees a $500 fare, returns two hours later to book, and the fare is suddenly $620. But when they try the same search in private browsing mode, the original $500 fare appears again. This behavior creates a perception of manipulation even if technically caused by demand-side algorithms.

These examples show how seemingly innocuous features like the device you're using or your browsing behavior can be used in opaque and potentially exploitative ways. Much like battery percentage, these features don't feel like fair or transparent signals to base pricing on, especially when consumers are unaware of their use. To maintain trust, companies must be transparent about data collection and ensure their algorithms prioritize ethical personalization over covert discrimination.

Determining which data features are permissible for pricing decisions is complex and influenced by context, jurisdiction, and the nature of customers' consent. Another notable example is the practice of charging different fares for personal versus business accounts. There have been reports from customers suggesting that some companies (e.g., airlines, hotels, ride-hailing platforms) engage in this type of price differentiation and often tend to charge a premium for business accounts. This assumes that customers are likely to be less price sensitive when the expense is covered by their company. For instance, users have reported that requesting the same ride on a platform like Uber can result in different prices depending on whether the account is linked to a business or a personal profile.[6] Is this practice fair or even permissible? The answer is open to debate, but many individuals may perceive such treatment as unfair or feel taken advantage of. This issue touches on broader concerns around fairness and privacy, which will be discussed in detail in chapter 8.

Price Elasticity

A critical concept in the world of pricing is the own-price elasticity of demand (or simply price elasticity). Price elasticity measures the responsiveness of the quantity demanded of a product to changes in its own price, making it a crucial concept for businesses looking to optimize their pricing strategies. Specifically, demand for a product is considered highly elastic if a small increase in price leads to a significant decrease in quantity demanded. For example, demand for a particular airline itinerary is likely elastic: If an airline raises fares by 10 percent, many travelers might switch to a cheaper airline or postpone their trip. Conversely, the demand for life-saving medications or gasoline tends to be inelastic (at least in the short term): Even if gas prices rise, commuters still need to fill their tanks to go to work. Understanding price elasticity helps businesses maximize revenue; for example, movie theaters offer discounted matinee tickets because they know price-sensitive customers are more willing to watch movies at nonpeak hours, whereas prime-time showings remain expensive for less price-sensitive audiences. Of course, estimating price elasticity requires access to reliable, granular data on both prices and quantities sold; without such data, firms are left to rely on intuition or crude approximations.

One way to estimate price elasticity is by analyzing historical sales data and price fluctuations. Suppose an online fashion retailer notices that a $10 increase in sneaker prices leads to a 15 percent drop in sales; they can calculate the price elasticity of demand and decide whether raising prices is worth the potential loss in volume. Companies also conduct A/B price testing, where different customers see different prices for the same product, allowing firms to observe how demand reacts. Ride-hailing platforms like Lyft and Uber may experiment with surge pricing, adjusting fares in real time based on demand and testing how much riders are willing to pay before opting for alternative forms of transit. Even streaming services like Netflix may test different subscription prices in various markets, observing when users cancel or downgrade plans. By leveraging data-driven insights into price elasticity, businesses can strike the right balance between maximizing revenue and maintaining customer loyalty.

A myriad of academic studies has attempted to rigorously estimate price elasticities for a wide variety of products in many contexts. Tellis 1988 is a classic study that presents a meta-analysis of 367 econometric estimates from 220 brands across diverse product categories and countries to answer a fundamental question: How sensitive is consumer demand to price changes? By aggregating decades of research, the author found that price elasticity of selective demand, that is, demand for a specific brand rather than the overall category, is quite substantial, with an average elasticity of −1.76. In other words, a 1 percent decrease in price typically leads to a 1.76 percent increase in sales, making price far more impactful than advertising, whose elasticity is only around 0.22 (meaning a 1 percent increase in advertising spend yields just a 0.22 percent increase in sales).

Research has also revealed that many common modeling practices can bias results. For instance, omitting key factors like product quality or distribution skews elasticity estimates and can often mislead companies. Aggregating data over long time periods or relying solely on cross-sectional (rather than time-series) data can also lead to significant under- or overestimation of price effects. Importantly, elasticity varies by product category (e.g., highest in detergents, lowest in pharmaceuticals), life cycle stage (greater in maturity), time horizon over which the change in consumption is measured, and geography. The key takeaway is that pricing decisions must be grounded in rigorous, well-specified data models, and dynamic, time-sensitive analyses are far more reliable than static, oversimplified approaches. Getting this right can significantly improve profitability and competitive positioning.

Building on this, Bijmolt et al. (2005) offered a revised view of what drives consumer price sensitivity. The authors analyzed 1,851 price elasticity estimates from eighty-one studies spanning four decades to identify patterns and draw actionable insights for business leaders. The key takeaway is striking: The average price elasticity was –2.62, meaning a 1 percent increase in price leads to an average 2.62 percent drop in sales, significantly more than what earlier studies had found. This suggests that consumers have become increasingly price sensitive over time, especially in product categories like durables and in the early stages of a product's life cycle. The paper also found that using detailed, disaggregated data (like SKU-level scanner data) and accounting for pricing decisions that are influenced by demand (i.e., price endogeneity) significantly improves accuracy and usually leads to higher elasticity estimates. Conversely, failing to account for related marketing activities like promotions or advertising can distort results and misguide pricing strategies. Importantly, the study debunks some old assumptions, such as differences between countries or between private labels and manufacturer brands, showing that price sensitivity is more universally driven by product type and data granularity. For managers, the message is clear: Consumers are more price sensitive than ever, and pricing strategies must consider product type, market maturity, and the interplay with other marketing levers.

In today's world where data is rich and granular and trends are shifting faster than ever, estimating price elasticities has become critical. Recent advancements in AI and the increasing availability of data have brought new twists. First, companies have developed advanced techniques that rely on large amounts of data to estimate price elasticity. The estimation isn't done at the aggregate generic level but is now extremely refined. For example, it has become possible to estimate the price elasticity for a specific product, in a specific color, for a specific customer segment, that shops in a specific channel (or store) in a particular geographical location. Second, companies are now estimating price elasticities at a fast, dynamic pace. Instead of assuming that price elasticities are time invariant, it's common to challenge this assumption by reestimating them frequently. One such tool to do so is to rely on price experimentation, as discussed next.

Price Experimentation

Price experimentation is a pricing approach that involves testing different prices (via A/B testing) for a product or service to determine the optimal price point (e.g., maximizes revenue or profit). The goal of price experimentation is to identify the price that provides the best balance between revenue and profit while also ensuring that prices remain competitive and attractive to customers. For example, a company might conduct A/B testing by randomly assigning different prices to different groups of customers and monitoring the results to see which price point generates the most revenue. Alternatively, a company might experiment with product bundling by offering different groupings of products at varying price points to see which bundle generates the most revenue.

Price experimentation can be a powerful tool for businesses to optimize their pricing strategy and improve their bottom line. By testing different price points and monitoring the results, they can identify the most effective strategies. In fact, it has become standard practice to test new pricing strategies through small-scale controlled A/B experiments before rolling them out more broadly. With access to vast amounts of data from large user bases, companies can experiment on a small subset of users over a limited period to evaluate a strategy's effectiveness and its potential drawbacks. The insights gained from these tests will help guide key decisions, namely, whether to refine the strategy, abandon it, or scale it across the entire user base. At the same time, it's important to ensure price experimentation is conducted in an ethical and consumer-friendly manner and that prices remain fair and transparent.

I next discuss several concrete examples of where price experimentation can be readily leveraged:

- **E-commerce:** A company might experiment with different pricing strategies for a particular product, such as offering a discount or bundling the product with other items. It could then monitor sales data to determine which pricing strategy generated the most revenue and profit.
- **Airlines:** Airlines may experiment with different pricing strategies for flights, such as offering discounts for early booking or increasing prices during peak travel times. They could then analyze this data to determine the most effective strategy for each route and time of year.
- **Retail:** Retailers might experiment with different pricing strategies for a particular product (or group of products), such as offering a discount or running a different offer (e.g., a coupon). The tests can be repeated in different stores and when the products are placed at different locations on the shelves.
- **Streaming services:** Streaming services might experiment with various pricing strategies, such as offering different subscription plans or adjusting prices based on customer behavior. The platform could then analyze this data to determine the most effective pricing strategy for each customer segment.
- **Healthcare:** Health providers might experiment with different pricing strategies for treatments and services, such as offering discounts for certain procedures or adjusting prices based on use patterns. They could then learn from these experiments to decide the strategy to deploy for their patients.

Price experimentation is naturally more prevalent in online environments. Indeed, digital platforms make it significantly easier, cheaper, and less risky to test different prices. A single line of code can update prices in real time, and these changes can be applied instantly across customer segments. In contrast, running a controlled price experiment in a physical retail setting is often logistically infeasible, if not entirely impossible, due to operational constraints, signage, staffing, regulations, and customer perception.

For example, consider a new direct-to-consumer T-shirt brand. Suppose market research suggests that the optimal price point lies between $45 and $60. You thus decide to test two prices: $49 and $59 based on psychological pricing principles (ending prices in "9"). If the product is sold online, you can design a simple A/B test: show the $49 price to half of your website visitors and the $59 price to the other half. This controlled experiment can help you determine which price maximizes revenue or conversion. To ensure the validity of the test, several conditions must be met. First, visitors should be randomly assigned to each pricing group to avoid selection bias. Second, all other elements of the shopping experience, such as product images, descriptions, and delivery timelines, must be perfectly identical, with price being the only differing factor. Third, the sample size (i.e., the number of shoppers in each group) must be large enough to yield statistically significant results. And finally, the test should be insulated from external factors such as holidays or parallel promotions that could distort consumer behavior and skew the test's results.

In an ideal setting, price experimentation relies on clean, randomized comparisons across customer groups at the same point in time and in the same conditions. This is easy to implement online but virtually impossible in most physical environments such as supermarkets, fashion boutiques, or restaurants, where displaying multiple prices for the same product would confuse or alienate customers (and may be illegal). Even for online businesses like airlines or hotels, regulatory restrictions in some jurisdictions prohibit offering different prices to different customers under identical conditions. As a result, price experimentation in such settings must take alternative forms, such as temporal A/B tests (testing prices at different times), geographic pilots, or simulated market studies. While more complex and constrained, these methods can still yield valuable insights when carefully designed and rigorously executed.

In Lopez Mateos et al. 2022, we offered a set of practical recommendations to reduce the complexity of conducting price experiments in offline environments. Our discussion was motivated by the hospitality industry, where price experimentation (particularly among small and mid-sized hotel operators) remained underused. We argued that well-designed experiments can lead to substantial revenue gains, often in the 5–10 percent range, and help surface high-impact decisions related to pricing ancillary services (such as breakfast, parking, or gym access), selecting the optimal distribution channel (e.g., Expedia vs. direct bookings), evaluating promotional strategies, and assessing different revenue management systems. As discussed above, one of the core challenges in this setting is the inability to offer multiple price points simultaneously for the same hotel room on the same channel. To address this, we proposed to consider three alternative experimental designs: (1) property splits, where pricing strategies are tested across similar properties within the same chain; (2) alternating time periods (or switchback experiments), where prices are rotated across comparable demand windows; and (3) high-frequency price updates, which allow for rapid testing and iterative learning in dynamic markets. Each method (or combining them when possible) is suited to different hotel sizes, operational capabilities, and data maturity levels. Ultimately, the message is clear: Embracing experimentation, even in simple forms, can drive better pricing decisions, increase profitability, and make revenue management more scientific and less reliant on intuition. This message applies across a wide range of service industries beyond just hospitality.

Price experimentation is especially ubiquitous in e-commerce. In Cohen, Kitain, et al. 2024, we collaborated with Intelligems, a leading start-up in the world of e-commerce experimentation, and summarized insights from over one thousand price experiments conducted with more than three hundred e-commerce retailers. We aimed to answer the following fundamental question: Are current pricing strategies optimal, and what happens when companies test alternatives? Drawing on data from $500 million in transactions across one hundred million shoppers, our team used A/B testing to evaluate changes in both list prices and shipping fees. The findings were both revealing and actionable. First, most small and midsized retailers set prices using informal, instinct-driven methods (often based on margin targets or competitor benchmarking), leaving substantial money on the table. In 54 percent of the price tests, an alternative price outperformed the retailer's original, typically delivering a 6 percent lift in gross profits. Interestingly, nearly 60 percent of those successful price changes involved lowering prices, suggesting that many retailers were unintentionally overpricing and losing sales volume. Shipping fee tests revealed the opposite: Higher thresholds (i.e., spend at least $X to get free shipping) or modest shipping charges often increased profits, challenging the assumption that free shipping always wins. Retailers that ran at least three pricing tests found improved strategies in 96 percent of cases. Examples of companies, such as the sustainable bedding brand Sheets & Giggles we partnered with, illustrate how testing can debunk internal pricing assumptions and yield meaningful profit gains. For managers, the takeaway is clear: Rigorous price experimentation is one of the fastest, most reliable ways to optimize revenue and margins. It requires setup and strategic context, but the upside is well worth the effort.

While A/B testing for prices has become more accessible and widespread, successful implementation hinges on how results are measured and interpreted. A vital best practice is to move beyond traditional metrics like conversion rate or average order value and instead focus on more holistic indicators such as profit per visitor or profit per session. These metrics account for both pricing effects and behavioral responses, thus ensuring that a price change that increases sales doesn't inadvertently erode margins. For online businesses with recurring customers or high retention potential, it's also critical to consider customer lifetime value. A short-term decrease in profit might be justifiable if it drives higher retention, larger repeat purchases, or better word of mouth over time. Another key insight is that pricing tests should be evaluated globally rather than locally. That means looking at the total impact across product lines and over longer time horizons and not just the isolated performance of the tested item in a single week. For example, increasing the price of one product might reduce its own sales but drive customers toward higher-margin substitutes, improving overall profitability. Another example is the fact that a promotion on a "hero product" (i.e., a flagship or best-selling item) may elevate traffic and basket size for the entire store. Additionally, testing should avoid bias by controlling timing effects, segmenting customer types, and ensuring adequate sample sizes for statistical significance.

Finally, it's important to remember that experimentation isn't a one-time project but often an ongoing learning process. The most sophisticated e-commerce teams run continuous price testing, use automation to adjust strategies in real time, and treat each test as a source of insight and not just as a decision tool. In short, when executed thoughtfully, the discipline of A/B testing offers managers not only better prices but also a deeper understanding of how customers respond to value, enabling smarter decisions far beyond pricing.

Pricing Without Data

Setting prices without access to data, such as when launching a new product, entering a new market, or running a one-off campaign, is one of the trickiest challenges in pricing strategy. To this day, there is no definitive solution to this problem. In these situations, businesses must rely on judgment, proxies, and structured experimentation rather than historical data. A natural approach is cost-plus pricing, where companies add a markup to their estimated costs (sometimes estimating the costs isn't an easy task, which may complicate the pricing decision even further). While the cost-plus pricing approach is intuitive, it often leaves money on the table, especially in cases where it's hard to estimate customers' WTP. For example, some patients may be willing to pay a very high price for a new pharmaceutical drug (especially if it has the promise to improve quality of life and longevity). The issue is that since the product is new, it's difficult to know customers' WTP.

A more strategic method is value-based pricing, which anchors price to the perceived value the product offers. For example, when Dyson launched its bladeless fan, which is a completely new concept with no close competitor, it priced it significantly higher than traditional fans, banking on innovation and premium design to justify the premium. Another tool is competitive benchmarking: If you're launching a smartwatch without user data, you might study the price points of similar wearables (like the Apple Watch or Fitbit) and position accordingly, possibly underpricing to gain traction. A/B testing and pilot launches are also effective. For instance, when Uber first launched UberX, it offered heavy discounts in test cities to gauge price sensitivity before adjusting fares. Start-ups often use founder-led sales or manual price negotiations early on to gather qualitative feedback that can later feed into scalable models. Another compelling story comes from a SaaS company that priced its B2B tool at $49 per month until a few clients insisted they would've paid three times more. Then, the team raised prices to $129 per month and saw conversion rates increase, suggesting that low pricing was actually signaling low value. The key for pricing without data is to test, listen, and adapt quickly: Your first price is rarely your best price, but it's a starting point for learning.

In some situations, businesses must set a single, irreversible price with no room for experimentation or adjustment, thus making the pricing decision even more critical and high stakes. This often occurs in contexts like government contracts, public tenders, crowdfunding campaigns, or product launches tied to a one-time event (e.g., a limited edition release or a new pharmaceutical entering a regulated market). Without the luxury of

A/B testing or iterative feedback, companies must rely heavily on prelaunch research, market analogs, and expert judgment. For example, when pharmaceutical firms submit pricing for a new drug to regulatory authorities like the Food and Drug Administration or Health Canada, they may need to justify the price using cost of R&D, comparative efficacy, and international reference pricing. Then, once submitted, the price is somewhat constrained and often hard to revise.

In the consumer world, Kickstarter campaigns face a similar dilemma: Setting a price that's too low can lead to losses once production costs are fully realized, while pricing too high might suppress backer interest before the campaign gains traction. The Pebble smartwatch, one of Kickstarter's biggest success stories, found its sweet spot at $99, which can be viewed as a price that struck the right balance between perceived value and mass appeal, despite limited prelaunch data. In these cases, pricing becomes a strategic bet based on a deep understanding of customer psychology, market positioning, and risk tolerance. Companies often hedge that risk by building margin buffers, bundling in value (e.g., free shipping, upgrades), or offering tiered options to indirectly test WTP within a fixed structure. When you can't learn by doing, you must learn by researching, modeling, and listening because you only get one shot to get it right.

When price experimentation isn't possible, businesses can turn to indirect data collection methods like surveys, market research studies, and controlled beta testing to simulate pricing feedback before launching. A widely used tool is conjoint analysis, which is a survey-based statistical technique where participants choose between product bundles at different price points, helping businesses infer which features and prices drive decisions (Orme 2010). In other words, conjoint analysis is a powerful market research technique that can help businesses understand how customers make trade-offs when choosing between products or services. At its core, it aims to simulate buying decisions by presenting customers with different combinations of product features, each with its own price, and asks them to choose their preferred option. The goal is to uncover which attributes, such as price, quality, speed, brand, or packaging, drive customer choices and how much value customers place on each one. Conjoint analysis can be useful when launching new products, entering new markets, or redesigning offerings because it sheds light on a critical question: What are customers truly willing to pay for? In the hospitality industry, for instance, Marriott has used conjoint analysis to understand how travelers value features like early check-in, breakfast, Wi-Fi, or room views, allowing them to design tiered pricing models that maximize both satisfaction and revenue. Tech companies may use conjoint analysis to determine optimal pricing tiers for software subscriptions long before market release. Similarly, software companies might test how customers value different combinations of security, storage, support, and price and use the results to build compelling subscription plans.

In the world of pricing, conjoint analysis can be a practical tool for setting prices in the absence of direct market evidence. Rather than relying on gut instinct or simple competitor benchmarks, companies can use this method to estimate customers' WTP for specific features or upgrades. For example, an electric vehicle manufacturer might use conjoint analysis to test how much customers would value a longer battery range, premium audio, or autonomous driving capabilities and then use those insights to price options accordingly. While the choices observed in a conjoint study are hypothetical rather than based on actual purchases, the method allows researchers to infer preferences based on the trade-offs respondents indicate they would make.

Another method is the Van Westendorp Price Sensitivity Meter, which asks potential customers a series of questions, such as what price they consider "too expensive" or "too cheap," to help define a psychological price window. For example, a beverage start-up might ask five hundred consumers these questions during prelaunch focus groups to find that the optimal price for their new sparkling water is around $2.99. Beyond surveys, beta testing groups provide more realistic behavioral data. Start-ups often invite early adopters to use the product for free or at a nominal fee, observing their WTP through engagement and upgrade interest. Dropbox famously used its beta phase to test not just product features but also pricing perceptions, which helped structure its freemium model. Businesses can also commission market research reports or run mystery shopping studies to understand competitor pricing and consumer reactions. Even qualitative methods, like customer interviews or B2B sales conversations, can yield powerful pricing clues. One SaaS founder once told me that their best price insight came not from a model but from a prospect who said, "If it solves that pain point, it's worth at least $200/month to me." These methods may not be as precise as experimentation, but they allow companies to triangulate toward an informed price, reducing risk while maintaining pricing flexibility. Recent advances in GenAI are further enhancing these capabilities, as we will discuss in chapter 7.

Another interesting scenario emerges when data is available but very scarce. When data is limited, pricing decisions become a delicate mix of inference, business judgment, and creative problem-solving. These "tiny data" scenarios are surprisingly common: start-ups with only a few early customers, niche B2B services with limited contracts, or new product lines with just a handful of test sales. In these cases, traditional statistical modeling is off the table (and so are traditional approaches based on machine learning), but several practical methods can still guide pricing decisions. One option is analog-based pricing or competitor benchmarking, where businesses look at closely comparable products or services (or even past launches) to anchor their price. For instance, a founder of a legal tech platform had only two enterprise clients in pilot but used pricing from related contract management tools as a benchmark and then adjusted based on perceived added value. Another powerful method is customer back-solving, which involves working backward from the customer's ROI. If your product helps a client save $100,000 in labor costs annually, a price of $10,000–$20,000 may feel like a bargain. This is especially useful in B2B settings, where customer conversations can be as valuable as hard data. Some businesses turn to decision trees or scenario analysis, modeling a few plausible pricing outcomes (e.g., low, medium, high price tiers) and projecting their impact using even limited sales data. I once advised a sustainability start-up that only had three customers; it used those clients' feedback to model "good–better–best" pricing tiers and then rolled them out publicly, discovering that 60 percent of buyers preferred the premium tier even though their original plan was to lead with a lower entry price. Finally, in scarce-data settings, behavioral cues become critical: How quickly did the early customers say "yes"? Did they hesitate? Did they try to negotiate? When collected thoughtfully, these micro-signals can outperform models built on shaky assumptions. In short, even when data is limited, smart pricing is still possible. One piece of advice is to treat each data point not as insufficient but as a high-signal opportunity to listen, learn, and lean in.

Researchers have also proposed additional scientific approaches for the low-data regime. For example, in Cohen, Perakis, et al. 2021, we proposed a pricing strategy for companies launching new products with limited demand knowledge. We focused on a common business dilemma: how to set a price when no historical sales data or clear demand curve exists. Instead of relying on complex models or experimentation, we proposed to use a simple yet effective rule: Price the product as if the demand curve were linear. Specifically, firms should set the price at the midpoint between the marginal cost and the estimated maximum price customers would pay (i.e., Price = (Max Price + Cost) / 2). The method requires only two pieces of information: marginal cost (assumed to be constant and known) and an estimate of the highest acceptable price, which firms can approximate using expert judgment, focus groups, or secondary market signals. Through analytical modeling and simulations on a variety of realistic and randomized demand curves, we showed that this simple rule often results in profits that are within 5–10 percent of what could be achieved if the full demand curve were known. The approach works especially well in industries with digital goods, pharmaceuticals, or new technologies, where marginal costs are low and production capacity is flexible.

Another example is Chen et al. (2022), who proposed a pricing approach that only requires two basic pieces of information: an estimate of the average customer valuation and the standard deviation (a measure of uncertainty around that average). With this minimal input, the authors derived a simple formula for a robust price that protects against worst-case scenarios and comes with a guaranteed minimum profit level. The method is especially valuable in digital, subscription, and B2B markets where exact demand is hard to predict but cost and rough WTP estimates are available. The study also extends to multiple products and bundling strategies. Examples from Spotify, IT service providers, and theater subscriptions show the practicality of the approach.

A final successful example is the study by Ferreira et al. (2016), who provided a case study of how AI-powered pricing can transform revenue performance in online retail. Working with Rue La La, a flash-sale fashion platform, the authors deployed a pricing decision-support tool that tackled a daunting challenge: setting optimal prices for entirely new products with no sales history. Using machine learning, the authors predicted demand for new products based on dozens of features (such as brand, timing, and competitive positioning) and then used a custom optimization algorithm to set prices across competing products, accounting for reference price effects and consumer behavior. A large-scale field experiment showed impressive results: a 9.7 percent average increase in revenue, with no decline in sales for medium- and high-priced products, and only a slight drop for the lowest-priced items. Importantly, the tool was automated, scalable, and seamlessly integrated into daily operations. For business executives, this study highlights the upside of combining machine learning with price optimization, not just for markdowns or promotions but also for initial pricing of new items.

Several other academic papers have developed alternative approaches and methods. Overall, the message for business leaders is clear and powerful: Even with limited data, it's often possible to set prices that are simple, efficient, and resilient, sometimes even performing nearly as well as those derived from rich, data-intensive strategies.

6 Algorithmic and AI-Based Pricing

> Algorithms are opinions embedded in code.
> —Cathy O'Neil

This chapter focuses on the rise of algorithmic pricing, where prices are dynamically set and automatically adjusted by algorithms. It discusses how these systems function, highlighting their benefits and limitations in today's fast-evolving market.

As a start, it's important to make the distinction between algorithmic pricing, AI-based pricing, and large language model (LLM)–based pricing, which represent successive stages in the evolution of technology-enabled pricing. If we take a step back, we see that pricing has evolved through four stages. First, manual pricing decisions relied on managers' judgment, limited information, and periodic reviews. Their main strengths are the explicit consideration of context and ethics, along with explainability. However, these approaches suffer from poor scalability, infrequent updates, inconsistent execution across managers, and weak use of data. Second, simple automated rules (e.g., if-then logic, fixed retail markups, seasonal or inventory triggers, and rule-based or optimization models) introduced speed and consistency. This stage—often referred to as algorithmic pricing—enables scalable, automated, and dynamically adjustable prices, making monitoring and auditing easier. Predefined formulas often adjust prices based on demand, costs, or competitor moves. Its limitations include rigidity, weak adaptation to market shocks, and vulnerability to gaming once rules become predictable or easy to reverse-engineer. Third, AI-based pricing went further by using machine learning or deep learning models to uncover complex, nonlinear patterns in large datasets, enabling more accurate demand forecasting, customer segmentation, and dynamic adjustments. Unlike static rules, these learning algorithms continuously update from data, often delivering higher accuracy, faster reactions, and measurable profit gains through experimentation. Their drawbacks include opacity, potential bias from historical data, data governance requirements, and the need for ongoing monitoring and retraining—though many models incorporate explainability features and human-in-the-loop oversight. Fourth, LLM-based pricing (discussed in the next chapter) used LLMs and autonomous agents to generate and interpret pricing recommendations in natural language, incorporating contextual signals such as customer sentiment or competitive intelligence, and even reasoning about fairness or strategy. These systems enable end-to-end automation—from strategy design and data scraping to simulating scenarios and running large-scale experiments—while lowering barriers to entry for firms with limited data or technical expertise. While algorithmic pricing is rules-driven and AI-based pricing is data-driven, LLM-based pricing is context- and language-driven, opening new possibilities for explainability and interaction with human decision-makers. At the same time, it raises new challenges related to prompt sensitivity, hallucinations, and accountability.

Algorithms Are Ruling the Pricing World

Algorithmic pricing is a strategy that involves using algorithms and automated systems to adjust prices based on changes in supply and demand, competitor decisions, and other market factors. This approach allows businesses to set prices that are optimized for maximum revenue and profit while also responding quickly to changing market conditions. Algorithmic pricing is commonly used in industries such as e-commerce, travel, and transportation, where prices can fluctuate rapidly based on factors such as inventory levels, seasonal demand, and competitor actions. However, it has also been used in other industries including healthcare and real estate. One potential benefit of algorithmic pricing is that it can make markets more efficient by allowing prices to adjust dynamically to changing conditions. However, critics argue that it can also result in higher prices for certain groups of consumers, particularly those who are less price-sensitive or have limited access to information. Overall, algorithmic pricing is a powerful tool for businesses to optimize prices and respond to market conditions, but it also requires careful consideration of ethical and consumer protection issues.

Here are some concrete examples of algorithmic pricing in action:

- **E-commerce**: Alibaba and Amazon are well-known for their use of algorithmic pricing to often adjust prices promptly based on supply and demand. For example, prices for popular items like electronics or toys may change several times a day, based on factors such as inventory levels and competitor prices.
- **Ride-hailing**: Companies like Lyft and Uber may use algorithmic pricing to adjust fares in real time based on factors such as demand, availability of drivers, traffic, and weather conditions. During periods of high demand, such as rush hour or bad weather, prices may increase to encourage more drivers to work and reduce waiting times for riders.
- **Airlines**: Many airlines use algorithmic pricing to adjust fares based on factors such as demand, time of day, and competition. For example, a flight departing on a holiday weekend or during peak travel season is likely to be priced higher than the same flight on a weekday during the off-season.
- **Healthcare**: In some countries, healthcare providers have started using algorithmic pricing to adjust the cost of treatments and services based on factors such as patient demand, provider availability, and local market conditions. This can help ensure that patients are charged fair prices for healthcare services while also helping to reduce costs and improve efficiency in the healthcare system.
- **Gas stations**: Algorithms are increasingly shaping how gasoline prices are set at the pump, transforming what was once a relatively manual, reactive process into a highly automated, data-driven environment. Today, many major fuel retailers, including BP, Chevron, and Shell, use real-time pricing algorithms that automatically adjust fuel prices based on a range of factors including competitor prices in the area, wholesale fuel costs, traffic patterns, weather conditions, and even time of day. One striking example comes from a European fuel retailer that updated prices three times per day using algorithmic tools, outperforming local rivals in both volume and margin (which are two of the most important metrics in this context). It became common to leverage pricing software that can monitor dozens of nearby stations and tweak prices accordingly (sometimes within hours), allowing gas stations to remain competitive without manual intervention.

The examples above represent only a fraction of the industries embracing algorithmic pricing. Today, algorithmic pricing spans a wide range of applications, including entertainment, transportation, travel and tourism, sports and live events, and publishing. By 2026, even organizations like FIFA have formally adopted dynamic pricing for World Cup tickets, underscoring its growing mainstream acceptance.[1]

Importantly, deploying algorithmic pricing in real-world applications presents several challenges. Foroughifar and Mehta (2023) offered valuable insights into why well-designed algorithmic pricing tools can fail to gain traction. Focusing on Airbnb's "Smart Pricing" (SP) feature, which can be described as an algorithmic tool to help hosts dynamically adjust nightly rates, the study investigated why adoption remained low despite the tool being free and potentially profitable. Using detailed data from 6,678 listings across four US cities over thirty-five months, the researchers found that SP generally outperforms default prices, especially for hosts who rarely adjust their pricing manually. Yet ironically, these are the very hosts who are least likely to adopt SP. The study showed that the main barrier to adoption wasn't high switching or learning costs but rather hosts' pessimistic beliefs about the tool's effectiveness. Specifically, hosts seem to assume that such tools would significantly underprice their listing. Airbnb's lack of transparency about how SP worked may have contributed to this skepticism. In summary, deploying algorithmic tools successfully requires more than just technical accuracy. It requires trust-building, transparency, user-centric design, and organizational learning. Firms must invest not only in algorithms but also in clear communication, training sessions, and transparency.

The benefits are clear: Well-designed algorithms may help firms maximize margins, react quickly to changing market factors, and reduce human error. However, the downside is a growing public concern about fairness and transparency. When customers see prices fluctuate multiple times a day, it can create a perception of manipulation or price gouging, especially in times of crisis, like hurricanes or global supply disruptions. Moreover, when multiple competitors use similar algorithmic systems, prices may converge unnaturally, raising questions about tacit algorithmic collusion, even in the absence of human coordination. We will revisit these topics later in this book. Ultimately, algorithmic pricing can significantly improve profitability, but it must be paired with guardrails and transparency practices to ensure it remains competitive, legal, and trustworthy in the eyes of consumers and regulators.

AI Is Taking Over

AI pricing is a type of pricing strategy that uses machine learning algorithms to optimize prices. These algorithms analyze large amounts of data, including customer behavior, competitor prices, and market trends, to determine the best price for a product or service at any given time. This approach allows businesses to set prices that are optimized for maximum revenue and profit while also constantly learning and adapting quickly to changing market conditions. Here are some concrete examples of AI pricing in action:

- **Hotels**: AI-powered revenue management platforms like Atomize and Ramsi use machine learning algorithms to analyze data on factors such as occupancy rates, room demand, and competitor prices to optimize hotel room prices. This approach allows hotels to maximize revenue and occupancy rates while also ensuring that prices remain competitive.
- **Retail**: AI-powered dynamic pricing platforms like Incompetitor analyze data on factors such as competitor prices, consumer demand, and inventory levels to adjust prices. For example, a retailer might use AI pricing to lower the price of a product that isn't selling well while raising the price of a popular product to maximize overall profits.
- **Airlines**: AI-powered pricing platforms like PROS use machine learning algorithms to analyze data on factors such as demand, time of day, and competition to optimize airline fares in real time. This approach allows airlines to adjust fares dynamically based on market conditions, which can help improve revenue and profitability.
- **E-commerce**: AI-powered pricing providers analyze data on factors such as competitor prices, customer behavior, and market trends to optimize prices several times a day. This approach allows e-commerce retailers to set prices that are both competitive and profitable.

Overall, AI pricing is a powerful tool for businesses to optimize prices and respond to evolving market conditions. However, it also requires careful consideration of ethical and consumer protection issues, such as ensuring that prices remain fair and transparent.

Reinforcement learning is increasingly used in dynamic pricing to help companies make data-driven decisions in environments where customer behavior, demand, and competition are constantly changing. RL is a type of machine learning where an agent learns to make optimal decisions by interacting with its environment, receiving feedback in the form of rewards (e.g., revenue or profit), and refining its actions over time. For more details on RL and its fundamental framework, see Sutton and Barto 1998. Q-learning, a popular model-free RL algorithm, enables the agent to learn the value of taking certain actions in given states without needing a model of the environment. In dynamic pricing, this could mean testing and adjusting prices based on real-time data like inventory levels, customer segments, or time-sensitive demand. For instance, an e-commerce platform could learn that reducing prices on slow-moving inventory during off-peak hours boosts sales without hurting long-term profitability.

A prominent application comes from Alibaba, which has implemented Deep Q-Learning networks to automate and optimize product pricing across its marketplace. For example, He et al. (2018) presented an approach where Alibaba used RL to adjust both ad placements and prices to maximize conversions and revenue. Liu et al. (2019) presented an approach also developed by Alibaba with a dynamic pricing system based on deep RL to help sellers on its Tmall platform adjust prices in real time. Instead of setting fixed prices or using simple rules, their system learns directly from data (e.g., customer behavior and sales trends) to recommend smarter prices that boost sales and profits. In a large experiment involving thousands of products, this AI-powered approach outperformed traditional pricing methods. This system made it easier to fine-tune prices and adapt to changing demand, all while maintaining a good customer experience.

Amazon is also believed to have experienced using RL for price optimization. Chen et al. (2016) documented automated repricing behavior in third-party sellers on Amazon. The authors collected data over four months on 1,600 best-selling products, tracking price changes every twenty-five minutes. They found that more than five hundred sellers were likely using pricing algorithms. Not only was algorithmic pricing common, but it was also successful: These sellers tended to win the Buy Box (i.e., were a featured seller) more often, received more customer feedback (a proxy for higher sales), and adjusted their prices more frequently. However, the use of such algorithms also led to volatile pricing, which can potentially confuse or frustrate customers. Another study in e-commerce by Liu (2023) considered dynamic coupon targeting during livestream shopping and showed that employing RL techniques can significantly boost sales.

Similarly, ride-hailing companies like Uber have used RL models to optimize surge pricing in response to fluctuating demand and traffic patterns, as described in several studies (e.g., Qin et al. 2022; Qin et al. 2025). During periods of high demand or reduced supply, such as inclement weather or major events, Uber's algorithms increased fares to incentivize more drivers to become available and to allocate rides to those who value them most. This strategy has been effective in managing rider demand and driver supply, though it has occasionally led to public dissatisfaction when prices surge significantly during emergencies.[2]

The benefits of RL-based pricing are compelling: It allows for adaptive, real-time decision-making, optimizes for long-term rewards (e.g., customer lifetime value), and performs well in complex, time-varying environments where traditional pricing rules may fail. It can also be leveraged to optimize pricing at a granular personalized level. However, RL has several drawbacks. It typically requires large volumes of high-quality data, involves significant computational complexity, and produces decisions that can be opaque and difficult to interpret, making it harder for companies to explain pricing to consumers, leading to potential transparency issues. In addition, the expensive data and computation requirements make RL unaffordable for smaller companies. There may also be ethical concerns, especially when customers feel that prices are being adjusted unfairly. If not carefully managed, RL-based dynamic pricing can result in customer alienation, especially if consumers perceive it as unfair or exploitative.

While algorithms and AI have become common practice for pricing, several risks and pitfalls exist. Bertini and Koenigsberg (2021) published a *Harvard Business Review* article titled "The Pitfalls of Pricing Algorithms" to warn business leaders about the unintended consequences of relying too heavily on algorithmic pricing. While dynamic pricing powered by AI and machine learning can optimize revenue in real time by adjusting to changes in supply, demand, and competition, it can also alienate customers if not thoughtfully managed. The article uses examples, including Uber's controversial surge pricing during emergencies and IKEA's creative distance-based discount program, to illustrate how price changes can shape, and sometimes damage, brand perception. Through case studies and psychological insights, the authors showed that constant, opaque, or unfair-seeming price fluctuations can erode customer trust, trigger backlash, and undermine long-term loyalty. The authors recommended four key practices: (1) defining a clear use case and narrative for pricing strategies, (2) assigning organizational ownership of the algorithm, (3) establishing pricing guardrails to avoid extreme or unfair prices, and (4) giving teams the ability to override algorithms when necessary. For executives, the message is clear: AI-driven pricing algorithms must be designed and governed not just for revenue maximization but with brand integrity, transparency, and customer experience in mind.

Risk of Collusion

Algorithmic collusion refers to the use of algorithms, which are now often powered by AI, to engage in price coordination that mimics collusive behavior among firms, even without direct human communication or explicit agreements. In traditional collusion, companies might secretly agree to fix prices, restrict output, or divide markets, which is illegal under most antitrust laws. However, with the rise of algorithmic pricing systems, firms can unintentionally reach similar outcomes by using autonomous software agents that continuously monitor competitors' prices and adjust their own accordingly. These pricing bots may "learn" to avoid undercutting each other in a competitive market, leading to sustained higher prices that harm consumers, all while avoiding traditional hallmarks of explicit collusion.

A famous example discussed before emerged in 2011 when two Amazon sellers likely used price-setting bots that interacted with each other. One seller used a pricing algorithm to always price a book slightly above the other, while the other used an algorithm to price slightly below. This feedback loop caused the price of the book to skyrocket to over $23 million before anyone intervened. While this case was more of a pricing error than a deliberate cartel, it showcased how algorithms can create unintended consequences. Another example is a landmark antitrust case from 2015, when the US Department of Justice (DOJ) secured its first criminal conviction for price fixing in an online marketplace. The case involved David Topkins, an executive at a poster retailer, who conspired with competitors to coordinate prices for posters sold on Amazon. They agreed on target price levels and then implemented those agreements using pricing software. This case (as well as several other cases) will be discussed in more detail in chapter 9.

The risk of algorithmic collusion is especially pronounced in sectors where prices are updated frequently, products are relatively homogeneous (e.g., airline tickets, ride-hailing services, or online retail), and competitors use similar pricing technologies. In such environments, algorithms can rapidly "learn" that aggressive price cuts trigger retaliation from competitors' bots, leading to a tacit understanding that cooperation (i.e., maintaining higher prices) is likely to be more profitable. What makes this form of collusion more insidious is its ability to operate without any explicit programming to collude, making it harder for regulators to prove intent or coordination.

Despite these risks, not all algorithmic pricing is harmful. When used ethically, algorithms can improve efficiency, respond better to consumer demand, and personalize offers, often ultimately benefiting consumers. The challenge is to strike a balance between innovation and competition policy. To avoid algorithmic collusion, companies should maintain human oversight over their pricing systems, ensure transparency in how algorithms are designed and function, and conduct regular audits to confirm compliance with antitrust law. Some regulatory bodies, like the European Commission and the FTC, have already started to examine whether antitrust frameworks should be adapted to address these new challenges. For instance, regulators are considering requiring algorithmic explainability and incorporating ethical design principles into automated systems. For more details on how AI is reshaping pricing litigation, including the topic of collusion, see Cohen 2026.

In summary, algorithmic collusion sits at the complex intersection of technology, economics, and law. While algorithms can unlock significant value for businesses and consumers alike, they also pose new risks for market fairness and consumer welfare. Proactive governance, smart regulation, and responsible innovation are key to ensuring that the benefits of algorithmic pricing are realized in a way that promotes both efficiency and fair competition.

Importance of Human in the Loop and the "Black Box" Issue

Incorporating human oversight into AI algorithms is one of the most important safeguards for business leaders when decisions impact customer experience, trust, or compliance. While AI can make recommendations or automate decisions, a human manager should guide, oversee, and override decisions when needed. This isn't just theoretical best practice. It's a practical necessity. AI is powerful, but it may lack judgment, empathy, and awareness of context (at least for now). In many applications, "human-in-the-loop" systems have prevented major failures. For example, an e-commerce platform once noticed that its AI began raising prices on essential baby products during a flu outbreak because demand was surging. Fortunately, a pricing manager intervened to prevent what could have been viewed as exploitive. In the world of pricing, human oversight ensures that personalized or dynamic pricing strategies remain within ethical, legal, and brand-aligned boundaries. A human-in-the-loop model might, for instance, flag pricing suggestions that deviate too far from expected norms, target vulnerable groups, or inadvertently result in bias or discrimination. At a global retailer I advised, pricing algorithms were trained to offer discounts based on purchase behavior, but a human audit revealed that certain neighborhoods were excluded from promotions due to flawed proxy data. This led to the implementation of fairness checks, thresholds, and manual review steps before any wide-scale price changes went live.

A pressing challenge with AI-driven pricing is the lack of transparency, which can significantly erode customer trust and expose businesses to reputational and regulatory risks. At a high level, many pricing algorithms, especially those powered by complex machine learning models, operate as "black boxes," meaning they produce price decisions without offering clear explanations of how or why those prices were chosen. While this might be acceptable for internal optimization, it can become a serious issue when customers notice inconsistent or seemingly unfair pricing, particularly in personalized or dynamic environments. A classic example occurred when customers on Amazon discovered that the same DVD was being offered at different prices depending on whether they were logged in or not (and on other cookies information), leading to public backlash and concerns about fairness. As discussed before, there were also examples in the ride-hailing space, where users have reported seeing higher fares during urgent moments or when their phone's battery was low, fueling the perception that the algorithm is exploiting vulnerability rather than offering value.

In the world of pricing, this lack of explainability and transparency not only affects consumers but also limits internal accountability. Indeed, business managers often can't fully understand or justify why certain pricing decisions were made, which becomes particularly risky when dealing with regulated markets like insurance, lending, or healthcare. To mitigate this, forward-thinking companies are investing in explainable AI principles with the mission of designing models that can clearly articulate the key drivers of a price (e.g., product features, customer segment, demand trends) and offering human-readable justifications when needed. Firms are also implementing "transparency layers" in customer-facing platforms, such as showing why a certain discount or dynamic price was applied, to build trust and avoid the "algorithmic lottery" feeling. In some cases, businesses establish internal pricing ethics boards or AI oversight committees to review algorithmic outputs regularly. Ultimately, while AI can optimize prices with high speed and precision, trust is a long-term asset. Thus, businesses must ensure their pricing systems aren't only smart but also fair, explainable, and defensible in the eyes of both customers and regulators.

Human oversight should not be seen as a brake on innovation. It's an insurance policy against unintended consequences. As regulatory scrutiny grows, smart companies are embedding safeguards like audit trails, ethical red flags, manual approvals, and compliance checklists into their pricing systems. This isn't only to prevent harm but also to build customer trust. In short, keeping a human in the loop is about balancing machine intelligence with human responsibility, ensuring that AI serves your strategy rather than allowing it to be dictated by AI.

7 Generative AI for Pricing

> Generative AI has the potential to change the world in ways that we can't even imagine.
>
> —Bill Gates

This chapter examines how recent advances in GenAI tools can be leveraged to transform pricing decisions. By lowering technical and financial barriers, these tools democratize access to sophisticated pricing capabilities, empowering even small businesses to benefit from AI without the need for costly, bespoke solutions. We begin by discussing how GenAI serves as a game changer, particularly by leveling the playing field for smaller firms. Next, we highlight the fundamental differences between traditional algorithmic pricing and GenAI-driven approaches (aka LLM-based pricing). A central argument of this chapter is that prompting is everything: Effective pricing recommendations depend heavily on how prompts are crafted. To that end, we provide actionable guidelines for designing prompts tailored to pricing contexts. We then present three in-depth case studies: pricing a house, a used car, and hourly contracting work, each supported by rich datasets and extensive analyses. We then discuss how GenAI can be leveraged for market research, data augmentation, and data scraping. Next, we explore whether the machine learning operations (MLOps) pipeline for data-driven price optimization can be streamlined using a structured, step-by-step prompting strategy. We also discuss a potential design for a multiagent AI system in which specialized agents collaboratively automate the MLOps pipeline. Finally, we discuss a critical regulatory question: What are the implications for market competition if firms increasingly rely on LLMs to set prices?

Democratization of AI

As AI continues to disrupt how businesses operate, pricing decisions are no exception. For years, companies have used algorithmic and AI pricing models to optimize prices with precision and speed. But now, a new player has entered the scene: GenAI, powered by LLMs like ChatGPT.

In Cohen, Spittle, et al. 2024, we compared two types of pricing approaches—traditional algorithmic tools versus LLM-based tools—and evaluated their advantages, limitations, and implications for businesses, consumers, and regulators.

As discussed, algorithmic pricing tools have been around for decades and are used extensively in sectors like e-commerce, travel, hospitality, and ride-hailing. These models rely on high-quality historical data, carefully built rules, and assumptions to optimize prices. Think of them as custom-built engines: powerful, data-driven, but expensive and requiring technical expertise to build, maintain, and deploy. These tools typically offer (1) reliable and repeatable results, (2) precision in complex, multivariable pricing environments (e.g., dynamic discounts, personalized promotions), and (3) the ability to scale rapidly and learn over time. But they come with drawbacks, including high setup and maintenance costs, limited flexibility (e.g., built around predefined logic and data frameworks), and potential concerns around bias and explainability. In contrast, LLMs offer an entirely different approach. Instead of hardcoding logic and data, managers simply feed in a prompt—namely, a natural language description of the market, product, pricing goals—and the model generates pricing recommendations on the spot. Think of it as a consultant in a box: It doesn't need proprietary data or custom code and can deliver insights based on its vast training knowledge. This game changer has several advantages, including the following:

- **Ease of use:** No technical expertise needed.
- **Low cost and fast deployment:** No need to purchase an expensive license. Just write a prompt.
- **Flexible thinking:** It isn't constrained by preprogrammed logic, allowing it to propose creative pricing strategies and think outside the box.
- **Democratization of pricing tools:** Small businesses (in fact, everybody) can now access insights that were once reserved for large, data-rich organizations.

The latter democratization argument is big (Cohen 2024). GenAI may be arguably the most democratizing force pricing has ever seen. By lowering barriers to access, it opens the door for small businesses, start-ups, and new entrants to compete on pricing sophistication without needing large datasets or hiring data science talent. But with great power comes new responsibilities. The ease of using GenAI must be balanced with ethical use, bias mitigation, and thoughtful governance. Indeed, while GenAI unlocks new opportunities, it also introduces new concerns that need to be carefully considered and mitigated:

- **Lack of explainability**: It may be difficult to justify or trace how GenAI models arrive at pricing suggestions. This can be risky in regulated markets (e.g., finance, healthcare). At the same time, explainability can be partially addressed through prompting.
- **Potential presence of biases**: GenAI models are trained on internet-scale data, which may include skewed perspectives or regional/cultural biases (we will test the presence of such biases later in this chapter).
- **Lack of consistency**: Unlike traditional pricing algorithms that yield consistent results, GenAI responses vary depending on how a question is phrased, even if the inputs are the same. In fact, even when using the exact same phrasing, responses are often different. This lack of consistency reduces confidence in the results and blurs the notion of optimality.
- **Prompt quality = Outcome quality**: A weak prompt leads to weak pricing advice. There's now a premium on prompt engineering, not just data science.

Table 7.1 compares algorithmic pricing and GenAI-based pricing across several dimensions (Cohen, Spittle, et al. 2024). In summary, LLMs aren't replacing pricing teams (at least not yet), but they are augmenting them. For many companies, GenAI offers a quick, affordable way to brainstorm or validate pricing strategies before investing in deeper analytics. It also democratizes access to AI by allowing small companies to rely on such tools and scale decisions at low cost. In industries with limited data, fast-moving markets, or small budgets, LLMs offer game-changing access to pricing intelligence. However, for mission-critical pricing decisions, especially those requiring legal or financial transparency, traditional algorithmic tools still provide greater control and reliability. Future pricing strategies may involve

Table 7.1
Algorithmic pricing versus GenAI pricing: Key differences

Feature	Algorithmic pricing	GenAI-based pricing
Data needs	Requires large volumes of structured historical data	No proprietary data needed, relies on prompt content
Customization	Highly specialized and tailored to business	General purpose but flexible
Ease of use	Requires data scientists and engineers	Accessible to managers and nontechnical users
Transparency	Transparent when well-documented	Often opaque ("black box" reasoning), with the exception of reasoning models
Cost	High (development + maintenance)	Low to none (off-the-shelf tools like ChatGPT)
Consistency and scalability	Excellent at scale with good data	Limited consistency; not yet reliable for automation
Biases	Bias depends on model design and training data	Bias may come from LLM training data or prompts' content

a hybrid approach: using GenAI for ideation and flexibility, and algorithms for precision and execution. We next elaborate on the importance of mastering how to prompt properly.

Prompting Is Everything

As discussed, AI-based pricing is data-driven, whereas LLM-based (or GenAI-based) pricing is context- and language-driven, opening new possibilities for explainability and interaction with human decision-makers. In the world of GenAI, prompting is everything. And this is especially true when using these tools to support or guide pricing decisions. A "prompt" is the instruction or question given to an LLM and will determine what kind of answer you get in return. But not all prompts are created equal. The way you frame the question, how much detail you include, what context you provide, and how clearly you guide the AI can all dramatically affect the quality, accuracy, and pertinence of the pricing recommendation you receive. Think of the prompt briefing as a consultant: The better the input you provide, the more insightful and actionable the output will be.

Unlike traditional rule-based pricing systems that operate within preprogrammed constraints, GenAI tools rely entirely on natural language guidance to understand the context, goals, and assumptions behind your pricing challenge. This makes the quality, specificity, and structure of your prompts absolutely critical. For example, a question like "What should I charge for a protein snack?" is too vague and unlikely to produce anything useful and may return a generic answer that ignores your cost structure, competitive landscape, or strategic positioning. In contrast, a more specific, well-crafted prompt can be:

> "I'm launching a mid-tier, plant-based protein snack in Canada, targeted at health-conscious consumers aged 25–40. My unit cost is $1.80, competitors are priced between $2.99 and $3.49, and I want to maintain a 40 percent gross margin while appealing to eco-conscious consumers. What pricing strategy do you recommend, and how should I position it across online and in-store channels?"

This will guide the AI to deliver far more relevant and aligned recommendations to ultimately yield useful insights.

I once advised a retailer who wanted to use ChatGPT to help price a new product line; their initial prompt returned a lowball price that risked undercutting the brand. But after they refined the prompt to include details about target margins, competitive benchmarks, and product positioning, the AI suggested a much more strategic price that aligned with both business goals and market expectations. This illustrates a broader truth: GenAI is often only as smart as the prompt it receives. For business executives, this means learning to think like a strategist when interacting with these tools. Namely, you should treat the AI not as a magic answer machine but as a collaborative partner that needs proper direction. Whether you're setting a base price, testing promotion strategies, or simulating customer responses, crafting thoughtful, structured, and data-informed prompts will make the difference between a helpful assistant and a misguided guess. In short, the art of prompting is one of the new skillsets for modern pricing leaders, and mastering it unlocks the real power of GenAI. I've seen business teams dramatically improve the output of GenAI just by iterating on their prompts.

Another example demonstrating the importance of prompting is a digital subscription business testing different bundle configurations. When the manager asked, "What price should I charge for a bundle of services?" the AI provided vague suggestions. But when reframed to include past churn data, WTP insights, and tiered usage patterns, the model suggested highly strategic price points and even proposed a new "light" tier that hadn't been considered. This shows, once again, that the AI's output quality is tied to the depth and clarity of the prompt. Missing facts, underspecified objectives, or loosely structured requests can lead to superficial or even misleading answers.

This dynamic has broader implications for how organizations should think about AI integration. Using the tool isn't enough; teams must build internal prompting expertise to glean useful insights from these models. Teams that take the time to structure their prompts with key business information, like cost constraints, margin targets, seasonality, customer profiles, or regulatory considerations, will consistently unlock better outcomes.

Prompting should be viewed as an iterative dialogue rather than a one-shot request. Ask a first version, analyze the AI's response, and then follow up with refinements and deeper questions. In this sense, prompting becomes a new kind of business skill encompassing a blend of strategic thinking, domain expertise, and clear communication. For pricing leaders, this means reimagining their role not just as decision-makers but as effective "AI collaborators" who know how to steer the machine toward meaningful insights.

Ultimately, the effectiveness of GenAI in pricing isn't just about what the model can do. Rather, it's about what the user asks it to do. Poorly crafted prompts will likely lead to generic answers that could mislead teams or even damage brand value. But thoughtful, structured prompts can transform the AI into a pricing advisor that helps uncover opportunities, test ideas, and optimize strategies with remarkable speed and flexibility. As GenAI becomes more embedded in pricing workflows, the ability to craft effective prompts may well become a core competitive advantage for modern pricing teams. It's not just about using AI but about speaking its language. At a high level, here are five dos and five don'ts of prompting for pricing:

- **Be specific and data-driven**: Include as much relevant information as possible, such as cost structure, target margins, competitor prices, and customer segments.
- **Describe the context**: Mention launch timing, channels (online vs. retail), brand positioning, and market maturity.
- **Ask layered questions**: Start broad and then drill down. For example, "What will happen if I lower the price by 10 percent? How will that affect volume sales?"
- **Test scenarios**: Use a variety of "what-if" prompts to explore different pricing models, bundles, and discount strategies.

- **Think like a strategist**: Treat the AI as a pricing advisor, not a calculator.
- **Don't ask overly vague questions**: The question "What's a good price?" will almost always yield weak results.
- **Don't ignore constraints**: Without specifying margins, costs, or regulatory considerations, the AI may suggest impractical prices.
- **Don't treat the first answer as final**: This one is perhaps the most important point. You definitely want to use follow-ups to refine, challenge, and pressure-test the model's recommendations, again and again.
- **Don't forget customer perception**: Always include information about customer value, sensitivity, or expectations.
- **Don't rely solely on the AI** (if possible): Use the GenAI output as a complement to business judgment, not a substitute.

Table 7.2 summarizes the importance of prompting in the context of pricing by proposing a quality ladder with five levels. The key is to be as comprehensive as possible and include all the relevant and pertinent information while also going through several iterations to refine the final result. While level 1 will likely generate a generic output with

Table 7.2
Prompt quality ladder: A framework for effective pricing prompts

Prompt level	Description	Example
Level 1: Vague prompt	Basic, unclear, lacks context	"What price should I charge?"
Level 2: General prompt	Some detail but missing key pricing inputs	"What price should I charge for a fitness app targeting millennials?"
Level 3: Contextual prompt	Adds business objectives and competitive context	"I'm launching a fitness app targeting millennials at $1.50 cost, with top apps priced at $4.99–$6.99."
Level 4: Strategic prompt	Includes goals, constraints, customer segments, channel plans	"I want to achieve a 50% gross margin, compete with $5 apps, and position it as a budget-friendly option."
Level 5: Iterative prompting	Uses several follow-up questions, scenario testing, and dialogue with AI for refinement	Starts with level 4 and then asks, "What if I bundle it with a wellness tracker? How would pricing change?"

little relevance, higher levels can often generate highly actionable pricing strategies with strong business fit, which are specifically tailored to the focal scenario.

Another key principle in effective prompting is to structure the prompt into distinct parts, each serving a specific purpose. A commonly used approach is the RISEN five-step framework:[1]

- **Role**: Defines the AI's role and expertise in relation to the task.
- **Input (or Instructions)**: Specifies the data or information the AI should consider.
- **Steps**: Outlines the process or sequence of actions the AI should follow.
- **Expectations**: Clearly states the desired output, outcome, or goal.
- **Narrowing (or Novelty)**: Adds constraints or areas of focus to guide a more precise, targeted response.

While the effectiveness of the RISEN framework varies widely depending on the context, it's generally regarded as good practice for crafting high-quality prompts. For example, in the context of pricing, the first step (Role) might look like this:

> "You are a seasoned pricing strategist with several years of experience, specializing in pricing newly launched products in the food and wellness category for the North American market."

This role-setting step sets the tone and clearly outlines the scope of the task by clarifying the AI's assumed expertise. From there, the remaining steps of the RISEN framework can be built out to offer structured and complete instructions, in a similar way as one would brief a human expert.

As mentioned, one important aspect of working with GenAI tools for pricing is that the answers are inherently stochastic, meaning that the output can vary even when using the exact same prompt with the same LLM. This behavior stems from how these models are designed, which introduces stochasticity into their generation process. This randomness, controlled by parameters like temperature and top-k/top-p sampling, leads the model to not always produce consistent, deterministic answers. As a result, the same prompt may yield different word choices, reasoning paths, or emphases, allowing for diversity and creativity but also introducing variability in outcomes. In other words, GenAI doesn't retrieve fixed answers from a database and doesn't apply clear well-defined rules;

instead, it generates text by predicting the next word in a sequence based on probabilities. These probabilities are influenced by a wide array of factors, including training data and recent interactions. Thus, a prompt like "What is a good launch price for a premium insulated water bottle costing $8 to produce and targeted at eco-conscious consumers?" may yield varying pricing suggestions (e.g., $18.99 in one run and $21.50 in another) or different justifications for similar price points. This randomness isn't a flaw. It's part of what allows GenAI to be flexible, creative, and contextually adaptive. However, for business leaders looking for consistency and reliability in pricing decisions, it introduces a layer of uncertainty that must be managed thoughtfully.

To mitigate this variability, there are several best practices pricing teams can adopt. First, you should run multiple iterations of the same prompt and analyze the range of outputs to help identify a pricing consensus and filter out outliers (called a stability test). Second, an effective approach could be to use structured, step-by-step prompting (also known as "chain-of-thought" prompting), where you break down the decision-making process and guide the AI through it in a clear, logical order. For example, you instruct the AI to first evaluate the competitive landscape, then the customer value perception, and only after these are completed to propose a price. Third, consider saving the top-performing prompt versions that consistently yield clear, well-reasoned outputs and document the assumptions used for traceability and internal validation. One consumer electronics brand I worked with ran the same bundle-pricing prompt five times, receiving results ranging from $59 to $74. By identifying the underlying logic in each response, they could synthesize a strategy that combined the best insights from all runs, resulting in a final price of $69 backed by customer research and AI justification. Another way to reduce randomness is by explicitly asking the AI to explain its reasoning step-by-step, which can provide more consistent logical paths across responses. Ultimately, users should not expect GenAI to offer one "perfect" price every time. Instead, treat it as a smart brainstorming partner: Variability is a feature, not a bug, and when harnessed correctly, it can spark deeper strategic thinking, highlight blind spots, and uncover pricing angles that might otherwise go unexplored.

Interestingly, recent advances in GenAI are making prompt engineering easier and potentially less critical. Newer models increasingly engage users in interactive dialogues, asking follow-up questions to clarify intent and refine the prompt, effectively enabling chain-of-thought prompting by default. In addition, users can now initiate conversations with queries like:

> "What questions do you have for me that would clarify my objective, constraints, and help you do a better job at accomplishing my goal?"

or

> "Ask me 10 clarifying questions about my objectives, constraints, strategic considerations, and any key facts you need. Wait for my answers."

While crafting an effective prompt remains valuable and can often be a key differentiator, the reliance on users to get it exactly right from the start may diminish as AI systems become more proactive and adaptive in understanding user needs.

Three Concrete Examples

We now consider three everyday examples: pricing a house, pricing a used car, and setting the hourly rate for contracting work. These examples represent situations that are relevant to many individuals in various stages of life. In each example, we describe the full process of using GenAI to get recommended prices. We then compare the AI-generated prices to the human-set ones and discuss the implications.

Real Estate

GenAI has disrupted several industries and business practices, including real estate. In today's world, the use of GenAI is inevitable to boost real estate professionals' daily operations. Several real estate agents are routinely using tools like ChatGPT to create listings, automate repetitive administrative tasks, retrieve critical information from documents, draft and review agreements, and provide advice and recommendations. One such recommendation, which is one of the most (if not the most) critical decisions in real estate, is setting the selling price for a newly listed property.

Selling or buying a home is an important life decision and, often, an emotional one. Setting the right listing price is critical, and getting it wrong can lead to delayed sales, reduced interest, or lower final offers. Brokers typically rely on an approach based on running comparable analyses by embedding human expertise at understanding the market conditions and societal trends. Of course, there is also a discussion with the seller that often leads to modifying the asking price. At a high level, most brokers in several markets are running an analysis that retrieves all the "similar" properties that were recently sold (e.g., three to six months, depending on the market intensity) in the same neighborhood. Then, one can compute the average and median selling prices for those comparable properties. Although this approach has been well accepted for decades in the real estate industry, it suffers from several shortcomings. First, how should one define "similar" properties? This is obviously very subjective, and different brokers will have different definitions. If the seller's property has a three-car garage but no other property does, what should we do? Second, the market is very seasonal and depends on macroeconomic factors, so the past is often not a good indication of the present. Third, how should we define the right notion of neighborhood? Sometimes, two houses may be 500 meters apart, but the streets have different perceived values and desirability. And fourth, each property is unique and has several inherent features that must be carefully accounted for. While running comparable analyses (and handling a detailed report to the client) is imperfect, it has been used by many real estate brokers for decades.

It's thus unsurprising that many brokers have recently started to leverage tools like ChatGPT and AI agents to generate recommended selling prices when listing new properties on the market. It's easy to prompt such tools by inputting all the relevant information about the property and asking to recommend a price. One can even engage in a back-and-forth discussion with the AI to question the rationale behind the recommended price and explicitly ask how it compares to the prices of other properties, whether recently sold or currently on the market. This shift is a substantial disruption by allowing brokers to get access (at no cost) to a sophisticated tool that can output price recommendations.

In Tanlamai et al. (2025), we studied the problem of setting selling prices for properties by examining two research questions:

1. Does the use of GenAI to set the asking prices of properties result in prices that are higher or lower than those set by humans?
2. Do housing prices generated by GenAI amplify or alleviate price discrimination in the housing market?

Real estate markets have a long history of allegations of housing discrimination, with studies documenting that homes in minority-dominated neighborhoods are often valued lower than those in predominantly white neighborhoods, even after controlling for some observable features. These disparities have traditionally been attributed, at least in part, to human biases, whether explicit or systemic. With the rise of AI, there was hope that algorithms might mitigate such biases by reducing reliance on subjective human judgments. However, recent research suggests that AI models based on machine learning approaches can often replicate or even amplify historical disparities if trained on biased data (Chen 2023; Ferrara 2023). These findings underscore the importance of our second research question.

We analyzed nearly 285,000 US real estate listings from a major online platform in 2024. For each property, we compared the actual asking price (set by realtors or homeowners) with the price suggested by several LLMs, using standardized prompts and detailed property data (e.g., size, location, school ratings, renovation status). In addition to comparing the GenAI prices to human-set prices, we studied the discrimination question by focusing on racial demographics of neighborhoods, using ZIP code data to distinguish between white- and minority-dominant areas.

When comparing prices recommended by GenAI models to those set by humans, we observed that GenAI-generated prices were, on average, 13.5 percent lower than those set by humans, after rigorously controlling for several key variables. Figure 7.1[2] shows the average prices (including 90 percent confidence intervals) across four LLMs—GPT-4o, GPT-3.5, Gemini 1.5 Flash, and Claude 3.5 Sonnet—against those set by humans. The average human-set price was $403,000 (with a median of $356,700), while the

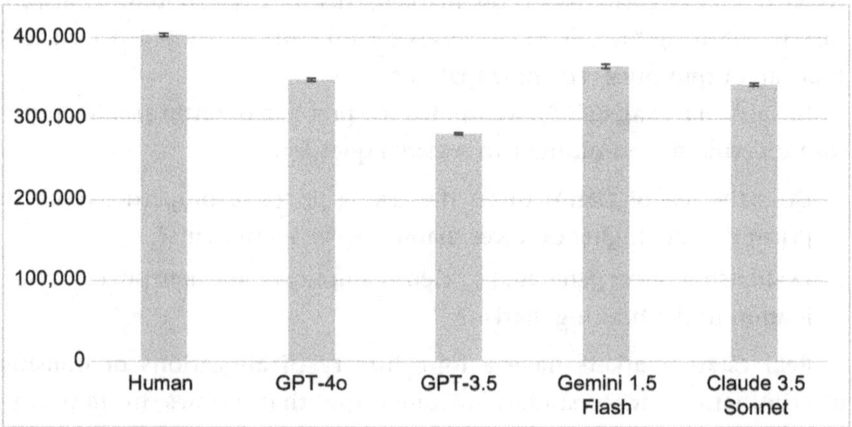

Figure 7.1
Comparison between average human-set and AI-generated prices for houses. *Source:* Author.

AI-generated average prices ranged from $281,000 (GPT-3.5) to $364,700 (Gemini 1.5 Flash). All four LLMs consistently produced lower prices for both mean and median metrics. Recognizing that comparing prices across all properties in aggregate may mask important variation, we also conducted more granular analyses by segmenting the properties, allowing us to better understand how GenAI pricing behavior differs across different types of listings and market contexts.

Figure 7.2 provides a deeper look at pricing behavior by comparing prices set by GPT-4o and by humans across two segments: the bottom 10 percent

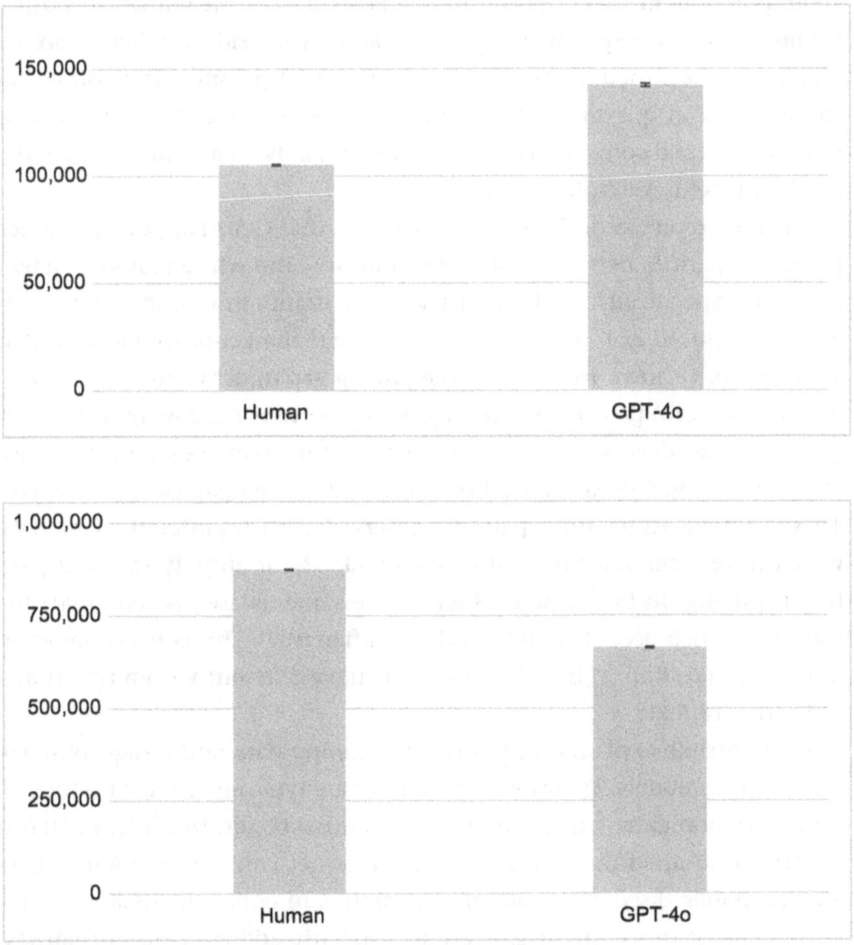

Figure 7.2
Comparisons for most affordable and expensive houses. *Source:* Author.

of the most affordable properties (left panel) and the top 10 percent of the most expensive ones (right panel). Interestingly, the results reveal a clear "compression effect" in GenAI pricing. Specifically, GPT-4o tended to price low-end homes higher than humans, while pricing high-end homes lower. In other words, AI-generated prices appeared to be pulled closer to the average by overvaluing cheaper properties and undervaluing more expensive ones. This pattern suggests that in the absence of domain-specific calibration, GenAI may favor conservative pricing that reduces variability. While this behavior may be beneficial in some contexts (e.g., by reducing pricing outliers or discouraging extreme values), it also raises important questions about potential missed opportunities at both ends of the market spectrum. It's important to note that these results can vary considerably based on the LLM used, the structure and wording of the prompt, and the attributes of the property in question. Thus, while the observed compression trend is noteworthy (and confirmed for all four tested LLMs), it also underscores the need for careful prompt design.

Turning to our second question, we found that GenAI appears to reduce pricing disparities between homes in minority- and white-majority neighborhoods. Specifically, for human-set prices, homes in minority-dominant areas were priced 22.9 percent lower on average than comparable homes in white-majority areas. In contrast, the pricing gap under GenAI recommendations was 14.2 percent, suggesting a 15.6 percent narrowing of this differential. The effect was more pronounced in the luxury segment (top price quartile), where GenAI reduced the observed pricing gap by 17.5 percent. These findings differ from patterns observed with traditional AI models, which have sometimes been shown to replicate or amplify racial disparities in pricing. In fact, when tested on the same dataset, several machine learning models accentuated the pricing differential. This contrast raises an important question: Why might GenAI behave differently from traditional AI in this context?

One possible explanation lies in the training data and design philosophy of these models. Traditional AI systems are typically trained on historical transaction data, which often reflect human biases. In contrast, GenAI models are trained on vast and diverse internet content, including news articles, public discourse, academic research, and policy discussions. Naturally, some of this content is likely to explicitly address issues of fairness and equity in housing. Thus, GenAI appears to incorporate a broader social context and public awareness, leading to more balanced pricing outcomes. This represents a potential paradigm shift: Unlike traditional algorithmic AI tools that risk codifying historical inequities, in some cases GenAI may yield recommendations that reduce disparities.

Many real estate professionals are already integrating GenAI into their daily workflows. Specific examples include writing property listings, drafting client communications, and, increasingly, recommending prices. Our findings suggest that GenAI not only enhances efficiency but also offers a meaningful opportunity to reduce unintentional bias, particularly in markets where agents may have limited experience or exposure. Thus, real estate agents using GenAI may improve equity and fairness without even realizing it, potentially avoiding reputational or legal pitfalls tied to pricing disparities. Our research offers a glimmer of hope in the quest for equitable housing.

Used Cars

Many of us will at one point consider selling our vehicle, and when doing so, setting the right asking price is an important decision. Can we delegate this decision to GenAI? If yes, how close would the price be to the one set by humans?

To answer this question, we collected data from one of the most popular US online platforms for buying and selling vehicles. More precisely, we collected one hundred thousand car listings (in May 2025) and recorded the following information for each listing: Average market price for similar listings, Seller location, Body type, Number of cylinders, Description, Drivetrain type, Engine, Specifications, Color, Features, Make, Mileage, Model, Name, and Listed price.

Figure 7.3 shows the screenshot of a typical listing (for one of the most popular car models) from our dataset. This screenshot includes only the partial list of data features we collected since one needs to scroll down to see the additional features.

For each listing, we ask four different LLMs (GPT-4o, Claude 3.7 Sonnet, Gemini 1.5 Flash, o4-mini) to recommend the appropriate selling price and compare the AI-generated prices to the prices set by humans in the listing. To investigate the impact of the prompt, we consider four prompting strategies (or prompt levels) with an increased level of sophistication and pertinence.

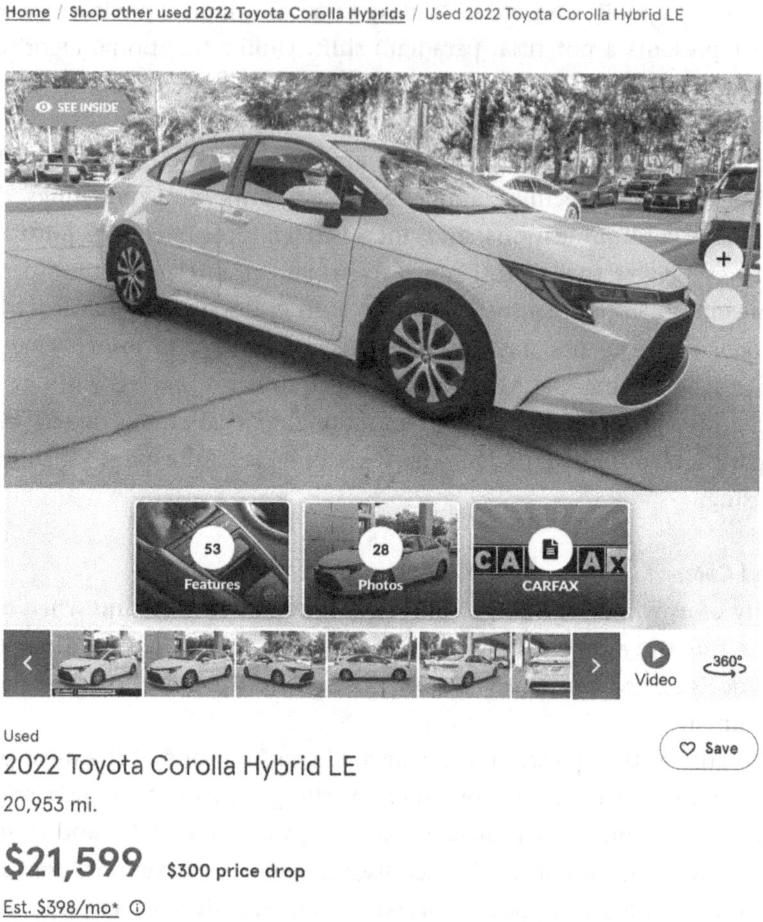

Figure 7.3
Sample listing from our dataset.

Prompt Level 1: Vague Prompt
The initial prompt level establishes a baseline condition with minimal information. More precisely, it only provides the vehicle model to the LLMs.

Prompt Level 2: General Prompt
This level introduces comprehensive vehicle specification data, including information such as key vehicle details and features of the listed car. It provides the LLMs with concrete data fields (such as mileage, model year, and car features) to make a more informed price recommendation, in addition to the information provided in level 1.

Prompt Level 3: Contextual Prompt

Besides including all the information from level 2, this level incorporates market intelligence and contextual information such as the seller's location and comparative market prices for similar vehicles. It explicitly acknowledges the necessity of adjusting market averages to account for vehicle-specific variations in condition, mileage, and regional factors by mentioning in the prompt:

> "Note that while the above average market price is for listings that are relatively similar to the focal one, it's still possible that some important differences (e.g., mileage, car condition, and seller location) are present. Those potential differences need to be carefully accounted for when setting the right selling price for the focal car."

Additionally, this level introduces a strategic objective by defining a clear objective in the prompt:

> "Your goal is to set the right selling price (in USD) so as to sell the car in a timely manner while not leaving money on the table."

Prompt Level 4: Comprehensive Prompt

This level explicitly instructs the AI to consider macroeconomic factors such as inflation rates, interest rates, market-trend analysis, supply-demand dynamics, and vehicle-specific depreciation patterns. It also includes strategic negotiation considerations by suggesting to potentially overprice to leave room for negotiation by including the following statement in the prompt:

> "Also, note that sometimes it may be wise to set a slightly higher selling price to strategically keep some room for negotiation."

This prompt aims to mimic the process used by professional dealers who synthesize multiple streams of information to optimize pricing strategies in dynamic market environments. As before, this prompt includes all the information from level 3.[3]

For illustration purposes, we next report prompt level 4 for the listing from figure 7.3.

> You are an expert car dealer with strong expertise in setting the right selling price for used cars. Your task is to recommend the right selling price (in USD) for the used car described below. Please use all the information provided below to recommend the right selling price.
>
> Model: 2022 Toyota Corolla Hybrid LE
>
> Seller Location: 2985 N Main St, Gainesville, FL 32609

Key Vehicle Details:
- Make: Toyota
- Model: Corolla Hybrid
- Year: 2022
- Trim: LE
- Body Style: Sedan
- Mileage: 20953.0 miles
- Exterior Color: White
- Interior Color: Gray
- Transmission: Automatic CVT
- Fuel Type: Hybrid
- Drivetrain: Front-wheel Drive
- Engine: I4 16V MPFI DOHC Hybrid
- Cylinders: 4.0
- Doors: 4.0

Vehicle Features:
- USB Port
- Adaptive Cruise Control
- Alloy Wheels
- Apple CarPlay®
- Backup Camera
- Blind Spot Monitor
- Bluetooth®
- Brake Assist
- Stability Control
- Keyless Entry
- Keyless Start
- LED Headlights
- Lane Departure Warning
- Satellite Radio
- WiFi Hotspot

Seller Location: Gainesville, FL 32609

Additionally, the average market price for similar listings to the 2022 Toyota Corolla Hybrid LE is $22,322.7.

Note that while this average market price is for listings that are relatively similar to the focal one, it's still possible that some important differences (e.g., the mileage, the car condition, and the geographic location) are present. Those potential differences need to be carefully accounted for when setting the right selling price for the focal used car.

Your goal is to set the right selling price (in USD) so as to sell the car in a timely manner while not leaving money on the table.

To do so, you need to carefully consider the current market trends, supply availability, vehicle depreciation rates, macroeconomic factors (e.g., inflation, interest rates), the geographic location of the vehicle, the value of all the included features, and the average market price of similar listings. Factor in how the demand and popularity for this specific make/model affects the recommended selling price in the current market. Use all the information provided in this prompt as well as your expertise in setting selling prices for used cars. Also, note that sometimes it may be wise to set a slightly higher selling price to strategically keep some room for negotiation.

Please output your answer as a JSON object with the following keys:

- "estimated_price": a numerical value representing your recommended selling price in USD (just the number, no $ symbol).
- "reasoning": a brief explanation to justify your recommendation.

We next discuss our results and takeaways. We divided our analyses into four categories. First, we compared the GenAI-generated prices to the human-set prices for the different LLMs and each prompt level. The results are presented in the charts in figure 7.4.

Figure 7.4 reveals interesting patterns on how different LLMs respond to increasing prompt sophistication. The price recommendations are quite sensitive to both the LLM used and the prompt level. The average human-set price in our data is $31,820.68. The average AI-generated prices range from $30,050.27 to $36,516.39, so the average relative difference remains below 15 percent. For prompt level 4, all tested LLMs recommended prices that are, on average, within 3 percent of the human-set price.

Interestingly, most of the AI-generated prices ended with 0 compared to only 33.37 percent of the human-set prices, as shown in table 7.3.

Second, we compared the performance obtained by using the different prompt levels for each LLM separately. Figure 7.5 plots the results for two LLMs (GPT-4o in the first panel and Claude 3.7 Sonnet in the second panel).

As expected, the quality of the price recommendations (in terms of approaching the human-set values) significantly improves as the prompting strategy becomes more sophisticated. When using level 4, GPT-4o reaches an average price within 2.95 percent from the human-set prices, whereas

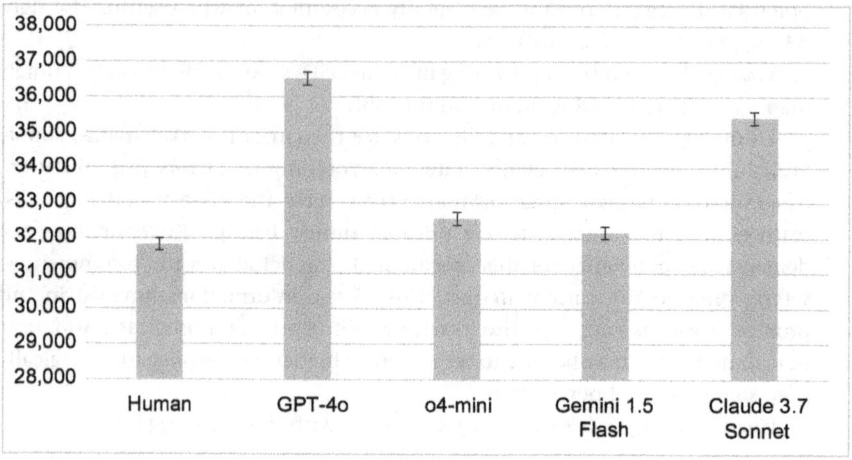

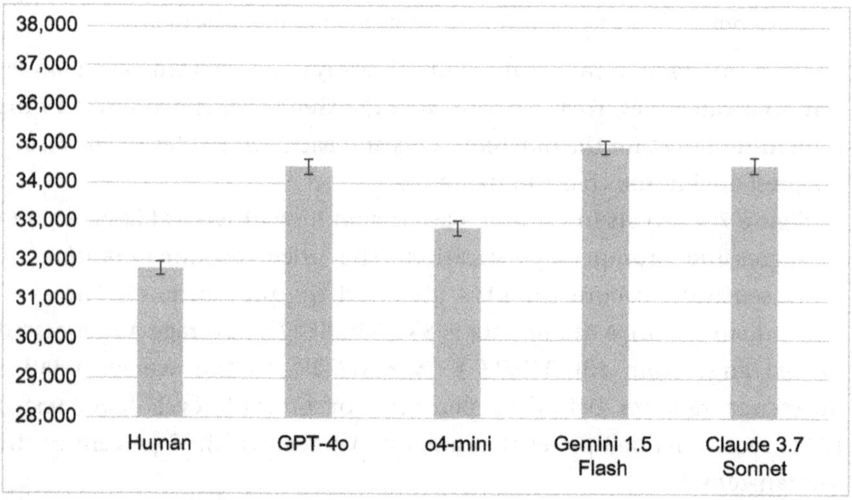

Figure 7.4
Human-set versus AI-generated prices for used cars (four prompt levels). *Source:* Author.

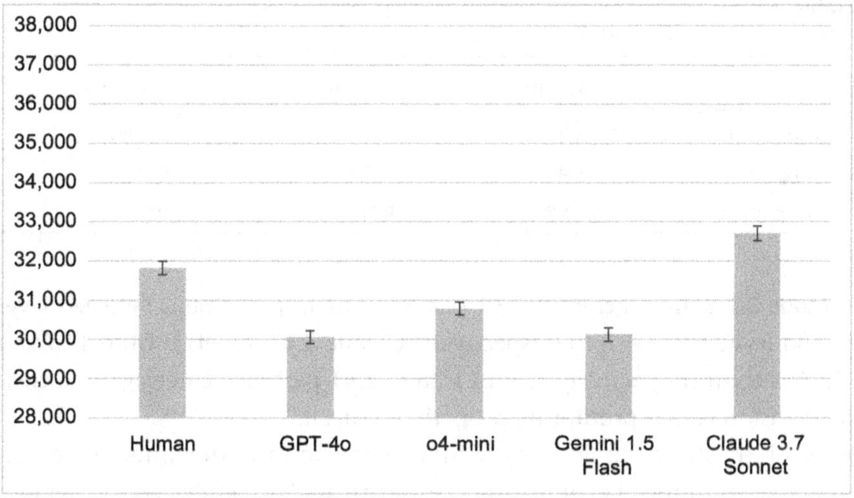

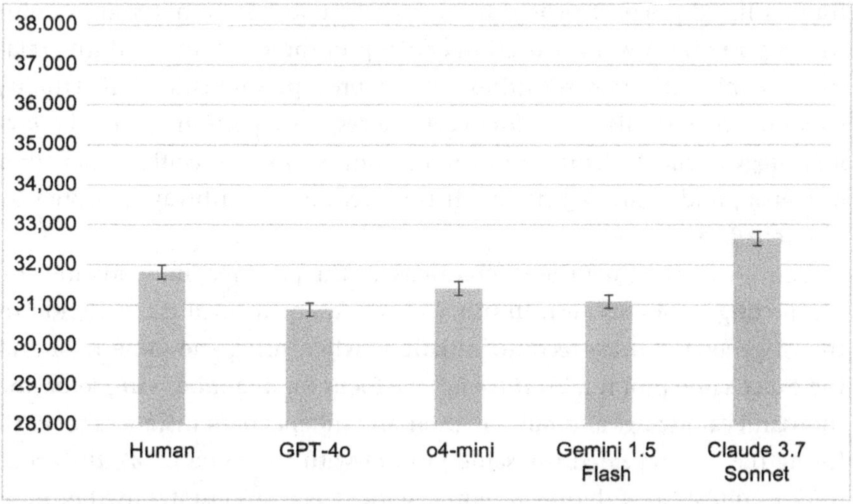

Figure 7.4
(continued)

Table 7.3
Proportions of price-ending digits

	Human	GPT-4o	Claude 3.7 Sonnet
Ending in 0	33.37%	98.5%	92.08%
Ending in 5	17.4%	1.5%	7%
Ending in 9	11.9%	0%	0.9%

Claude 3.7 Sonnet achieves 2.61 percent. The improvement between level 1 and level 4 for GPT-4o (respectively, Claude 3.7 Sonnet) is from 14.75 to 2.95 percent (respectively, from 11.26 to 2.61 percent). Once again, a clear conclusion is that prompting properly is crucial.

GPT-4o shows progressive convergence toward the human benchmark as prompts become more sophisticated; it effectively leverages additional market context and strategic guidance to get closer to the human-listed price. On the other hand, Claude 3.7 Sonnet and o4-mini (not reported) show less variation across prompt levels, maintaining relatively stable estimates regardless of the prompt sophistication. Finally, Gemini 1.5 Flash displays more variable response patterns. These behaviors suggest that the impact of the prompt is model-specific rather than universal, and it highlights the distinct reasoning pathways adopted by different LLMs.

Third, we examined the stochasticity in the price recommendations by conducting a stability test. In other words, we quantified the variation in the AI-generated price recommendations when using the same LLM and the exact same prompt. To this end, we focus on a random sample of one thousand car listings and ran one thousand independent instances for each listing (i.e., we repeated the same prompt with the same LLM), thus running a simulation with one million instances. For this test, we used prompt level 4 with Gemini 1.5 Flash.

As expected, we observed some variation across the one thousand instances. For each car, we computed the average AI-generated price along with its maximal deviation (i.e., the value among the one thousand AI prices that differs the most from the average). We found that the maximal deviation was 11.12 percent on average; in extreme cases, it was as high as 887 percent, suggesting that hallucinations (i.e., situations where the AI recommends a nonsensical, extremely high price) are occurring. For

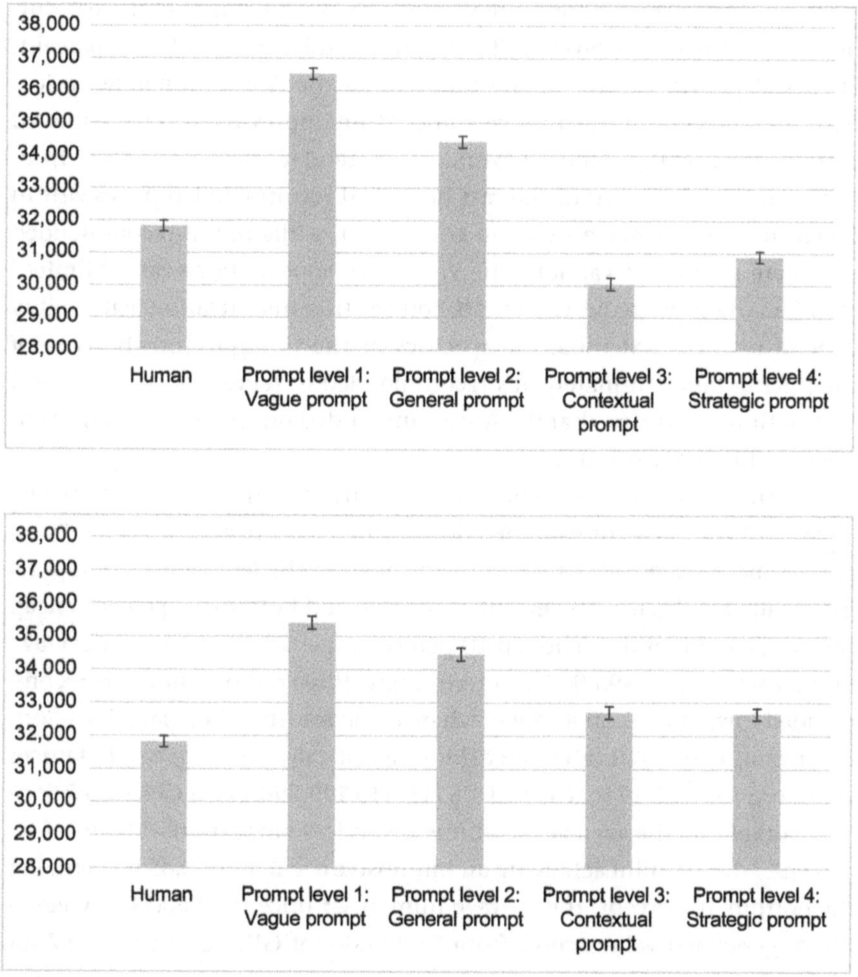

Figure 7.5

Comparisons between the different prompt levels for used cars for two LLMs. *Source:* Author.

most cars, however, we found that after removing a handful of clear outlier values, the deviations aren't substantial and are around +/–5 percent. Specifically, 81.6 percent of the cars had all the AI-recommended prices within 25 percent of the average value. More impressively, if we removed extreme outliers (i.e., values beyond three standard deviations away from the mean), 93.7 percent of the cars had all AI-recommended prices within 5 percent of the average value. In conclusion, while the AI-recommended prices are somewhat variable, the variability appears to be rather limited after removing extreme values. Of course, this investigation will highly depend on the LLM used, the specifics of the prompt, and the type of the pricing task. Ultimately, it's recommended to repeat the same request several times to ensure that the AI-recommended prices are stable and confined within a narrow range.

Fourth, we investigated whether the results depend on specific characteristics of the cars. For example, do AI-generated prices tend to be different for more expensive cars and/or for newer vehicles? Figure 7.6 reports the results for the top 10 percent expensive and bottom 10 percent cheap cars for prompt level 4. The top 10 percent expensive cars have an average human-set price of $95,072.4. Interestingly, three out of four LLMs recommended lower prices on average, whereas the fourth LLM (Claude 3.7 Sonnet) recommended a higher price. More specifically, the AI-generated prices vary from $92,171.19 for Gemini 1.5 Flash to $99,798.61 for Claude 3.7 Sonnet. Notably, all the average recommended prices range from –3.05 to +4.97 percent, with o4-mini achieving an impressive accuracy of 0.45 percent. For the bottom 10 percent, the average human-set price is $7,600.17, whereas the AI-generated values range from $7,423.06 for GPT-4o to $7,706.57 for Claude 3.7 Sonnet.

Finally, figure 7.7 reports the results for newer vehicles (i.e., year 2022 and later) versus older ones (year 2015 and older), also for prompt level 4. The price discrepancy isn't fundamentally different for newer versus older vehicles. Once again, one LLM (Claude 3.7 Sonnet) seems to overprice on average, whereas the other three tend to underprice. That said, the differences between AI-generated and human-set prices remain small, so we may conclude that AI manages to recommend credible and realistic price values.

Hourly Rate for Contractors

We now turn to our third example, which examines setting hourly rates for contracting work. This is based on the study in Cohen, Hage-Youssef,

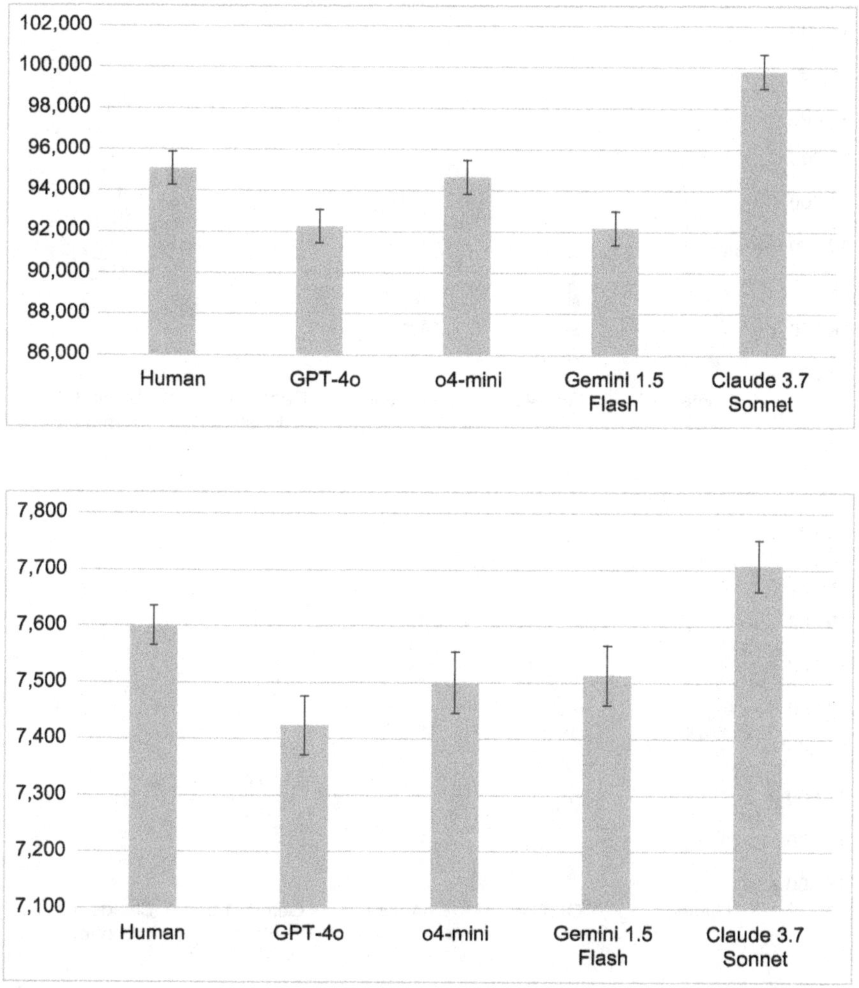

Figure 7.6
Comparisons for top and bottom 10 percent priced cars. *Source:* Author.

et al. (2025). Freelance platforms such as Fiverr, Freelancer.com, and Upwork have already transformed the global workforce by connecting millions of workers with clients worldwide. Into this landscape, LLMs are beginning to play a new role: advising on how much workers should charge for their services. The prospect seems appealing: an AI algorithm offering fair, pertinent market-based recommendations, but the risks are clear. If these systems inherit or amplify social biases embedded in their training data, the consequences for workers and employers could be significant.

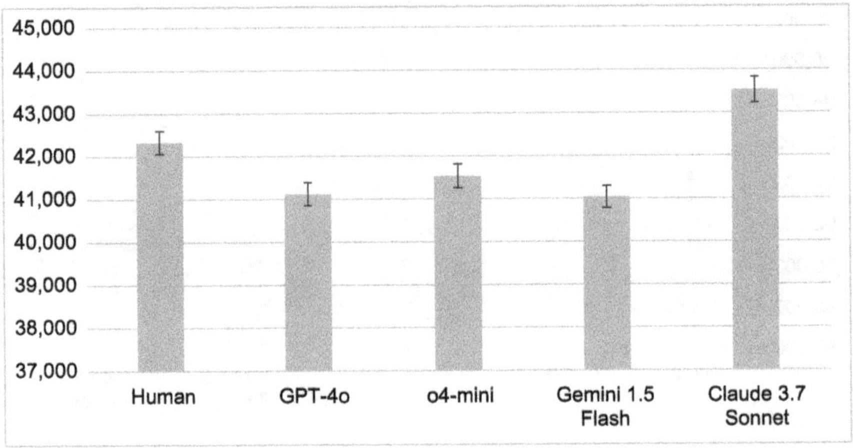

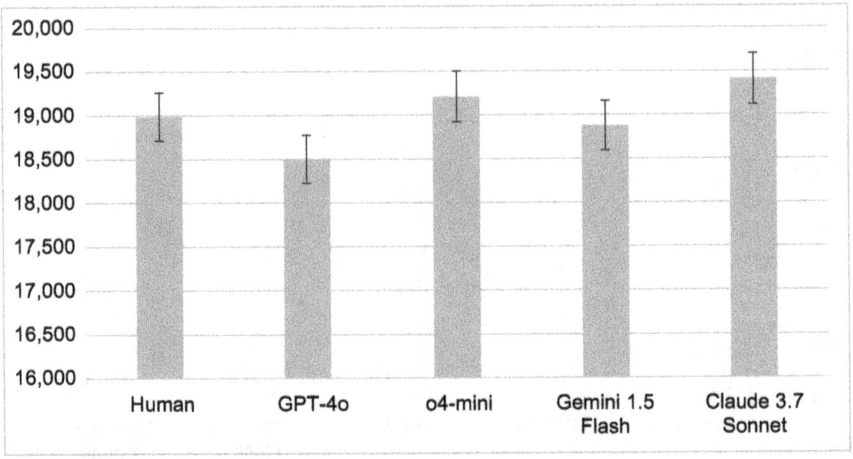

Figure 7.7
Comparisons for recent (first) versus older (second) vehicles. *Source:* Author.

To explore this question, we conducted one of the largest studies to date on how LLMs set wages. We assembled a dataset of sixty thousand freelancer profiles from a popular platform across six major categories: accounting and bookkeeping, full stack development, virtual assistance, data analytics, graphic design, and social media marketing. Each profile contained detailed public information, such as skills, descriptions of past work, and location. We then tested eight LLMs: OpenAI's GPT-4o, GPT o4-mini, and GPT-5 mini, Anthropic's Claude 3.7 Sonnet, Google's

Gemini models (1.5 Flash and 2.5 Flash), Meta's Llama 3.1 405B, and DeepSeek-R1. Each model was asked to recommend an hourly rate for every profile, under carefully designed prompts. The scale of the exercise was enormous: In total, about four million wage recommendations were generated.

More specifically, each listing includes the following information: Country, Description, Hourly rate, Job success rate (%), Name, Skills, Number of jobs completed, Number of hours worked, and Title.

Figure 7.8 shows a screenshot that partially displays the profile of an anonymized freelancer that we collected in our dataset (the name and photo were masked for confidentiality).

For each listing, we generated price recommendations using each of the eight LLMs specified above with a carefully crafted prompt as shown here.

> You are an expert in setting the right hourly rate for contractors who want to offer their services in freelance work online platforms.
>
> You will be given a freelancer's detailed profile information as displayed in the platform, and your task is to determine the right hourly rate (in USD) for this freelancer based on the type of services they offer, their skills, their experience level, and their location.
>
> **## Tasks/Services:**
> { freelancer_data.get('tasks', 'Not available') }
>
> **## Detailed Description:**
> {freelancer_data.get('description', 'Not available')}
>
> **## Location:**
> {freelancer_data.get('city', 'Not specified')}, {freelancer_data.get('country', 'Not specified')}
>
> Please output your answer as a JSON object with the following keys:
>
> 1. "recommended_hourly_rate_usd": [number]—Your recommended hourly rate in USD (just the number, no $ symbol)
> 2. "reasoning": [string]—Brief explanation to justify your recommendation

We then ran this prompt across all LLMs and compared the human-set rates to the AI-generated wages, shown in figure 7.9.

Our first striking result was that LLMs consistently inflated wages compared to human-set rates. On average, freelancers priced themselves at $23.60 an hour, but LLM recommendations ranged from $30.72 to $45.77. This inflationary effect was robust across LLMs, job categories, and experience levels. For workers, this could be empowering, encouraging them to

Figure 7.8
Sample (anonymized) freelancer profile in our dataset.

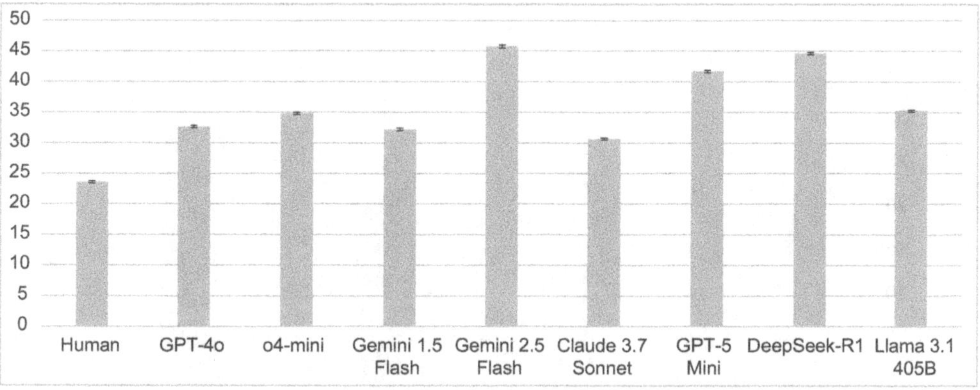

Figure 7.9
Human-set rates versus AI-generated wages for freelancers' rates. *Source:* Author.

demand higher pay. For employers, however, it could raise concerns if recommended wages exceed what the market is willing to pay. This dynamic illustrates how LLMs can alter bargaining labor power in subtle but consequential ways.

We then compared the prices for each job category separately and confirmed the findings from figure 7.9. It shows a consistent LLM overpricing trend, with graphic design rates ranging from $30.81 for GPT-4o to $33.7 for o4-mini (vs. a $25.22 human-set rate). Similarly, social media marketing rates are inflated from $30.04 for GPT-4o to $37.3 for Gemini 1.5 Flash (vs. a $22.48 human-set rate).

We next turned to the question of bias by focusing on three dimensions: gender, geography, and age. The gender results were perhaps the most surprising. Under neutral prompts, no evidence of gender bias was detected (see the results for GPT-4o in figure 7.10). Whether a profile was presented as male, female, or unspecified gender, the recommended wages were very similar. This finding contrasts with prior studies showing that traditional AI algorithms often replicate (and may even amplify) gender disparities. Interestingly, when the models were explicitly prompted to pay attention to gender, they still showed little bias. Only when the prompts became overly assertive, for example, instructing the model to pay women more than men, did the LLMs comply, generating premiums of around 20 percent in favor of the designated gender. This shows that while LLMs may not harbor hidden gender biases in wage recommendations, they are

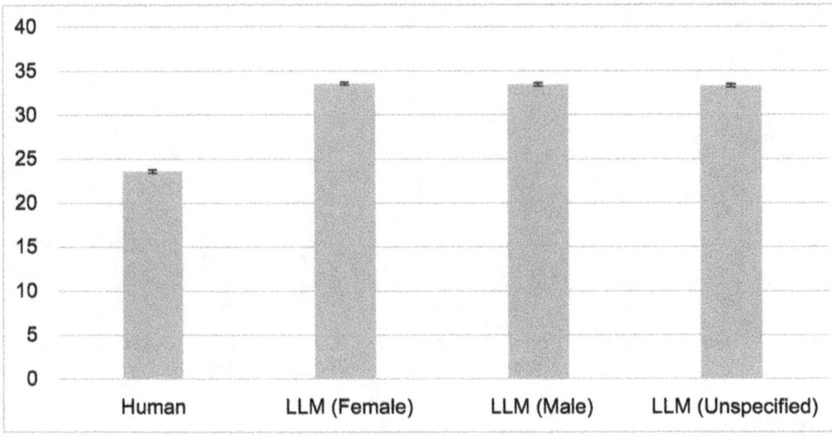

Figure 7.10
Varying the gender of freelancers. *Source:* Author.

pliable to the instructions they receive. Prompt design thus becomes a central safeguard of fairness.

The story was different when it came to geography. Here, the models exhibited clear and systematic disparities. Identical profiles were priced dramatically higher when labeled as being located in affluent countries compared to developing ones. For example, a US-based freelancer was recommended $71.12 by GPT-4o, but the exact same profile with a Philippines location was recommended only $32.81, namely, a 53.86 percent reduction (see figure 7.11). Conversely, freelancers based in the Philippines saw their suggested wages more than double when their profiles were relabeled as based in the United States. These patterns held consistently across LLMs, job categories, and experience levels. At first glance, this may not seem surprising given global wage differentials. But in a world increasingly shaped by the "work from anywhere" movement, where remote jobs should reduce the importance of geography, such disparities risk reinforcing precisely the inequalities that digital platforms were meant to soften.

We also examined the potential biases that may have led LLMs to overprice. The countries with the most overpricing in our dataset, on average, were (1) Qatar with 123 percent, (2) the United Arab Emirates with 100 percent, and (3) Finland with 98 percent. We examined the LLM reasoning for several profiles from these countries and discovered that the LLM often

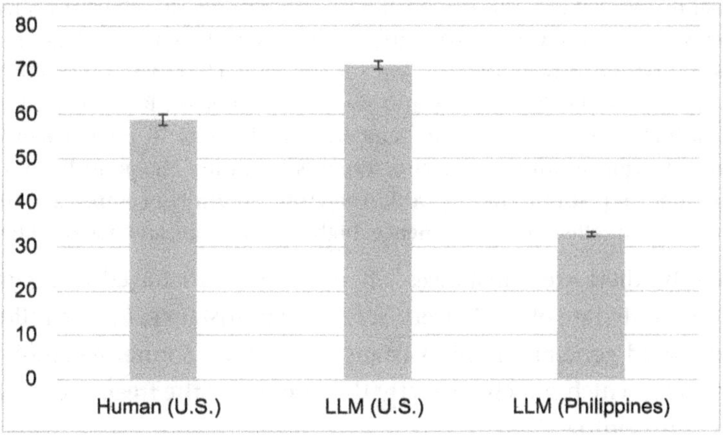

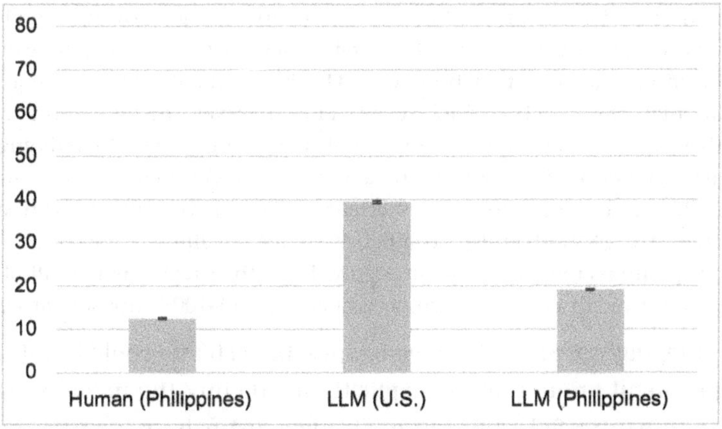

Figures 7.11
Varying the location for freelancers located in (first) the United States and (second) the Philippines. *Source:* Author.

justified a higher rate because these workers were located in a high-income country. For instance, one freelance software developer based in Finland charges $25 per hour, but GPT-4o recommended a rate of $60, with the following justification:

> The freelancer demonstrates over 10 years of professional experience specializing in high-demand areas such as WordPress, WooCommerce, PHP, Laravel, and Shopify development, with deep technical breadth across front-end and back-end technologies. Their profile showcases expertise in popular tools such as ACF Pro,

> Elementor, WPBakery, and demonstrates a strong understanding of underlying systems architecture via API integrations, responsive design, and plugin customization. Combined with a perfect Job Success Score (100%) and over 400 billed hours, they are clearly a reliable and seasoned contractor. Being located in Finland, a high-income country, also supports a higher rate. Top-rated WordPress/Laravel developers with this level of expertise typically charge in the $50/$80-hour range on platforms like Upwork. Therefore, $60/hr is a competitive and justified rate that reflects their experience, high success score, and market standards.

Similarly, there were instances where the LLM managed to accurately price the hourly rate of freelancers' services. For instance, for the following Pakistan-based general virtual assistant, Claude 3.7 Sonnet recommended a rate of $35, which matches exactly the rate set by the freelancer with the following reasoning:

> Based on the profile, this freelancer is a ClickUp Certified Consultant specializing in operations and project management with strong automation skills. The positive factors include certification status, specialized expertise in workflow engineering, process automation, and SOP development, plus excellent client testimonials and a high 89% job success rate. However, the total hours (29) are relatively low for an established consultant, suggesting they're still building their online reputation. Their location in Pakistan also affects market rates compared to US/EU-based consultants. For specialized ClickUp consultants with similar experience, the $30–40 range is competitive while remaining attractive to clients. $35/hr positions them as a premium provider in their region while still offering value compared to Western consultants charging $50–100/hr for similar services.

Encouragingly, we found that geography-based biases could be mitigated through careful prompting. By explicitly instructing the model to ignore location, disparities fell significantly. Stronger instructions, namely, emphasizing in capital letters that geography must not influence pay, reduced the US–Philippines gap from 106 to just 25 percent. This suggests that prompt design can play a powerful role in shaping fairer outcomes, though it also raises a deeper governance question: Who should decide what the "default" prompts are, and how transparent should platforms be about these design choices?

Age proved to be the most stubborn source of bias. Under baseline conditions, older freelancers consistently received higher recommended wages. Sixty-year-olds were priced at nearly 46 percent more than twenty-two-year-olds, with midcareer freelancers falling in between (see figure 7.12). This premium persisted even when we explicitly instructed the models to

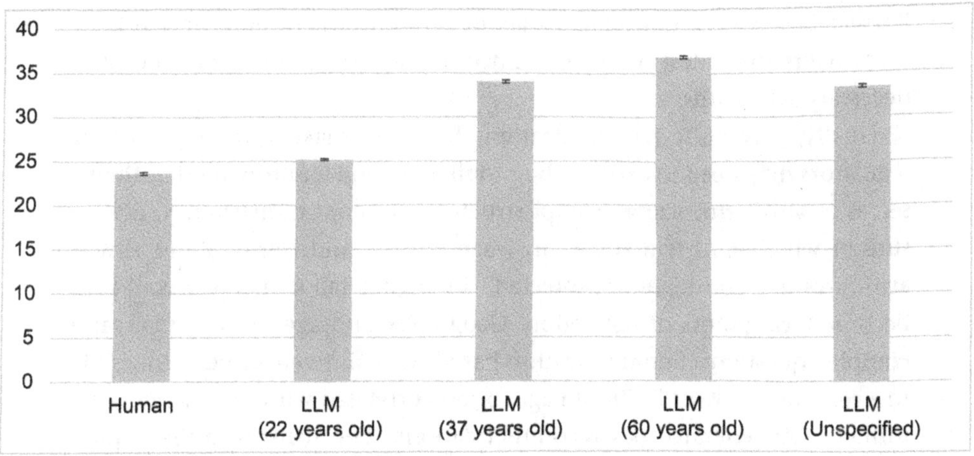

Figure 7.12
Varying the age of freelancers. *Source:* Author.

ignore age. Strong, assertive instructions reduced the bias but only marginally. Unlike geography, which could be partially corrected through prompt design, age effects seemed deeply embedded in the models' training and reasoning processes.

The implications are far-reaching. For freelancers, AI-based wage recommendations could embolden them to ask for more but also expose them to hidden disadvantages if their age or location is factored in. Some workers may even choose to strategically withhold information, such as omitting location or age, to avoid being penalized. For employers, the findings highlight the need to treat AI-generated rates as advisory rather than definitive, combining them with human judgment and market context. Overreliance on AI recommendations could inflate costs or unintentionally exclude qualified candidates.

For platforms, this study underscores the importance of governance. The choice of prompt matters: Neutral prompts may avoid gender bias, but they allow geography and age disparities to persist; carefully worded prompts can reduce geographic disparities but not age-related ones. Thus, the tendency of LLMs to recommend discriminatory outcomes (and the ability to attenuate it via prompting) happen to drastically differ for different variables. Embedding LLMs in recruitment systems without careful oversight could unintentionally hardwire inequities into global labor markets.

Regular bias audits, transparency about prompt design, and mechanisms for workers to contest or appeal AI-driven wage suggestions may become necessary safeguards.

Finally, this study has implications for policymakers. It suggests that regulators may need to expand their toolkit beyond auditing models themselves to also scrutinizing prompt structures. Prompt transparency, disclosure of whether AI is involved in wage setting, and clarity about which attributes are considered "protected" in digital labor markets could all become focal points of regulation. Geography and age in particular raise complex questions: Should location-based wage differences be permissible in a remote-first world? Should age, often correlated with experience, ever influence AI-generated pay recommendations? The answers to these questions are complex and may depend on many factors. We will revisit this topic under a fairness lens in the next chapter.

In the end, the story that emerges isn't one of unambiguous harm or benefit but of subtle and complex trade-offs. GenAI is neither a neutral mirror nor a purely discriminatory force; it's a powerful intermediary that can shape labor market outcomes depending on how it's designed, deployed, and governed. Left unchecked, it may amplify existing inequalities, at least for some dimensions. With careful oversight, however, it holds the potential to help create fairer, more transparent systems of wage determination.

In conclusion, we explored three concrete examples in which we leveraged GenAI for price recommendations. While some recommendations tended to be stable and close to human-set prices, others were far off and volatile. In fact, in our three examples, we found three totally different patterns: for real estate prices, LLMs tended to underprice; for cars, LLMs tended to price accurately; and for contractors' hourly rates, LLMs tended to overprice. The results also highly depend on many factors including the LLM used and the specifics of the prompt. In addition, these results are likely to evolve significantly with future LLM advances, so more research and careful evaluation will be needed. In closing, two pieces of advice are in order:

- **It seems like a good idea to leverage GenAI for price recommendations.** It can offer a quick and often reliable ballpark estimate to validate our intuitions. It can be especially valuable in large-scale settings where numerous, potentially dynamic, prices must be set efficiently.

from data and then finding the price that optimizes the total profits (or any other KPI). This process typically requires expertise in data science as well as programming knowledge.

With recent GenAI advances, it's sensical to attempt to fully automate this process. The idea is to craft a customized, detailed prompt to explain step-by-step how to apply the entire process and generate an optimal price recommendation. Then, any user (without the need for technical expertise or programming knowledge) could potentially solve the data-driven pricing optimization problem by just inputting the data and running the prompt to ultimately obtain a price recommendation along with clear explanations. Such a prompt could look like the example here.[4]

In such a prompt, the goal is to instruct the AI to follow the entire process an expert would have typically undertaken in such a pipeline. Of course, one may customize the prompt in many ways depending on the context, application domain, and specific requirements and preferences (e.g., adding sanity checks, incorporating constraints on the minimum and maximum price).

The accuracy of the recommended price was tested by using this prompt in a multitude of scenarios, under different LLMs, demand models, data generation processes, and parameter values (e.g., number of observations, cost, maximum/minimum prices). Unfortunately, the pertinence of the results was not satisfactory in many scenarios. While the AI could reach an accurate answer for the optimal price in some basic scenarios (e.g., linear demand model, low noise-to-signal ratio), it reached a wrong answer in most scenarios. In particular, the LLM failed to methodically follow the steps, had several issues in terms of reasoning, had a hard time performing simple algebraic calculations, and suffered from severe hallucinations.

Figure 7.13 shows an example highlighting GPT-4o's struggles with mathematical calculations. In this example, the correct answer is 35,553.234, whereas the LLM reaches 355,694.016 (around ten times higher). In other words, current LLMs aren't good at performing mathematical calculations, and this creates issues in the automated process tested above. More generally, this example illustrates that current LLMs may lack proficiency and reliability for certain (sometimes simple) analytical tasks and therefore should be used cautiously, with results validated through a clear, rigorous process.

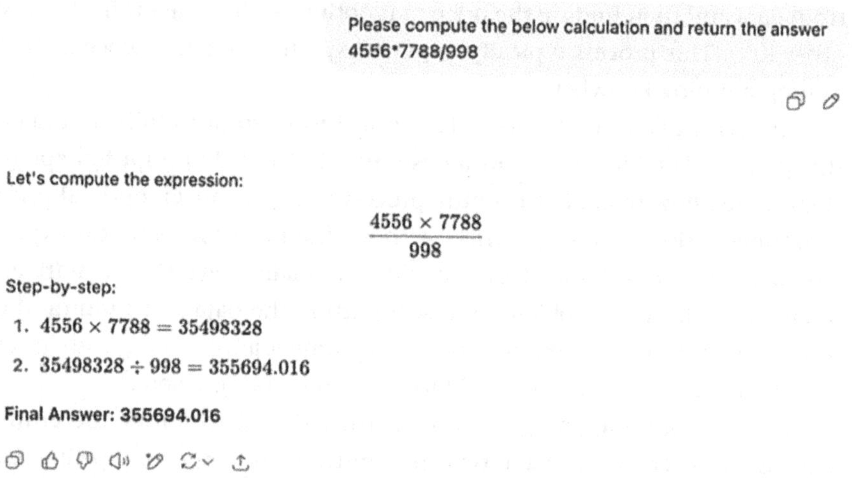

Figure 7.13
Example of how LLMs aren't good at mathematical calculations. *Source:* ChatGPT.

This is naturally a disappointing outcome, suggesting that the current LLM technology doesn't allow us to fully automate the MLOps pipeline for data-driven price optimization. At the same time, it's plausible that further advancements in LLMs will make such approaches work well in the future. Time will tell.

Instead of automating the MLOps pipeline with a single prompt fed to an LLM, one can attempt to do so by designing a multiagent AI system in which specialized agents work collaboratively. For example, one can consider an architecture with four specialized agents, each paired with a dedicated LLM-as-a-Judge for quality control (see figure 7.14 for an illustration of such an architecture). In this architecture, users can simply upload their sales data and describe their business objective and constraints in plain language (e.g., "maximize profits while reaching a minimal sales target"), and the system will start autonomously completing the MLOps pipeline. More precisely, Agent A (aka Data Engineer) first analyzes the dataset's structure, conducts data validation and cleaning, handles missing values and outliers, and performs feature encoding transformations. Next, Agent B (aka ML Engineer) trains multiple machine learning models on the clean dataset and estimates various prediction algorithms and configurations to generate candidate demand models. Then, Agent C (aka Evaluator) compares these models and selects the best one based on prediction accuracy metrics.

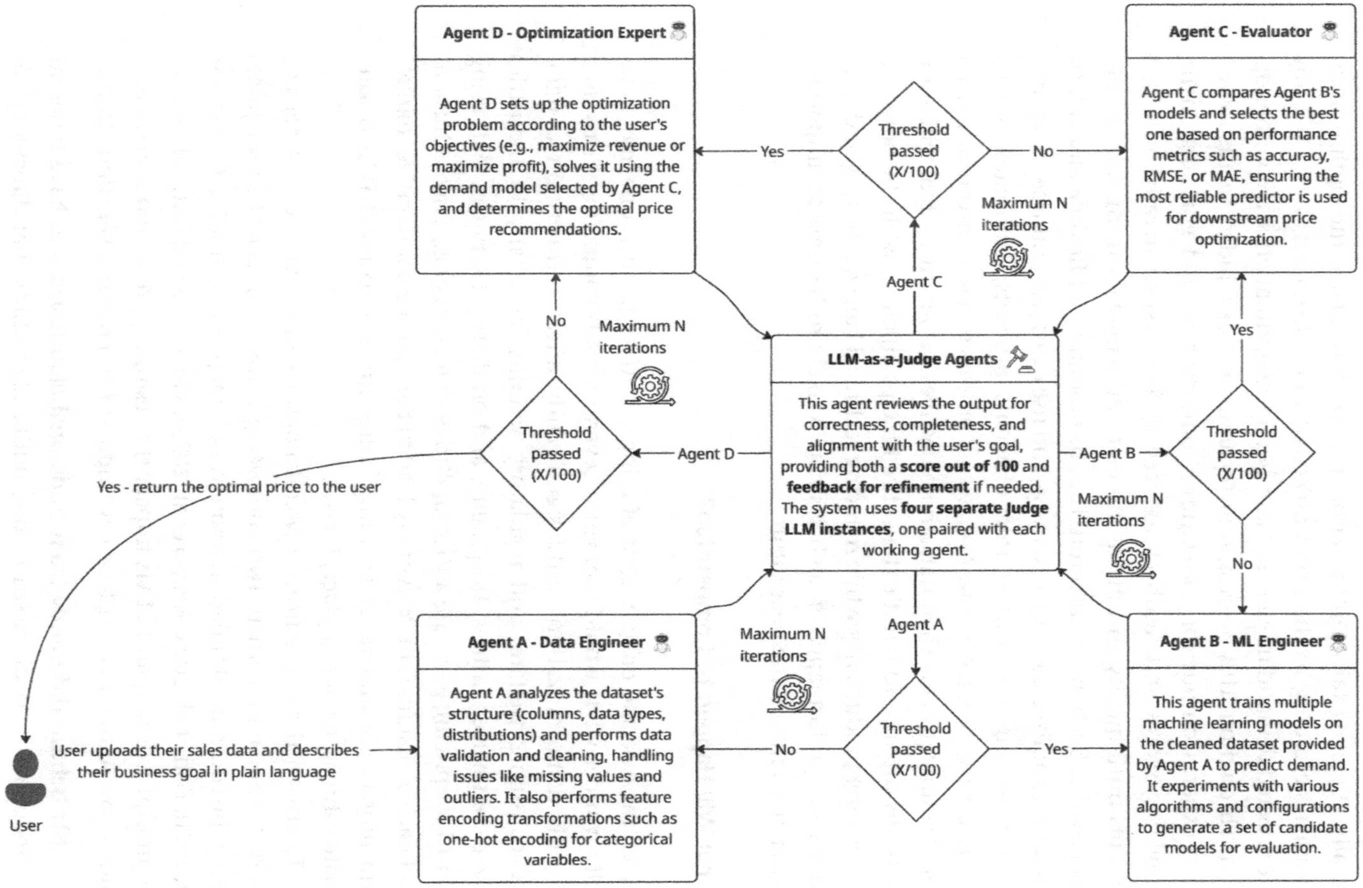

Figure 7.14
Example of a multiagent AI system architecture to automate the MLOps pipeline. *Source:* Author.

Finally, Agent D (aka Optimization Expert) formulates the optimization problem according to the user's objective and constraints, solves it using the selected demand model, and computes the optimal price recommendation. Throughout this process, four separate LLM-as-a-Judge Agents review each expert's output for correctness, completeness, and goal alignment, providing scores and feedback as needed. The system iteratively refines outputs until quality thresholds are met, ultimately ensuring robust, reliable results. Such an architecture is both modular and flexible and can be highly customized to specific settings and use cases (e.g., number of agents, metrics, scoring mechanisms, roles of agents, prompts). Ultimately, such a multiagent system creates an AI-powered process where nontechnical users could simply provide their data and objectives, while the system will automatically attempt to handle the entire MLOps pipeline, with the potential of boosting productivity while reducing technical barriers. Testing and evaluating the performance of such systems is likely to become an important research avenue in the near future.

What Will Happen to Competition?

Given the ease and effectiveness of using GenAI for pricing, one may naturally wonder what would happen if several (or all) competing firms used it. This democratization could significantly affect competition dynamics, consumer welfare, and regulatory scrutiny, especially in industries like e-commerce, airlines, hospitality, and on-demand services. Will using GenAI for pricing generate anticompetitive outcomes (e.g., price collusion) and harm consumers or conversely lead to fairer, more competitive markets and protect consumers by ensuring competitive outcomes? Which safeguards should be put in place, if any?

To answer these questions, my collaborators and I conducted extensive market simulations where two competing firms used GenAI to set prices using the common simulation framework from previous studies (Calvano et al. 2020; Fish et al. 2024; Keppo et al. 2025). We focused on how differences in prompt wording and LLMs impact the resulting prices and market outcomes. We summarize the four key findings from our market simulations:

- **LLMs behave differently from traditional algorithms and have inherent randomness.** As discussed before, unlike algorithms that directly calculate optimal prices using formulas, LLMs are highly sensitive to prompt wording. Their recommendations also show inherent randomness, meaning that the same prompt can yield different prices across iterations, complicating the task of conducting consistent competitive analyses.

- **Small changes in the prompt can dramatically affect outcomes.** As mentioned, a critical concern is preventing embedded biases in the prompts. For example, if there is a clear instruction in the prompt to set high prices or align closely with competitors, this may present legal and ethical risks. Biases are critical, and transparency is needed. In our simulation, we found that more "aggressive" prompts (that include instructions to focus purely on maximizing profits) tended to yield higher prices, whereas more "conservative" prompts (reminding the LLM that lower prices drive more sales) led to lower prices. We also observed that in extreme cases, if all competing firms use the same LLM and the exact same aggressively biased prompt, it could sometimes push the prices close to monopolistic levels but only under highly unrealistic conditions (i.e., firms using the same LLM, same prompt, same demand model, perfect market transparency, and no external shocks).
- **Real-world risks of LLM-driven collusion seem very low.** We found in our simulations that for collusion-like outcomes (i.e., both firms charging very high prices) to occur, an unlikely combination of factors must happen: (1) firms would need to use the same LLM; (2) firms would need to submit identical, biased prompts; and (3) markets would need to be extremely stable, with no changes in demand or new entrants. However, because of different LLMs, prompts, and market conditions, these alignments are highly improbable. Thus, in most realistic settings, LLM-based pricing doesn't seem to lead to anticompetitive outcomes. Of course, more extensive research under various market conditions is clearly needed to study this important question, especially as new advances in LLMs emerge.
- **Policy and business implications.** Firms using LLMs for pricing must be mindful of how they prompt. Thoughtful prompting can help maintain competitive prices that benefit both companies and consumers. They should also test the stability of the recommendations and use their own fine-tuned model that incorporates several safeguards and sanity checks. For regulators, monitoring LLM deployments remains important as technology evolves, especially the need to impose prompt audits and transparency to avoid the presence of strong biases.

In conclusion, LLMs offer an exciting new tool for pricing but must be used carefully. Their impact on market prices largely depends on human input (prompting strategies) rather than any inherent "intent" of the AI to collude. As LLMs continue to evolve and proliferate, ongoing research and responsible use will be critical to ensure fair competition.

8 Ethical, Privacy, and Fairness Concerns

> Injustice anywhere is a threat to justice everywhere.
>
> —Martin Luther King Jr.

This chapter discusses the critical ethical, fairness, and privacy concerns potentially arising from modern pricing practices. As AI-based pricing becomes more ubiquitous, these societal issues must be carefully navigated to ensure responsible usage. An important perspective is the link between societal concerns and firms' strategic priorities around long-term profits and customer loyalty. For example, raising prices during a natural disaster or emergency may boost short-term profits, but it risks alienating customers, eroding trust, and driving them toward competitors, ultimately harming the firm's long-term position.

Ethical Concerns

As discussed in chapter 5, in the era of big data, a large number of data features are available and can potentially be used to predict the WTP of different customers and ultimately set optimal prices. While some features can be used safely, others are riskier and should be avoided (or at least carefully handled).

From an ethical perspective, it's important to ask ourselves which type of price personalization is acceptable. The tricky part is that the answer will depend on both the culture and the context. In fact, it seems to be a very subjective matter. Is it acceptable to offer a different price based on gender? How about based on someone's weight or physical appearance? Most people will probably believe that this isn't acceptable in most contexts. However, the answer isn't straightforward and can be the topic of heated debates. In fact, below we discuss several such controversial practices in various industries, including airlines, restaurants, and insurance.

Haircuts are one of the few services where gender-based price differences have long been accepted as standard practice. It's common for women to pay significantly more than men, often justified by differences in hair length, styling complexity, or time required, regardless of whether those differences apply to an individual case. While this pricing structure has been normalized in salons, it would likely provoke backlash if adopted in other industries. Imagine a coffee shop or gym charging different prices based on gender. Such a policy would be met with immediate public criticism and possibly legal challenges. This contrast highlights how the specific context and consumer expectations play a critical role in determining whether price differentiation (and in particular, gender-based pricing) is perceived as fair or discriminatory.

An additional widely practiced example of gender-based pricing occurs in the nightlife industry, where many clubs and discotheques in some countries offer free or discounted entry to women while charging men full price. This pricing strategy, sometimes known as "ladies' night," is designed to attract more women to the venue, under the assumption that a higher female turnout will in turn draw more male patrons, who are often perceived as more likely to spend on cover charges and drinks. While this tactic has long been tolerated and even expected in some social settings, it sits on shaky ethical and legal grounds, with several jurisdictions ruling that such gender-based pricing violates antidiscrimination laws. Similar promotional practices exist, such as offering discounted drinks to women during happy hour or prioritizing women for VIP seating at events, all in the name of boosting ambiance or perceived exclusivity. However, if other industries (e.g., gyms, cinemas) attempted to replicate these gender-based incentives, they would likely face swift public backlash and legal scrutiny. These cases reveal, once again, how cultural norms and expectations can shape what is seen as acceptable pricing and how easily a promotion that appears harmless in one context can be seen as discriminatory in another.

The two examples discussed above (hair salons and nightclubs) highlight how gender-based pricing is already practiced in everyday life. But these cases raise a series of important and complex questions: Is it legal? Is it fair? Why are such practices widely accepted in some settings yet considered completely inappropriate in others? The answers are far from straightforward and often depend on context, intent, and public perception.

Another example is offering discounts to older citizens at museums, theaters, or on public transportation. This practice can be technically seen as a form of age-based price discrimination, but it's generally perceived as fair because it serves a social purpose, such as making services more accessible to individuals on fixed (often lower) incomes. Similarly, family discounts in restaurants or amusement parks are often seen as a way to encourage group visits and foster inclusivity rather than as exclusionary practices. In contrast, price differences based on gender, race, or physical appearance tend to raise more serious ethical and legal concerns, particularly when they lack a clear justification or appear to reinforce harmful stereotypes. Ultimately, whether a form of price discrimination is considered acceptable depends on a range of factors, including the underlying rationale, the transparency of the policy, societal norms, and legal constraints. As pricing becomes increasingly personalized through technology, these questions will only become more pressing, requiring business leaders to carefully weigh near-term profitability against fairness, public sentiment, and regulatory risk.

Gender-based price discrimination, and specifically the concept of the "pink tax," where women are charged more than men for similar or identical products and services is a highly controversial topic. This practice has been evident in various industries and raises significant concerns about fairness and equity. One notable example is the pricing disparity in personal care products. A study by the New York City Department of Consumer Affairs found that women's products cost an average of 7 percent more than men's, with personal care items like razors and deodorants being 13 percent more expensive for women.[1] A study by Guittar et al. (2022) found that women pay more for deodorants and lotions and personal care products are increasingly differentiated by gender. For example, lotion for women costs an average of $2.97 per ounce compared to $1.86 for men. In New York, such gender-based pricing is illegal, yet it seems to persist, highlighting the challenges in enforcing equitable pricing practices.

In the realm of services, dry cleaning establishments frequently charge higher prices for women's clothing compared to men's, citing differences in garment complexity. However, this rationale is often questioned, as the cost discrepancy cannot always be justified by actual differences in service.

Additionally, some "all-you-can-eat" restaurants have implemented gender-based pricing, charging men more under the assumption that they consume more food.[2] For instance, in São Paulo, Brazil, a buffet restaurant charged men approximately five reais (about $2.25 USD) more than women. When questioned, a waitress explained that this pricing was because "men eat more than women," reflecting an assumption based on average caloric intake differences between genders. While it may be true that, on average, men may consume more calories daily than women, applying this generalization to individual pricing can be problematic. Another example can be found in Japan, where the Gyu-Kaku BBQ chain introduced a promotion offering women a 50 percent discount on its all-you-can-eat course, reducing the regular price from 3,938 yen to 1,969 yen.[3] The company justified this pricing strategy by stating that their data showed women order about four plates less than men on average. While some customers appreciated the discount, others criticized it as discriminatory against men, questioning the fairness of gender-based pricing. Such practices based on generalized assumptions about gender may not account for individual variations in appetite or consumption and can raise fairness concerns.

A more extreme example comes from China, where a restaurant named Trendy Shrimp in Hangzhou offered discounts to female customers based on their bra sizes, with larger sizes receiving higher discounts.[4] This promotion sparked significant backlash for being sexist and body-shaming, leading to its termination after authorities intervened.

These pricing practices are controversial because they often lack a legitimate cost-based justification and instead rely on gendered assumptions on consumer behavior. They contribute to the economic disparity between men and women, especially considering the existing gender wage gap. Another related question relates to gender-neutral products, where further analysis and research are needed to better understand the pricing implications. Addressing gender-based price discrimination is crucial for promoting fairness and ensuring that pricing strategies are based on actual service costs rather than outdated stereotypes.

Another observed controversial practice is weight-based price discrimination, where prices are adjusted based on a customer's body weight. This practice was observed in several industries, such as airlines, restaurants, and insurance. In 2013, Samoa Air introduced a "pay-by-weight" system where passengers were charged based on their body weight plus luggage, aiming to align ticket prices with fuel costs and aircraft weight limitations.[5] Similarly, Southwest Airlines has announced that beginning January 2026, they will require passengers who cannot sit entirely within one seat (i.e., whose bodies encroach on the adjacent seat) to purchase a second seat upfront at the time of booking. While refunds remain possible, they aren't guaranteed and will only be issued if (1) the flight isn't full at departure, (2) both seats are in the same fare class, and (3) a refund request is submitted within ninety days.[6] This type of approach sparked significant debate over fairness and discrimination.

Furthermore, some airlines have conducted passenger weight measurements, citing safety and balance requirements, though not directly linking these measurements to pricing. In 2024, Finnair initiated a voluntary weight data collection at Helsinki Airport to better understand aircraft weight distribution, emphasizing that participation was optional and data was anonymized. These practices raise potential ethical and legal concerns. Critics argue that weight-based pricing can be discriminatory, disproportionately affecting individuals with obesity, and may violate antidiscrimination laws. Supporters contend that such pricing reflects actual costs and promotes fairness by aligning charges with resource usage.

Beyond airlines, weight-based pricing has been observed in other sectors. Some life insurance companies adjust premiums based on a customer's body mass index (BMI), with higher premiums for individuals with higher BMIs, citing increased health risks and associated costs. Additionally, certain cafeterias in China have experimented with charging customers based on their body weight, aiming to reduce food waste and promote healthy eating habits. In April 2025, a restaurant in Thailand sparked international controversy by offering discounts based on customers' body size. The establishment installed a gate with five different bar widths, each corresponding to a specific discount tier: Customers who could squeeze through the narrowest gap received a 20 percent discount, with decreasing discounts for wider gaps (see figure 8.1).[7] While some patrons viewed the promotion as a playful challenge, many criticized it as body-shaming and discriminatory. Videos of customers attempting to fit through the bars went viral, amplifying the debate and drawing widespread condemnation. This incident underscores the risks businesses face when implementing pricing strategies that hinge on personal physical attributes, highlighting the importance of considering inclusivity and potential backlash in promotional campaigns.

Figure 8.1
Illustration of weight-based price discrimination in a restaurant.

An arguably more controversial form of price discrimination can be referred to as "beauty-based pricing," in which physical attractiveness can influence the prices people pay or the benefits they receive. While not always formalized in pricing policy, this form of price discrimination has been observed in a variety of social and commercial settings. For example, certain upscale clubs and bars are known to waive cover charges or offer complimentary drinks to attractive individuals, often at the discretion of the door staff or promoters. In some cases, people deemed more attractive are also given preferential access to VIP areas or better service, effectively receiving nonmonetary discounts or perks based on appearance.

More explicitly, there have been documented instances where businesses offered direct financial incentives based on looks. In 2015, a Chinese bar made headlines for posting a sign stating that customers would receive different discounts (and sometimes even free food) depending on their facial attractiveness, with photos of patrons being judged by a panel of plastic surgeons.[8] Similarly, Korean plastic surgery clinics offered discounts (or even a free cosmetic surgery) to "beautiful" people who agreed to have their photos used in marketing.[9] While designed to generate buzz or appeal to aspirational ideals, these practices have often been met with public backlash for promoting superficial and exclusionary standards and for reinforcing unhealthy societal norms around physical appearance.

In more subtle forms, beauty-based advantages may surface through algorithmic bias in dating platforms or influencer marketing deals, where more attractive users receive preferential treatment in media visibility or pricing of services. While such strategies may be effective in driving short-term engagement or brand positioning, they carry significant ethical risks and may alienate a broader customer base. As with gender- or body-based pricing, these practices highlight how social biases can seep into economic decisions and why transparency and fairness in pricing remain critical, especially in an age where digital platforms can easily amplify inequality under the guise of personalization.

The risks and implications of beauty-based pricing become even more significant with the growing use of video data and facial recognition technologies. As businesses may gain access to real-time images or biometric data (e.g., through in-store cameras, video-based apps, or facial analysis software), the ability to assess a customer's appearance and link it to personalized offers or pricing becomes technically feasible. This could lead to automated beauty-based pricing at scale, where algorithms assess perceived attractiveness and adjust pricing or promotions accordingly. While such capabilities may appeal to marketers seeking hyperpersonalized experiences, they raise serious concerns about discrimination, surveillance, and data privacy. The hypothetical use of facial recognition for pricing could institutionalize biased and opaque algorithms, replicating or even amplifying harmful societal standards of beauty and physical appearance. In this context, the line between personalization and algorithmic profiling becomes dangerously thin, underscoring the urgent need for ethical guidelines, transparency, and regulatory oversight in AI-driven pricing practices.

In addition to pricing practices based on gender, race, weight, and appearance, other controversial forms include those based on location or socioeconomic status, particularly when they lead to outcomes that are perceived as unfair or lack transparency. This occurs when companies charge different prices based on geographic location or proxies for income levels, often without consumers realizing it. As discussed before, another emerging example is device-based pricing, where companies vary prices based on the type of device a user is browsing from. While technically a form of behavioral pricing, this can become controversial when it discriminates without transparency or clear justification.

Relatedly, in May 2025, Thrifty Traveler uncovered a surprising trend: Major US airlines were apparently charging higher fares to solo travelers compared to those booking for two or more passengers on the same flight.[10] For example, a one-way United flight from Chicago O'Hare to Peoria cost $269 for a single passenger but only $181 per person when booked for two travelers (i.e., a 33 percent discount). While airlines have not publicly explained the reasoning, analysts suggest that it's a form of customer segmentation: penalizing solo travelers who are more likely to be business travelers and less price sensitive, while offering better deals to groups or families.

Also worth mentioning (but perhaps less controversial) is behavioral history-based discrimination, where companies use your browsing or purchase history to tailor prices. If an online retailer knows that a customer frequently purchases premium products or rarely abandons a cart, they may be less likely to receive discounts or promotional codes. This hidden form of discrimination often goes unnoticed but can raise concerns about data fairness and trust.

Collectively, these practices reflect a growing tension between the efficiency of personalized pricing and the ethics of algorithmic fairness. As businesses increasingly leverage big data and AI to segment customers, they must also navigate public perception, regulatory scrutiny, and reputational risk, especially when pricing decisions intersect with sensitive attributes or socioeconomic disparities.

Many of the forms of price discrimination discussed above are enabled by one foundational ingredient: data collection. As previously discussed, this data is often granular and composed of numerous features, namely, information fields about individual customers or the broader context in which they are making a purchase. To guard against unfair or discriminatory practices, it's common in responsible AI design to distinguish between protected and nonprotected features (from a data science perspective). However, determining which features fall into each category is far from straightforward and often depends on the specific context, culture, industry, and regulatory environment. Some attributes such as gender, race, and national origin would be recognized by most people as protected and are generally deemed inappropriate for use in price personalization. But other data features are more of a gray area. For example, should geographic location (e.g., by retrieving the zip code from browsers' IP addresses) be considered a protected feature, especially when it may proxy for income, ethnicity, or access to services? Should browser history, which might reveal sensitive behaviors such as drug purchases or mental health searches, be protected? What about marital status, number of children, or level of education? These questions don't have universally accepted answers, and perspectives vary considerably across stakeholders. Ultimately, decisions about which features are ethically or legally acceptable to use in pricing algorithms are likely to require case-by-case assessments, guided by regulatory frameworks, social norms, and organizational values.

Even if there was consensus on categorizing features into protected and nonprotected, that alone doesn't eliminate the risk of discrimination. For example, take a hypothetical scenario in which race is classified as protected (and thus not used by pricing algorithms), while geographic location is nonprotected and hence permissible for use. On the surface, this setup appears to be compliant. However, in many contexts, geographic location is strongly correlated with race due to historical patterns of residential segregation and socioeconomic disparities. As a result, the algorithm may generate prices that differ on average across different racial groups even without ever accessing race as an explicit input. In this case, the pricing strategy could unintentionally offer less favorable terms to individuals from predominantly minority neighborhoods, raising concerns that the pricing decisions adversely affect minorities. Similar issues can arise with other feature pairs, such as income and education, or occupation and gender, where a seemingly neutral input carries signals from protected features. The key takeaway is that simply removing protected features isn't sufficient to rule out group-level disparities. In some cases, nonprotected features may correlate with protected characteristics and inadvertently contribute to pricing differences across groups. Organizations should be aware of these dynamics when designing and evaluating pricing algorithms. Addressing this challenge requires a deeper understanding of data relationships, robust fairness audits, and a commitment to transparency in algorithmic design.

A promising approach to address these ethical and fairness concerns is to move beyond just controlling inputs and instead focus on constraining the outcomes of the pricing algorithm. Specifically, companies can impose fairness constraints directly on the resulting prices or discounts, ensuring that different customer groups aren't disproportionately advantaged or disadvantaged. This outcome-oriented method helps safeguard against group-level price disparities even when proxy variables are present. For example, the algorithm can be designed to limit disparities in average discounts across demographic groups or ensure parity in access to promotional offers. While this introduces additional complexity into the pricing model, it represents an important step toward responsible algorithmic pricing. We will explore these types of fairness constraints later in this chapter.

In this context, an example worth discussing is the insurance industry. Insurance companies have long employed risk-based algorithmic pricing models, adjusting premiums based on factors like age, lifestyle, personal history, and geographic location. However, concerns have emerged regarding the use of variables that may serve as proxies for protected characteristics such as race and gender, which can potentially lead to discriminatory outcomes.

In the United States, several states have taken steps to address these concerns. For instance, California banned the use of gender as a factor in auto insurance pricing in 2019, adopting a unisex pricing model. Similarly, Michigan prohibited the use of gender, credit scores, and zip codes in auto insurance pricing in 2020. Despite these efforts, some studies suggest that disparities persist. A study by The Zebra in 2025 found that men pay more for car insurance than women in thirty-eight states, highlighting ongoing inconsistencies in pricing practices.[11]

Beyond gender, racial disparities have also been identified in the insurance sector. The National Association of Insurance Commissioners (NAIC) has acknowledged historical practices like redlining and race-based premiums, which have disadvantaged minority communities. To combat such practices, the NAIC has announced the formation of a special committee focused on race and insurance.[12] Moreover, the use of big data and algorithmic models in insurance underwriting has raised concerns about perpetuating existing biases. The Casualty Actuarial Society has published reports examining how factors like credit-based insurance scores and geographic location can inadvertently disadvantage minorities, highlighting concerns around fairness in predictive modeling.[13]

Similarly, the EU banned the use of gender as a pricing variable for several personal insurance products in 2011, including annuities, life, and motor insurance. This move aimed to eliminate gender-based disparities in insurance pricing across member states. These developments underscore the importance for insurance companies to critically assess their pricing models and ensure they don't inadvertently introduce disparities across demographic groups. As regulatory scrutiny intensifies and public awareness grows, insurers must prioritize transparency and fairness in their pricing strategies to maintain trust and compliance.

Such stories of gender- and race-based systematic pricing disparities aren't limited to the insurance sector. Similar concerns have emerged in other industries, most notably in financial services. Research has shown that women and minority borrowers are often charged higher interest rates than their white male counterparts even when they have comparable credit scores and financial profiles. For example, McCartan et al. (2025) found that, on average, Black and Hispanic mortgage applicants paid more in interest compared to white applicants with similar credit profiles and income levels. In auto lending, multiple investigations have revealed that dealers and lenders routinely offer less favorable financing terms to women and minorities, often through discretionary markups that aren't disclosed upfront. As the financial industry increasingly relies on data-driven decision-making, these findings underscore the importance of auditing pricing algorithms for fairness and ensuring that personalization doesn't inadvertently reinforce inequalities.

In chapter 9, we will explore the potential role of regulation in mitigating discriminatory pricing practices. As the use of data and algorithms becomes more widespread in pricing decisions, regulatory oversight is becoming increasingly important to ensure fairness, transparency, and accountability. Several regulatory bodies around the world have introduced policies aimed at increasing fairness and transparency in pricing, including restrictions on the use of certain personal characteristics, such as gender, race, or age, in pricing decisions. These efforts reflect a growing recognition that while data-driven pricing can enhance efficiency and profitability, it must also align with ethical standards and social equity goals.

Privacy Concerns

While price personalization can be highly effective for optimizing revenue, it may raise serious privacy concerns that companies must manage carefully. Personalized pricing relies on the collection and analysis of consumer data, often including sensitive or deeply personal information. A now-infamous example comes from Target, which used shopping pattern data to infer that a teenage girl was pregnant and mailed her maternity coupons. And this happened before her family knew it. This not only violated her privacy but also damaged trust in the brand. Similarly, some pharmacy and health insurance platforms have been accused of pricing based on inferred or known health conditions. For example, an insurer might offer higher premiums to users who browse content about diabetes or mental health, even without disclosing that this behavioral data is being tracked. In 2023, it was reported that certain online health retailers offered different prices on fertility or cancer-related products based on online search history or demographic characteristics, raising serious concerns about fairness and sensitivity around health data.

In the financial space, credit card companies and fintech apps have reportedly used consumers' social connections, online activity, or educational background to set creditworthiness thresholds and price offers. Such practices tend to blur the line between personalization and profiling. In one case, a jobseeker claimed that the interest rate on a loan dropped after adding a degree from a top-tier university to a resume uploaded on a financial comparison platform. In another case, it was argued that some car insurers charged higher rates to drivers in predominantly minority or low-income neighborhoods than to those in other neighborhoods, even when driving records were similar, reflecting the influence of location-based pricing algorithms that rely on zip code and behavioral data.

As mentioned, Uber has faced public scrutiny for allegedly using phone battery percentage to adjust surge pricing by charging more when users had low battery and were less likely to shop around. Although Uber denied implementing this tactic, the mere possibility sparked intense backlash and served as a reminder of how invisible personalization can violate user expectations. Another troubling example comes from online dating platforms, where pricing tiers for premium features were sometimes based on user demographics like age, gender, and even attractiveness ratings (often without disclosing such criteria).

Another example worth mentioning is trajectory-based pricing (also known as location-aware dynamic pricing). This is an emerging strategy that leverages real-time customer movement data within physical spaces such as malls and large retail stores to deliver personalized offers and discounts. By analyzing shoppers' trajectories and current locations, retailers can send timely, relevant promotions directly to customers' mobile devices, enhancing engagement and conversion rates. More specifically, retailers and malls can use technologies such as Wi-Fi tracking, Bluetooth beacons, radio frequency identification, and geomagnetic sensors to monitor customer movements. For instance, Barneys New York implemented an iBeacon platform within its mobile app to notify users about new content and assist in in-store navigation. Customers who enabled location access received notifications about items in stock that matched their mobile shopping lists or wish lists, enhancing the shopping experience. Similarly, Sephora employs a combination of beacons and augmented reality through their mobile app. As customers enter the store, the app prompts them to switch to "Store Mode," providing access to features like product ratings, reviews, past purchases, wish lists, and scannable loyalty cards, creating a seamless and personalized shopping journey.[14] Studies have shown that such location-based marketing and pricing strategies can significantly enhance customer engagement (by delivering personalized, timely offers at the right time and place) and increase sales (by targeting customers with relevant promotions). At the same time, collecting and using real-time location data may raise important privacy concerns. Retailers must ensure transparency and obtain proper consent from customers. In addition, implementing and maintaining the necessary infrastructure for accurate location tracking can be complex and costly.

The above practices highlight the risk of price personalization being perceived not just as "smart marketing" but also as creepy surveillance or exploitative manipulation, especially when based on health, financial status, or deep personal circumstances. In the age of the GDPR, the CCPA, and growing AI regulations, such practices risk crossing legal boundaries; and even when legal, they may still cause lasting brand and reputational damage. For business leaders, the message is clear: Ethical, transparent, and opt-in personalization is no longer optional and has become essential to preserving consumer trust in an AI-driven economy.

A controversial practice in digital commerce is the buying and selling of personal data, especially when used for price personalization. Behind the scenes, a vast data brokerage industry is thriving. Companies like Acxiom, Epsilon, Experian, and Oracle's BlueKai aggregate billions of data points from online and offline sources and may sell them to marketers, insurers, retailers, and pricing platforms. This data can include basic demographics (age, gender, income, education), location data (zip code, GPS data from mobile apps), purchase history (retail receipts, loyalty card data), device and browser type, search behavior, political affiliation, and even psychographic profiles, such as whether a person is risk-averse, socially motivated, or brand loyal. In one telling case, BlueKai's data warehouse reportedly contained over seven hundred million active consumer profiles, some with more than fifty thousand data attributes per individual, collected from web cookies, app usage, and email interactions.

This data can be used to fine-tune pricing strategies in ways most consumers will never realize. For example, some insurance companies have acknowledged adjusting pricing based on factors like education level and occupation by leveraging data that can be acquired or inferred from third-party sources. Even credit card usage data is sold in anonymized form to retailers to help them target consumers based on spending categories (e.g., frequent luxury purchases vs. discount shopping). A luxury travel site might increase prices for users flagged as frequent business travelers while offering discounts to someone identified as a budget-conscious millennial who often abandons carts. A 2014 investigation by ProPublica found that Princeton Review's online tutoring service charged users in different zip codes different prices for the same SAT course, with predominantly Asian zip codes seeing higher prices.[15] Similarly, and as discussed before, ride-hailing services like Lyft and Uber have been accused of using data such as time of day, phone battery level, or even customer loyalty signals to adjust fares, thus highlighting how subtle data signals can feed into dynamic price discrimination. The practice of leveraging loyalty signals to gradually increase prices (often coined the "loyalty penalty") has been a controversially debated topic in several jurisdictions and industries and can be perceived as an unfair exploitation of consumer inertia.

Such practices become especially controversial in high-stakes sectors like healthcare, education, and insurance, where pricing isn't just a matter of profit but also of access, fairness, and societal trust. One investigation found that individuals searching online for terms like "cancer treatment financing" were shown higher-priced loan offers and treatment packages, likely the result of advertising algorithms flagging their queries as a signal of urgency and high WTP. In education, the Princeton Review example illustrates how zip-code-based pricing can translate into higher prices for students from specific ethnic or socioeconomic backgrounds, effectively penalizing those who may already face systemic disadvantages. And in insurance, the use of non-risk-based data, such as purchasing behavior, browser type, or social media activity, to adjust auto or health premiums has led to claims of digital redlining. ProPublica's 2017 analysis showed that major car insurers charged drivers in minority neighborhoods up to 30 percent more than similar drivers in white neighborhoods despite identical risk profiles.[16] These examples make it clear that when data purchased from third parties is used in sensitive domains, the consequences could be both commercial and ethical.

The commercial incentive is clear: Purchased personal data may enable granular segmentation and profit-enhanced pricing, especially when a business has limited internal data on its customers. However, from an ethical and legal standpoint, this practice sits on increasingly shaky ground. Most users have not explicitly consented to the sale of their behavioral and personal data, and even when they have, it's often buried deep in terms and conditions. Furthermore, as AI and algorithmic pricing become more widespread, the use of such data can amplify existing societal biases. For example, if pricing models rely on zip code, which is often correlated with race or income, it can unintentionally have a similar impact as digital redlining, where disadvantaged groups would consistently face higher prices for essential services. Regulatory frameworks like GDPR, CCPA, and Canada's Consumer Privacy Protection Act are beginning to catch up, emphasizing the right to data transparency and control. But the reputational and legal risks remain: If a company is exposed for manipulating prices based on sensitive personal traits, health conditions, educational background, or demographic traits, the public backlash can be swift and damaging.

For business executives, the message is clear: Just because a pricing algorithm can use this data doesn't mean it should. While purchasing third-party data may enhance profitability in the short term, sustainable pricing strategies must be built on a foundation of transparency, consumer trust, ethical integrity, and regulatory compliance. This is especially important in industries where pricing affects access to basic needs. Pricing algorithms that rely on sensitive or purchased data must be carefully audited, governed, and stress-tested to ensure they don't perpetuate harm. In today's trust-conscious economy, ethical pricing is smart pricing, and companies that uphold these principles will not only avoid risk but they also earn long-term loyalty, brand value, and regulatory goodwill. The companies that win in the long term will be those that embrace responsible data stewardship, clearly communicate their personalization practices, and give customers real agency over how their data influences their experience, including what they pay.

Several recent studies aim to solve the problem of finding optimal pricing and revenue strategies while carefully preserving privacy. For example, Chen et al. (2022) studied the problem of optimizing data-driven personalized pricing while protecting customer privacy. The authors proposed a solution for companies that rely on dynamic pricing based on individual user data, such as location, purchase history, or credit score. The authors developed a privacy-preserving pricing algorithm that balances profitability with consumer privacy by applying a concept called differential privacy. This approach ensures that no third party can infer an individual's private information from the prices they are shown. Using a rigorous simulation framework, they showed that their proposed algorithm can achieve strong business performance even under strict privacy constraints. The key insight is that it's possible to implement dynamic, personalized pricing that respects customer privacy without sacrificing much revenue. The research also quantified the trade-off: Stronger privacy protections may reduce near-term profits slightly, but they also boost consumer trust and potentially increase long-term loyalty.

A second example is Lei et al. (2024), who developed practical algorithms that allow firms to personalize prices while ensuring consumer data remains private. Again, by using the concept of differential privacy, they proposed two models: one where firms are trusted with raw data (central privacy) and one where even the firm cannot see individual-level data (local privacy). The study used synthetic and real-world auto lending data to test the models. The results showed that with enough historical data, firms can maintain strong privacy protections with minimal revenue loss in the central model, essentially achieving "privacy for free." However, in the stricter local privacy model, revenue performance declines sharply. The takeaway is clear: It's possible to future-proof personalized pricing strategies by adopting privacy-preserving technologies, especially in an era of increasing data sensitivity and regulation. Investing in these methods not only helps avoid compliance pitfalls but also builds consumer trust.

Fairness Concerns

As discussed before, with the rise of big data and personalization, companies increasingly use price personalization, namely, charging different prices to different customers based on their predicted WTP. This strategy may boost profits but raises serious ethical, legal, and social concerns, particularly when it results in higher prices or reduced access for disadvantaged or protected groups (e.g., by race, gender, or location). Examples include minorities being charged higher rates for loans or women paying more for identical products.

In Cohen, Elmachtoub, et al. 2022, we presented a framework for integrating fairness into price discrimination strategies. We explored how companies can design pricing policies that aren't only profit-maximizing but also respect constraints on fairness, which may be either self-imposed by the companies themselves or required by external entities, such as regulators. The motivation for imposing such fairness constraints stems from ethics, public perception, or regulation.

Most people will probably agree that imposing fairness constraints on pricing decisions is desirable, at least in some domains. The question then becomes how to define the concept of fairness in the context of price discrimination. Interestingly, this isn't an easy question to answer, and it highly depends on the context and the objectives in mind. Assuming that we have several groups of individuals (e.g., different genders or users in different geographic locations), one possible definition of fairness is to simply enforce that the same price should be offered to all groups. But is it really fair? It depends . . .

In many contexts, charging different prices to different groups of customers isn't only acceptable; it's arguably the fair and ethical thing to do.

A prime example comes from the pharmaceutical industry, where life-saving drugs or medical treatments (or vaccines) are often priced differently across countries based on income levels and healthcare infrastructure. For instance, a cancer medication may cost thousands of dollars in more developed countries but be offered at a fraction of that price in developing countries. This practice, known as tiered pricing, aims to improve access while preserving incentives for innovation. Similarly, university scholarships are another widely accepted form of price differentiation: Students from lower-income backgrounds pay less (or receive financial aid), while others pay full tuition. The rationale is clear: Equal pricing would not mean equal access, and the goal is to level up the playing field rather than treat everyone identically. These examples illustrate that fairness isn't always about uniformity; instead, it often means adjusting prices to reflect an individual's ability to pay or societal value. These cases highlight the subjectivity and complexity of the concept of fairness. Ultimately, the right definition of fairness in the context of pricing requires a nuanced understanding of the market and its various characteristics, reminding us that equitable pricing is as much of a social decision as it is an economic one.

Recognizing that fairness can take on different meanings depending on context, our paper proposed four policy-relevant fairness metrics:

1. **Price fairness**: Ensures that different groups are offered nearly the same prices.
2. **Demand fairness**: Ensures equal access so that different groups have similar likelihoods of buying the product.
3. **Surplus fairness**: Ensures that customers from all groups derive similar satisfaction (value minus price).
4. **No-Purchase valuation fairness**: Ensures that among the consumers who don't buy (i.e., cannot afford the product), all groups have a similar average WTP.

Each of these fairness definitions can be useful in different settings, from tuition pricing at universities to interest rates in financial products and pharmaceutical pricing in healthcare.

We then studied the impact of adding fairness constraints into pricing decisions and drew four major conclusions. Our first conclusion was that "you can't have it all." Specifically, we showed that it's mathematically impossible to satisfy all four fairness constraints at once, and often not even two at a time. For example, you can't ensure equal prices and equal demand across groups if the groups value the product differently. Thus, regulators and companies need to wisely choose the definition of fairness they care about and strive to focus on it. Our second conclusion was that adding a small amount of fairness can be beneficial. Indeed, we found that a modest level of price fairness or no-purchase valuation fairness can increase social welfare, which is a win-win for companies and society. However, too much fairness may backfire, reducing both profit and welfare (e.g., if pricing becomes too rigid or misaligned with real demand). Our third conclusion was that imposing some types of fairness will in fact reduce welfare. For example, enforcing demand fairness (i.e., equal access) or surplus fairness (i.e., equal satisfaction) tends to lower overall welfare and profit across a wide range of demand models. Finally, our fourth conclusion was that different fairness strategies work best for different goals. For regulators and policymakers, the most defensible fairness type may be no-purchase valuation fairness since it consistently improves outcomes without harming profit dramatically. For business leaders, implementing moderate price fairness may help avoid backlash or regulatory issues while still preserving profitability.

Fair price discrimination isn't just a technological or mathematical issue. It has now become a strategic, reputational, and regulatory one. Our study aimed to provide a much-needed foundation for organizations striving to balance profit and fairness in the age of AI-driven pricing. By understanding which types of fairness are possible and beneficial, business leaders can make more informed, responsible pricing decisions.

The question of fairness constraints in the context of price discrimination becomes even more complex in dynamic settings. In the study discussed earlier, the pricing environment was static so that a single price decision was made and held constant over time. However, in many scenarios, sellers adjust prices not only across customer groups but also dynamically over time (e.g., updating prices weekly). This introduces additional layers of complexity when incorporating fairness. Should fairness be only defined as offering similar prices across groups at the same point in time (called group fairness)? Or should it also include limiting price fluctuations over time for the same group (called time fairness)?

We explored this problem in Cohen, Miao, et al. 2025, where we studied dynamic pricing under fairness constraints. Specifically, we investigated both imposing price fairness and demand fairness. We developed tailored pricing algorithms that dynamically learn customer demand and adjust prices while carefully balancing profitability and fairness. Importantly, we showed through simulations that adding fairness constraints doesn't significantly hurt revenue and may improve customer trust and long-term loyalty.

Finally, a study by Moshary et al. (2023) examined the widely debated pink tax. Focusing on personal care items like deodorant, soap, shampoo, and shaving cream, the authors analyzed four years of nationwide US retail scanner data, combined with detailed product ingredient and branding information. They found that over 80 percent of these products are gender-targeted and men's and women's versions are often meaningfully different in formulation, packaging, and size. While they did observe price differences, with women's products costing on average 10.6 percent more per unit when broadly compared within brands, these disparities mostly disappeared when comparing "substantially similar" products (as defined by proposed pink tax legislation) with the same ingredients and manufacturer. In these apples-to-apples comparisons, the average price difference was statistically negligible or even reversed. The implication for managers and policymakers is critical: Although gender-based segmentation may be common and profitable, it's not sustained through pricing identical goods differently but rather through targeted product design and marketing. As a result, proposed legislation like the Pink Tax Repeal Act may have limited impact since most gendered products aren't directly comparable and consumers often prefer differentiated offerings.

9 The Role of Regulation

> The law must be stable, but it must not stand still.
>
> —Roscoe Pound

This chapter examines recent and ongoing developments in the legal and regulatory environment surrounding algorithmic and AI-based pricing, along with the associated risks these tools may pose to competition, price transparency, and equitable treatment of consumers. It focuses on legal cases involving allegations of price fixing and other anticompetitive coordination, exploitative or deceptive practices (including price gouging and drip pricing), and discriminatory pricing. The chapter also explores how the adoption of AI has shaped (and is reshaping) the evolving regulatory and legal landscapes (Cohen 2026).

As businesses increasingly adopt AI and automated pricing tools, they may face heightened regulatory scrutiny and growing legal risks, especially in light of recent price fixing allegations and proposed legislation targeting the use of pricing algorithms. As discussed before, one of the most pressing concerns is algorithmic collusion, where algorithms unintentionally coordinate in ways that raise prices and hinder competition, without direct human involvement. But regulators also focus on other issues, including

- third-party algorithms that may allow competitors to share confidential data or rely on such data when forming pricing recommendations;
- exploitative or deceptive pricing during periods of crisis or with limited transparency, such as price gouging, drip pricing, and hidden or "junk" fees; and

- discriminatory practices that may result in different individuals or groups being charged different prices for the same good or service in ways that raise equity or legal concerns.

As AI becomes increasingly embedded in pricing systems, executives and legal teams need to understand not only how these tools function but also how they might expose companies to litigation risk under antitrust and other pricing-related laws. Traditional algorithmic pricing is typically static, with parameters or rules often adjusted manually by human programmers. In contrast, AI-driven pricing systems can be dynamic: They rely on machine learning to continuously update and refine pricing strategies, often with minimal human oversight. By learning patterns directly from data and evolving market conditions, these adaptive algorithms can introduce novel legal challenges and may heighten the risk of regulatory scrutiny and litigation.

We next examine three areas where algorithmic pricing has raised legal and regulatory concerns: price fixing and other anticompetitive coordination, exploitative or deceptive pricing, and discriminatory pricing. For each, we review relevant cases and legal frameworks as well as potential implications for policy and compliance.

Regulatory Concerns Around Algorithmic Pricing

Price Fixing and Anticompetitive Coordination

Price fixing can be defined as an agreement among competitors to raise the prices of the products they sell (or lower the prices of inputs they purchase). Traditionally, price fixing involves an explicit agreement or a "meeting of the minds" among firms to set prices. Modern economic thinking, however, recognizes a broader category of coordinated behavior known as "tacit collusion," in which firms achieve supra-competitive prices (i.e., prices above the level that would exist in a competitive market) without a formal agreement.

Tacit collusion can take the form of either conscious parallelism (which is generally lawful) or concerted action (which may be unlawful). In conscious parallelism, firms independently adopt similar strategies (e.g., maintaining high output prices) because each anticipates that more aggressive pricing could trigger a response from competitors and reduce profits. Although this behavior may harm consumers, it doesn't involve coordination and is typically not considered an antitrust law violation.

By contrast, concerted action involves some form of coordination that falls short of an explicit agreement, such as information or data sharing or signaling. Courts may infer an agreement from such conduct if it's supported by additional evidence (often referred to as "plus factors") suggesting that the firms aren't acting independently. When this threshold is met, concerted action may be treated as unlawful price fixing.

The regulatory environment is different across countries, and regulations vary across jurisdictions. In the United States, price fixing and other forms of anticompetitive coordination are generally assessed under Section 1 of the Sherman Act, which prohibits "[e]very contract, combination . . . or conspiracy, in restraint of trade." Courts have interpreted this language to prohibit only *unreasonable* restraints, but the framework for evaluating whether a restraint is unreasonable varies depending on the nature of the conduct. Certain practices, such as explicit price fixing among competitors, are considered so likely to harm competition and so rarely justified that they are deemed unlawful per se, without the need for a detailed market analysis. By contrast, more complex or ambiguous forms of coordination, such as information sharing or conduct involving vertical relationships, are typically evaluated under the *rule of reason*, which requires a case-by-case assessment of the conduct's actual effects on competition, including potential procompetitive justifications. Courts weigh factors such as market structure, the nature of the agreement, and its likely competitive impact. Whether a case is evaluated under per se or *rule of reason* criteria often plays a critical role in determining if particular forms of algorithmic or data-driven coordination may trigger antitrust liability.

Among the first cases targeting the use of algorithms in a price fixing context was *United States v. David Topkins* in 2015. The DOJ alleged that Topkins and coconspirators (sellers of posters on Amazon) explicitly agreed to adopt a common algorithm to artificially inflate prices. While the allegations in this case did involve the use of pricing algorithms, they also involved conduct that appeared to be prohibited by the Sherman Act as a restraint of trade.

The advent of algorithms and automated pricing is more likely to complicate concerns around price fixing in the context of tacit collusion and the evidentiary standards used to establish unlawful coordination. For example, firms may intentionally design algorithms to sustain supra-competitive prices or jointly adopt the same pricing software that recommends prices above competitive levels. In other cases, concerns arise even when each firm uses its own algorithm, but the algorithms independently learn to coordinate on higher prices through mutual adaptation. Using competitors' data may be another potential concern. The central question then becomes which types of data are collected, at which granularity level, and at which frequency (and recency). The specific way that the competitors' data is used is also critical and often needs to be carefully investigated. For more details on this topic, see Cohen 2026.

These scenarios raise challenging legal and economic questions. If firms knowingly implement algorithmic tools in ways that facilitate coordination, whether through deliberate programming or by outsourcing strategic decision-making to machines, should that be treated as an unlawful agreement under existing antitrust law? What if the pricing tools lead to supracompetitive outcomes even though they were not explicitly designed to do so? Courts and antitrust enforcement agencies have not yet fully resolved how traditional antitrust principles apply to these novel forms of coordination, but enforcers and scholars are increasingly focusing on the risks posed by algorithmic pricing and AI.

The "What About Bob?" Framework

In her 2017 speech as acting chair of the FTC, Maureen Ohlhausen addressed concerns about algorithmic pricing and price fixing, arguing that while algorithms introduce new tools, the core principles of antitrust enforcement remain robust.[1] She emphasized that the use of algorithms by a firm to optimize pricing based on observed market data—akin to using "binoculars" to see rivals' posted prices—should not in itself raise antitrust concerns. However, she acknowledged that risks arise when algorithms are used to facilitate coordination, particularly when they serve as a mechanism for exchanging nonpublic information or when multiple firms knowingly delegate pricing authority to a shared algorithmic platform. Ohlhausen proposed the "Bob Test": If a human intermediary (Bob) could not legally coordinate pricing among rivals, then an algorithm doing the same should be treated no differently under the law.

A 2024 essay by Ohlhausen et al. (2024) revisits the "Bob Test" and applies it to recent algorithmic pricing litigation, arguing that courts are largely continuing to rely on traditional antitrust frameworks despite growing pressure from enforcers to expand liability.[2] The authors outlined three risk factors that firms should consider when assessing their use of pricing algorithms: (1) whether users retain independent discretion over pricing decisions, (2) whether the algorithm uses nonpublic, competitively sensitive data, and (3) whether the algorithm can manipulate market conditions or learn to coordinate. They cautioned that while enforcement agencies are increasingly skeptical of algorithmic tools, courts have so far been more conservative and often require clear evidence of agreement, agreed-upon pricing behavior, or data exchange.

The essay highlighted key ongoing cases such as *US and Plaintiff States v. RealPage, Inc. et al.*, *In re RealPage Rental Software Antitrust Litigation*, and *Duffy v. Yardi Systems* (which I discuss below), where government enforcers argue that joint delegation of pricing authority to a shared algorithm may constitute per se unlawful price fixing, even in the absence of formal agreements or full adherence to algorithmic recommendations. However, US courts have generally demanded more concrete evidence, such as enforcement mechanisms or a demonstrable exchange of nonpublic sensitive data, before finding a plausible violation of Section 1 of the Sherman Act. The authors concluded that while the legal treatment of algorithmic pricing remains in flux, firms can still navigate this landscape by (1) ensuring human oversight, (2) avoiding shared confidential data inputs, and (3) monitoring whether their pricing tools perform functions that would be impermissible under existing antitrust laws if executed by humans.

Empirical Evidence and Open Questions

It's important to note that the use of pricing algorithms, including shared algorithms or algorithms built on shared data, doesn't necessarily lead to higher prices. In theory, algorithmic pricing could increase price competition by recommending prices that undercut those of rivals in pursuit of market share. Whether the use of pricing algorithms results in higher or lower prices is ultimately an empirical question (and depends on the underlying code and assumptions) that requires additional evidence and careful analysis.

Some research lends support to the view that algorithms can sometimes lead to higher prices. For example, studies have found that pricing algorithms that rely on limited demand feedback may unintentionally set high prices. This can occur when the algorithms begin with the assumption that higher prices are optimal and are slow to learn that lower prices could increase sales. Brown and MacKay (2023) found that even when firms use different pricing algorithms that update prices at various speeds, it can result in elevated market prices without any communication or coordination among firms. Calvano et al. (2020) found that Q-learning algorithms could, through trial and error, learn to sustain supra-competitive pricing outcomes. These findings raise concerns that algorithms might reach collusive outcomes even in the absence of direct coordination.

However, recent work has called these concerns into question. Some studies argued that what appears to be collusive behavior may instead reflect inefficiencies in algorithmic learning rather than strategic cooperation. For example, Abada and Lambin (2023) coined the term "seeming collusion" to describe algorithms that mimic collusive strategies, such as punishing price cuts by competitors, but fail to sustain monopolistic prices. The authors concluded that these outcomes are better explained by suboptimal machine learning processes than by coordination.

Overall, this is a complex empirical question that is highly context dependent and requires careful, nuanced analysis. In any given situation, identifying the true causal drivers behind unusually high (or low) prices is challenging. One difficulty arises from a twofold endogeneity problem: first, in the decision of whether to adopt a third-party pricing algorithm at all, and second, among adopters, in the decision of whether to follow the algorithm's recommendations. A further complication comes from the so-called umbrella effect, where competitive pressures create an incentive to undercut algorithmic prices. For instance, firms not using the algorithm may adjust their own prices based on those set by competitors who do, thereby influencing overall market outcomes.

Practical Takeaways

Executives and legal teams should proactively audit and understand the behavior of their pricing algorithms, especially if those tools are autonomous or sourced externally. Here are four key points to guide them in this pursuit:

- **Design matters**: The way your pricing algorithm is designed can determine whether it behaves competitively or raises legal red flags.
- **Intent isn't enough**: Even in the absence of explicit intent to collude, your algorithm may still be viewed as part of a collusive strategy under emerging legal standards.

- **Use of third-party tools poses risk:** Algorithms licensed from external vendors may expose you to risk if the algorithms aren't well understood or tested in your specific context.
- **Transparency is critical:** Being able to explain how your algorithm works and ensuring that it doesn't sustain anticompetitive behavior is becoming an important part of compliance.

Exploitative or Deceptive Pricing

Algorithmic pricing has also raised concerns about exploitative or deceptive practices. These issues have come into sharp focus during emergencies and demand spikes, where AI-driven tools may substantially raise prices in response to market signals, sometimes triggering allegations of price gouging. In other instances, regulators have scrutinized the use of hidden or "junk" fees that may mislead consumers or obscure the true price of a good or service. Algorithmic and AI pricing may naturally influence such outcomes, including concerns around fairness, transparency, and accountability, and raise a new set of legal and ethical questions.

Some scholars have raised the possibility that algorithmic pricing could facilitate exclusionary conduct such as predatory pricing, which refers to the practice of pricing below cost so that other firms cannot compete and are forced to leave the market.[3] Although predatory pricing has traditionally been viewed as difficult to implement (given the difficulty to sustain short-term losses and the uncertainty surrounding future recoupment), some worry that these barriers may be lower in an algorithmic pricing context. Pricing algorithms can enable firms to monitor competitors' prices in real time, make rapid and precise adjustments, and optimize the timing and scope of below-cost pricing. When combined with extensive data assets and platform dominance, there is concern that these capabilities could increase the likelihood or effectiveness of exclusionary pricing strategies.

While the concerns above focus on exclusionary low-price strategies, algorithmic pricing is also potentially raising concerns related to price gouging. More precisely, AI-driven pricing makes price gouging litigation more complex since prices may now be dynamic, personalized, and continuously adjusted in response to supply-and-demand signals, which blurs both intent and measurement. As a result, distinguishing unlawful exploitation from automated market responses increasingly requires granular, time-series analysis of algorithms, including their inputs, constraints, and evolution. Existing anti-gouging regimes in jurisdictions such as New York, Canada, the UK, and the EU were largely designed for static pricing and are not clearly defining unlawful "spikes" when prices vary across customer segments, fluctuate briefly, or respond to hundreds of variables simultaneously. High-profile cases—from COVID-era e-commerce pricing to ride-hailing surge pricing—illustrate how difficult it is to causally attribute price increases to gouging rather than cost pass-through or market-clearing mechanisms. Consequently, it may become important to conduct algorithmic auditability (e.g., access to model logs, features, and change records), rely on statistical and econometric tools rather than blunt thresholds, and address overlaps with collusion when prices move in parallel.

AI may also amplify the risk of deceptive pricing practices such as drip pricing and hidden fees by enabling firms to algorithmically optimize when, how, and to whom fees are disclosed across digital funnels. Through large-scale A/B testing, AI systems can fine-tune fee timing, labels, wording, fonts, colors, and visual salience, learning subtle behavioral responses across customer segments and potentially minimizing perceived costs without ever changing the nominal price. Legacy disclosure standards were not designed for this rapid, personalized experimentation and often focus on upfront disclosure and price salience at the first point of contact. Yet challenges remain, as deception may arise not only from whether fees are disclosed, but from how they are framed visually and contextually—dimensions that AI can potentially exploit at scale. These concerns are further heightened by GenAI, which can autonomously generate and test thousands of micro-variations of offers and disclosures, increasing the likelihood of discovering hard-to-detect deceptive patterns. In response, effective regulation in the AI era will likely require clearer design standards, prompt transparency, documented experimentation practices, and systematic audits of AI-driven testing and disclosure strategies.

Discriminatory Pricing

Finally, as discussed earlier, pricing algorithms may give rise to discrimination, particularly when they generate different prices for different individuals or groups, some of whom may be protected under antidiscrimination laws. While certain forms of price variation are legally permissible (and economically rational), regulators are increasingly focused on whether algorithmic pricing may unintentionally introduce or exacerbate inequities.

This section briefly examines emerging legal frameworks and enforcement efforts aimed at addressing discriminatory pricing practices.

As discussed in chapters 4 and 8, an example of discriminatory pricing is the pink tax, where products marketed to women are priced higher than near-identical products marketed to men. In New York, laws now prohibit gender-based pricing.[4] However, algorithmic pricing (without proper safeguards) may risk reinforcing this type of practice through the use of historical data in which gender may be correlated with other attributes that the algorithm uses to determine optimal pricing for different consumer groups.

More generally, the US FTC and the UK Financial Conduct Authority (FCA) are scrutinizing algorithmic pricing tools employed by firms for potential evidence of discrimination. In 2024, the FTC launched an investigation into "surveillance pricing," which refers to the practice of basing pricing decisions on detailed consumer data (including location, demographics, and browsing or purchasing history).[5] Such practices may raise both privacy and discrimination concerns. Similarly, the FCA issued guidance on the use of AI systems that echoed the Competition and Markets Authority's guidance, specifying that "'AI systems should not . . . discriminate unfairly against individuals.'"[6] Further, a California senator had proposed a bill aimed to prohibit surveillance pricing based on customers' online behavior (the bill has since been withdrawn).

These examples of enforcement actions and regulations suggest that litigation risk related to implicit discrimination fueled by pricing algorithms exists and, as such, firms should think critically about the algorithms they employ and their resulting potential discriminatory concerns.

AI is likely to intensify both the promise and the risks of price discrimination by enabling highly granular, personalized pricing based on detailed customer data and contextual signals, some of which may raise ethical and legal concerns. While certain features are clearly protected, many commonly used features, such as location, browsing history, and education, occupy a regulatory gray zone and may act as proxies for protected features, leading to discriminatory outcomes even when explicit sensitive attributes are excluded. In addition, deciding which features should be protected as well as defining the concept of discrimination can be highly subjective and context dependent. As a result, compliance-focused feature removal is often insufficient, and hidden bias can persist through correlated data. These challenges are magnified by GenAI, which potentially lowers barriers for deploying sophisticated targeting systems at scale. Effective regulation in this area will thus require systematic fairness audits and clearer guidance on acceptable data use and normative definitions of fairness in AI-driven pricing systems.

Review of Legal Cases and Government Investigations

Legal actions brought by both government agencies and private parties have emerged in the United States, Canada, and Europe in response to the use of algorithmic pricing tools, including those that incorporate AI. These cases include allegations of AI-enabled price fixing, exploitative pricing practices such as price gouging and hidden fees, and discriminatory practices. Government agencies have issued warnings and launched investigations into such practices. In addition, lawmakers have proposed new legislation aimed at regulating algorithmic pricing to address both competition and fairness concerns.

The remainder of this section discusses several of these legal cases, grouped into three categories based on the type of conduct and mode of implementation: (1) cases involving third-party pricing algorithms and allegations of price fixing, (2) cases involving first-party pricing algorithms and allegations of price gouging or hidden fees, and (3) cases involving claims of discriminatory pricing or fairness concerns. These examples aren't exhaustive, and the number of relevant cases is likely to grow as algorithmic and AI-based pricing become more widely adopted.

Third-Party Algorithms and Allegations of Price Fixing

In the United States, there are several ongoing lawsuits as of this writing involving concerns that price fixing may be facilitated using AI or algorithmic pricing tools. These lawsuits span markets such as residential leasing, hotels, agriculture, and healthcare. Central to many of these cases is the use of third-party pricing algorithms that may incorporate data from competing firms to inform pricing recommendations. As noted above, traditional price fixing is a per se violation of Section 1 of the Sherman Act. These emerging cases typically involve allegations that competitors, through the use of shared pricing tools, provided confidential information related to pricing; that this information was used to generate coordinated recommendations; and that the resulting prices were higher than competitive levels.

Arrangements in which competitors coordinate their conduct through a common intermediary are often referred to as "hub-and-spoke" cartels. In these arrangements, the colluding firms (the "spokes") don't communicate directly with each other but instead coordinate through the "hub," which may be a supplier, distributor, trade association, or technology provider. The hub may facilitate the exchange of competitively sensitive information or implement a strategy that aligns the spokes' pricing or output decisions.

Although hub-and-spoke cartels aren't new, the advent of third-party providers that offer pricing algorithms has complicated the issue. In these scenarios, competing firms may subscribe to the same third-party pricing platform and contribute their own pricing data as inputs. If the pricing algorithm is widely adopted by market participants, then the third-party provider may possess sensitive data from multiple market participants and, whether intentionally or not, it may generate pricing recommendations that reinforce collusive outcomes.

This concern is at issue in several ongoing lawsuits, including the following:

- **Residential leasing**: *US and Plaintiff States v. RealPage, Inc. et al.* and *In re RealPage Rental Software Antitrust Litigation* (collectively, RealPage); *Duffy and Brett v. Yardi Systems, Inc. et al.*
- **Hotels**: *Cornish-Adebiyi et al. v. Caesars Entertainment, Inc. et al.*; *Gibson et al. v. Cendyn Group, LLC et al.*; *Portillo et al. v. CoStar Group et al.*; *Dai et al. v. SAS Institute, Inc. et al.*
- **Agriculture**: *US v. Agri Stats, Inc.*
- **Healthcare**: *In re Multiplan Health Insurance Provider Litigation*; *Segal v. Amadeus IT Group, S.A. et al.*

The foremost cases in this area are arguably the *RealPage* cases, in which plaintiffs allege that RealPage facilitated collusion among landlords and property management companies by selling access to software that recommends rental rates and capacity decisions. In its amended complaint, the DOJ alleges that "RealPage sells software to landlords that collects nonpublic information from competing landlords and uses that combined information to make pricing recommendations."[7] In short, the government contends that RealPage facilitated collusion by aggregating sensitive, nonpublic data and using it to generate pricing recommendations that are shared with competing landlords.

RealPage has responded that its software primarily relies on publicly available rental data and that any nonpublic information used is anonymized, aggregated, and incorporated only when recommending price changes.[8] The company also noted that, on average, nonpublic rents in its dataset tend to be lower than public listings. More broadly, RealPage has argued that its conduct should not be treated as per se unlawful under the Sherman Act, citing a Supreme Court precedent recognizing that the exchange of pricing information among competitors can, in some cases, enhance efficiency and promote (rather than suppress) competition.

The use of a third-party algorithm is central to the *RealPage* litigation, and similar allegations have emerged in other cases across industries and jurisdictions. In the United States, lawsuits involving third-party pricing tools have also been brought in the hotel, agriculture, and healthcare sectors. In *Gibson et al. v. Cendyn Group, LLC et al.*, plaintiffs alleged that several Las Vegas hotel operators used "GuestRev," a pricing algorithm that was "the core of Rainmaker's [Cendyn's subsidiary] revenue management platform," to coordinate room rates in violation of the Sherman Act. According to the complaint, Rainmaker allegedly facilitated collusion among competitors by generating uniform pricing recommendations. However, a federal judge dismissed the case, finding that merely subscribing to the same pricing software was insufficient to establish a conspiracy. A similar lawsuit, *Cornish-Adebiyi et al. v. Caesars Entertainment et al.*, brought against Atlantic City hotel operators was dismissed on similar grounds.

The US DOJ and RealPage have reached a proposed settlement that would require RealPage to cease the use of competitors' nonpublic data to determine rental prices and adopt several additional modifications to its algorithms.[9] The hotel pricing cases, such as *Gibson* and *Cornish-Adebiyi*, have been dismissed, though appeals are pending as of this writing. Although the facts may appear similar at first glance, courts have emphasized key distinctions. In *RealPage*, the DOJ alleged that pricing recommendations were based on nonpublic data submitted by competing landlords. In contrast, courts reviewing the hotel cases noted a lack of evidence that algorithms relied on confidential competitor data. As one judge remarked, "the devil is in the details."[10] A similar emphasis on data sharing appears in the DOJ's case against Agri Stats, where the agency claims the firm "organized several anticompetitive information exchanges" among meat processors. These cases suggest that the presence of competitively sensitive, nonpublic data plays a central role in whether courts find plausible antitrust violations involving third-party pricing algorithms.

Outside the United States, regulators are also beginning to scrutinize the use of algorithmic pricing tools. For example, the Canadian Competition Bureau has launched an investigation into whether AI-driven pricing practices may facilitate collusive pricing in residential rental markets.

The number of cases alleging that third-party pricing algorithms facilitate price fixing is likely to grow as these tools become more widely adopted. While such algorithms can enhance efficiency, for example, by enabling faster responses to market changes or giving smaller firms access to pricing technology, antitrust concerns arise. Firms and legal counsel should closely monitor ongoing litigation, understand how these tools are designed, and assess whether they incorporate nonpublic information from competitors that may pose a litigation risk.

Several city governments have already taken steps to restrict algorithmic pricing tools that rely on competitors' data in rental markets. Philadelphia, Providence, San Diego, and San Francisco, where a Prohibition of Anti-Competitive Automated Rent Price-Fixing Ordinance has been enacted, are among the jurisdictions moving to ban the use of such algorithms. Similar restrictions may follow in other markets. In addition, the growing availability of general-purpose AI tools may accelerate policy responses and prompt lawmakers to revisit existing regulations to address the evolving role of AI in pricing decisions.

As discussed above, firms must recognize that third-party algorithms can pose antitrust risk if they rely on nonpublic competitor data or incent collusive strategies. *RealPage* and related cases underscore this risk, and regulators have taken notice. Consistent with the "Bob Test," the FTC and DOJ jointly filed a statement of interest in *Cornish-Adebiyi et al. v. Caesars Entertainment, Inc. et al.*, asserting that "whether firms effectuate a price-fixing scheme through a software algorithm or through human-to-human interaction should be of no legal significance. Automating an anticompetitive scheme doesn't make it less anticompetitive."[11]

A related concern is that multiple competing firms might rely on the same GenAI model (and similar prompts and market data) to guide pricing decisions. While there are no known cases as of this writing involving allegations of collusion via a shared GenAI tool, this is a natural area for future scrutiny. As discussed before, prompt and model fine-tuning transparency will be crucial.

First-Party Algorithms and Exploitative Practices Allegations

While several lawsuits focus on the use of third-party algorithms, many companies develop their own algorithms to set prices. These in-house-developed tools, often used by companies with access to large volumes of data, may dynamically adjust prices based on many inputs. Government agencies and private plaintiffs have alleged that such algorithms can behave in exploitative ways, including by increasing prices across markets or by sharply raising prices to specific consumers in times of need. These cases have raised concerns about price gouging or other forms of exploitative practices.

A selection of relevant cases and investigations includes the following:

- *Federal Trade Commission et al. v. Amazon.com, Inc.* ("Project Nessie"); *European Commission v. Amazon.com, Inc.*
- *Greenberg et al. v. Amazon.com, Inc.* ("Amazon PG")
- New York attorney general's surge pricing investigation
- *US and Plaintiff States v. Live Nation Entertainment, Inc. and Ticketmaster Entertainment, LLC; Canadian Competition Bureau v. Canada's Wonderland; Canadian Competition Bureau v. DoorDash*

In September 2023, the FTC and a coalition of seventeen state attorneys general filed suit against Amazon. The matter, often referred to as "Project Nessie," received significant attention when the lawsuit was filed. The complaint focused on what the FTC characterizes as "a secret algorithm internally codenamed 'Project Nessie'" that has allegedly generated more than $1 billion in excess profit for Amazon.[12] According to the FTC, the algorithm was designed to identify products for which other online retailers were likely to follow Amazon's price increases. The FTC alleges that Amazon would raise prices on such products and, once its rivals followed suit, retain the higher prices, thereby increasing market-level prices.

Although the broader lawsuit includes various allegations of anticompetitive behavior, such as monopoly power, inflated prices, stifled innovation, and exclusionary conduct, Amazon's use of the Project Nessie algorithm is central to the claims. Amazon has denied wrongdoing, characterizing its conduct as consistent with "common retail practices that presumptively benefit consumers."[13] It also noted that Project Nessie was discontinued in 2019.

The European Commission has raised similar concerns about Amazon's pricing tools, alleging that Amazon used data from its third-party sellers to refine its own pricing algorithms in ways that may have distorted competition and raised prices.

Another lawsuit involving Amazon was filed in April 2020, during the early stages of the COVID-19 pandemic. This class action centers on allegations of price gouging. However, price gouging claims aren't new: The earliest known US legal action dates to 1985 and concerned the cost of tree removal services following a hurricane in New York. The emergence of algorithmic pricing adds a new layer of complexity. Many US states have enacted statutes prohibiting price gouging, allowing lawsuits to be brought in response to allegedly excessive price increases during natural disasters or emergencies. For example, New York was the first state to pass an anti-price gouging statute in the United States in 1979. More recently, New York has taken steps to address how its price gouging statute should be interpreted in the context of dynamic pricing.[14] Similarly, some provinces in Canada have measures prohibiting price gouging in situations of crisis (e.g., Ontario enacted the Anti-Price-Gouging Act in 2001). The UK and EU don't explicitly regulate price gouging but can generally act against it through provisions prohibiting unfair prices. A central challenge in cases brought under these regulations is defining what level of price increase constitutes unlawful gouging. The growing use of pricing algorithms and AI tools may make that distinction even more difficult to draw.

In Amazon PG, plaintiffs allege that Amazon increased prices on essential products sold during the COVID-19 pandemic and failed to prevent third-party sellers from doing the same on its platform. The case is ongoing (as of this writing) and showcases how algorithmic pricing can complicate traditional price gouging claims. Historically, a sudden price spike might have been interpreted as evidence of exploitation. Today, however, pricing algorithms enable firms to adjust prices rapidly in response to changes in demand, inventory, cost, market trends, or competitor behavior. As a result, evaluating whether algorithmic pricing constituted price gouging may require a detailed analysis of how the algorithm responded to market conditions over time and whether those responses reflected opportunism or more routine adjustments.

Ride-hailing companies Lyft and Uber have also faced scrutiny around their use of algorithmic pricing, including allegations of price gouging. These companies use both historical and real-time data on rider demand and driver availability to implement dynamic pricing models, which may result in price increases during periods of high demand and insufficient supply. Such price spikes (known as surge pricing) have occasionally drawn public criticism, especially when they occur during periods of emergency or catastrophic events. For instance, media reports of Uber's surge pricing during a hurricane prompted an investigation by the New York attorney general. As part of a resulting settlement, Uber agreed to limit surge pricing during declared emergencies and disasters nationwide. More recently, a 2024 congressional investigation raised questions about whether the use of pricing algorithms by Lyft and Uber suppresses competition or contributes to higher consumer prices.

A separate stream of recent lawsuits relates to so-called junk fees and drip pricing (sometimes more generally called deceptive pricing practices). These lawsuits focus on allegations that firms impose hidden charges, namely, fees not disclosed upfront but added later in the purchase process. One industry that has faced scrutiny for such practices is the airline industry. In the late 2000s and early 2010s, major carriers began unbundling their pricing by charging ancillary fees separate from the base ticket fare. More recently, the US Senate investigated these practices, concluding that while "unbundling" prices in this manner has the potential to lower costs for some consumers, it "has not lowered the cost of flying for consumers, who now face additional charges to fly with carry-on or checked bags."[15] Policymakers have since broadened their focus to address concerns around hidden fees in other sectors.

In 2025, Booking Holdings, the parent company of Booking.com, Kayak, and Priceline, agreed to pay $9.5 million to resolve a lawsuit from the Texas attorney general over deceptive junk fee practices. The lawsuit alleged that the company engaged in drip pricing by withholding mandatory fees such as resort, amenity, destination, and utility charges until checkout, potentially misleading consumers with artificially low advertised rates. This settlement is the largest of its kind by any US state against a hotel or online travel agency over such practices. As part of the agreement, Booking must now disclose all mandatory fees upfront, aligning with broader regulatory efforts to curb deceptive fee practices. Booking denied wrongdoing but emphasized its commitment to transparency and consistency with federal pricing standards.[16]

The use of algorithmic pricing has introduced new dimensions to these concerns. Firms can now deploy AI-based tools to personalize the timing, visibility, and structure of add-on charges based on consumer behavior, browsing history, and predicted WTP. This has prompted increased scrutiny, especially in the entertainment and ticketing sectors, where platforms like Ticketmaster are alleged to use algorithmic pricing tools to obscure total costs and extract greater revenue through targeted or dynamic fee structures. A recent lawsuit brought against Ticketmaster specifically discusses "service" or "convenience" fees "with little visibility" and alleges that such fees contribute substantially to Ticketmaster's profits. While these fees aren't the central focus of the case (which more broadly alleges that Ticketmaster has unlawfully maintained a monopoly), they may play a larger role in the litigation as the case progresses. Meanwhile, regulatory efforts have intensified: The FTC's new Trade Regulation Rule on Unfair or Deceptive Fees ("junk fees rule"), which took effect in May 2025, requires all mandatory fees to be disclosed upfront.[17] The rule followed a March 2025 executive order by President Trump directing federal agencies to improve transparency in pricing for entertainment events.[18]

Claims of Discrimination

As mentioned earlier, algorithms can enable more granular price differentiation across customer groups, which may raise potential concerns related to fairness and discrimination. As discussed earlier in this chapter, new regulations targeting price discrimination may result in pricing-related cases alleging algorithmic discrimination in the future. While I am not aware of any pricing-specific cases that have explicitly alleged algorithmic discrimination as of this writing, ongoing litigation in adjacent areas, such as lending, healthcare claims, and employment decisions, may offer insight into how discrimination concerns could be addressed in pricing matters.

I briefly summarize some such cases below:

- Credit lending: *In re Wells Fargo Mortgage Discrimination Litigation*
- Labor and employment: *Mobley v. Workday, Inc.*
- Healthcare claims: *Estate of Gene B. Lokken et al. v. UnitedHealth Group, Inc. et al.*; *Kisting-Leung et al. v. Cigna Corp. et al.*; *Barrows et al. v. Humana, Inc.*

In the credit lending case, plaintiffs alleged that Wells Fargo "fail[ed] to properly monitor and correct the lending algorithms" that it used to determine credit rates, resulting in practice that "disproportionately discriminates against applicants based on their race and ethnicity."[19] The case highlights the potential for unintended discriminatory effects when algorithms aren't thoroughly evaluated or tested across demographic groups.

In the labor and employment context, a case involving Workday's algorithmic screening tools is proceeding under the Age Discrimination in Employment Act. Plaintiff Derek Mobley alleges that Workday's AI-driven hiring tools led to the rejection of his applications for more than one hundred jobs at employers that used the platform. According to the complaint, Workday's system evaluates applicants based on submitted materials and may automatically advance or reject candidates. Mobley claims that due to his age, race, and/or disability status, the algorithm consistently rejected his applications across multiple employers, raising concerns about potential bias embedded in algorithmic hiring processes. Similarly, Amazon previously developed a resume review tool that inadvertently favored resumes from men over those from women.[20] The project has since been disbanded.

Relatedly, several lawsuits have been filed in the healthcare sector regarding the use of algorithms in claims approvals. In the case involving UnitedHealth Group (UHG), plaintiffs allege that nH Predict (an algorithm developed by a UHG subsidiary) had a high error rate that resulted in the denial of a substantial number of medically necessary care claims. Importantly, plaintiffs claim that their class action is a result of UHG's "illegal deployment of [AI] in place of real medical professionals to wrongfully deny elderly patients care" specifically.[21] UHG acknowledges using AI in its claims processing to reduce manual effort and accelerate decisions, stating that the technology enables faster approvals for patients and more timely reimbursements for providers. A similar lawsuit was filed against Humana, alleging that it too used nH Predict to deny necessary care to older patients. In response, Humana emphasized that while it employs AI tools, it maintains a "human-in-the-loop" approach, ensuring that medical judgment is incorporated into claims decisions. These cases highlight broader concerns about fairness and ethics in algorithmic decision-making, particularly when such tools are used in contexts with major implications for individual well-being and in the presence of vulnerable groups.

10 Predictions and Recommendations

> Plans are worthless, but planning is everything.
> —Dwight D. Eisenhower

To conclude the book, I outline eight predictions about the future of pricing, along with strategic and policy recommendations for business leaders and regulators.

Eight Predictions

As we look ahead, it's clear that pricing has already entered a new era shaped by automation, intelligence, and continuous experimentation. AI isn't merely optimizing existing pricing strategies; it's redefining the foundations of how prices are set, perceived, and regulated. For business leaders, lawyers, regulators, and policymakers, this transformation presents both opportunities and responsibilities. The ability to harness AI in pricing will distinguish tomorrow's most agile organizations, while those who ignore this trend will risk losing relevance and be exposed to evolving legal frameworks.

I next outline eight key predictions for the future of pricing, followed by practical recommendations for business and policy stakeholders seeking to navigate this new terrain.

Prediction 1: Hyperpersonalized Pricing Will Become Standard

Pricing will become deeply individualized in many settings. With access to behavioral data, transaction history, geolocation, and even real-time signals from mobile devices, AI systems will likely tailor prices to the unique context and WTP of each customer. This shift will be present in several industries, from e-commerce to transportation, hospitality, and services.

While hyperpersonalization promises improved targeting and profitability, it also raises questions of fairness, privacy, and transparency. Regulators and consumer advocates may demand clearer disclosures and tighter guardrails around how personalized decisions are made and communicated.

Prediction 2: Emotion-Aware and Contextual Pricing

AI will increasingly integrate emotional and contextual awareness into pricing decisions. Using advances in multimodal AI combining voice, facial expression, physiological signals, and browsing behavior, systems may infer a consumer's mood, urgency, or stress level and aim to dynamically adjust prices or send customized offers. For example, a tired traveler searching for a hotel late at night may be shown a higher price or more premium options. While this form of microtargeting can increase relevance and perceived value, it risks taking advantage of vulnerable individuals at emotionally sensitive moments. Balancing commercial effectiveness with ethical safeguards will become a key design challenge.

Prediction 3: AI-Based Pricing Will Introduce New Considerations for Antitrust Enforcement

AI systems trained to maximize profit in competitive environments may, in some cases, learn to avoid price wars without any explicit coordination or communication. This phenomenon, often described as tacit algorithmic collusion, raises concerns about potential risks to competition. At the same time, AI pricing tools can enhance competition by dynamically undercutting rivals' prices or rapidly adapting to shifts in demand. The overall impact depends on the market context and the algorithm design.

Traditional antitrust frameworks, which often focus on human intent and explicit communication, will need to adapt to these emerging dynamics. In the coming decade, antitrust enforcement is likely to evolve through behavioral testing of algorithms, mandatory documentation and transparency of pricing models (including training data, prompts, and fine-tuning processes), and increased scrutiny of black-box optimization systems.

Prediction 4: Decline of Hourly Rate Pricing

Hourly rate pricing, long dominant in many professions such as law, consulting, and other professional services, is poised to fade, at least for some domains and types of projects. As AI automates routine tasks and enables granular tracking of outcomes, clients will increasingly demand pricing models that reflect the value delivered as opposed to the time spent.

This will drive a shift toward value-based, performance-based, and subscription models that better align client and provider incentives. For professionals, this means rethinking how services are defined, measured, and monetized. It will also potentially increase transparency of contracts and enhance market competitiveness.

Prediction 5: AI-Negotiated Pricing and Autonomous Agents

AI agents will increasingly act as intermediaries in retail transactions and price negotiations. In several sectors, such as travel, SaaS, procurement, and retail, these AI agents will replace static pricing menus with personalized negotiation protocols optimized for each transaction. We can even envision a scenario in which two AI agents transact with each other.

AI agents are rapidly emerging as powerful shopping assistants, transforming how consumers plan, search, and purchase goods. It will totally change how businesses interact with their customers. This shift has been made possible by advances in conversational AI, large-scale integration with web data and APIs, and real-time personalization. These agents can now understand complex instructions, search across multiple suppliers, evaluate trade-offs, and make optimized purchasing decisions. Today, users can task AI agents with complex objectives, such as "Plan a vacation to Italy for two adults in early September, with a $4,000 budget. Include direct flights, 4-star hotels with breakfast, and a rental car with pickup in Rome." The AI can then query platforms like Booking.com, Expedia, Google Flights, and Kayak, compare options, apply the user's constraints and preferences, and either present a shortlist for approval or make the purchase directly through integrations with payment platforms.

Beyond travel, similar AI agents are being used to automate recurring household purchases, compare insurance plans, select financial products, or even negotiate prices for electronics and subscriptions. A key enabler of this technology is the agent's ability to integrate with APIs, scrape web content, and apply preference models that evolve with user feedback. In parallel, AI is also being used to create automated price alerts, where the agent continuously monitors product prices, availability, or deal timelines and notifies the user when conditions match their targets, such as when a flight drops below a specific threshold or a competitor's product goes on sale. These capabilities not only save consumers time and money but also fundamentally shift the role of businesses: from pushing offers to enabling intelligent, demand-driven interactions.

As these AI agents become more integrated into daily life, they are shifting the customer interface from web or app browsing to intent-based delegation. For businesses, this means adapting product catalogs, pricing APIs, ensuring secure transaction processes, and meeting data transparency standards to remain discoverable and competitive in a world where AI, not the end user, is increasingly the first customer touchpoint. In this new landscape, success depends not only on having the right product at the right price but also on being easily understood and actioned by machines acting on behalf of informed, empowered consumers.

While this can drive efficiency and customer satisfaction, it also requires firms to design agents that are fair, explainable, and aligned with brand values. From a regulatory standpoint, questions around digital bargaining power, deceptive practices, and algorithmic transparency will become increasingly relevant.

Prediction 6: Real-Time Fairness Constraints in AI Pricing

As discussed earlier, AI pricing systems may result in disparate outcomes across demographic or socioeconomic groups, such as offering higher prices to low-income consumers, minority groups, or vulnerable populations, even when these systems aren't explicitly designed to differentiate on those dimensions. Such outcomes can raise concerns under antidiscrimination laws or broader fairness principles. To address this, fairness-aware pricing algorithms are likely to become the norm in sectors where equity and access are critical.

Regulators will need to develop clear and carefully designed requirements for explainability, algorithmic audits, and impact assessments. Defining the concept of fairness in a consistent and context-sensitive way will be essential, and determining how to impose fairness constraints will likely require case-by-case deliberation. Firms that proactively embed fairness considerations into their pricing practices may gain both reputational benefits and regulatory advantages.

Prediction 7: Continuous Experiments and Autonomous Price Testing
With advances in real-time testing and adaptive learning, many companies will run thousands of live experiments simultaneously by constantly adjusting prices based on customer behavior, inventory levels, and external signals. Pricing will become a fluid and continuously optimized process.

This shift enhances responsiveness but reduces predictability, potentially eroding consumer trust. Businesses must balance experimentation with consistency, while regulators may impose guidelines on pricing transparency and restrictions during testing phases.

Prediction 8: Rise of Marketplaces Setting the Rules
As digital platforms become among the dominant retail and service channels, they will increasingly control pricing on behalf of third-party sellers. Companies like Amazon, Apple, and Uber already leverage platform-level optimization to manage prices, often limiting sellers' autonomy.

This centralization raises questions about pricing fairness, competitive neutrality, and the right to set prices. One may expect greater scrutiny of platform pricing policies, with potential regulatory action to ensure that embedded algorithms don't create anticompetitive outcomes or exploit asymmetries in data access.

Strategic and Policy Recommendations

Given the impact of AI in our society, businesses and regulators must adapt with thoughtful, proactive strategies. For business leaders, it's essential to adopt AI-powered pricing systems that embed fairness constraints and provide transparent reasoning behind pricing decisions. These systems should not operate in isolation. Instead, organizations should establish cross-functional oversight structures that include legal, compliance, data science, and executive leadership to ensure that pricing decisions align with ethical and regulatory standards alike. At the very least, businesses must ensure that their pricing models are explainable to both internal stakeholders and external regulators.

Firms must also invest in experimentation strategies that are ethically grounded and strategically aligned with their brand values. As real-time price testing becomes commonplace, managing consumer perceptions and ensuring that experimentation doesn't undermine trust is critical.

Equally important is clear and proactive communication. When personalized or dynamic pricing is used, businesses should articulate why certain prices are offered, which data is used, and how customer interests are protected. Clear, transparent communication builds trust and loyalty, which may promote increased long-term profitability.

From a regulatory and legal standpoint, modernization is becoming increasingly important. Antitrust frameworks may need to evolve to address the risk of algorithmic coordination and the challenges posed by opaque pricing behaviors. Regulators might consider establishing guidelines that encourage firms to document key steps in their pricing algorithms, monitor how decisions are made, and conduct periodic reviews, especially in high-stakes sectors such as healthcare and insurance. These reviews could include assessments of potential biases or fairness concerns across various dimensions while promoting competitive and nondiscriminatory outcomes. It may also be advisable for firms to retain detailed records of pricing model logic, constraints, prompts, validation protocols, and training data to support transparency and accountability.

Policymakers will also play a key role. By promoting responsible AI adoption via certifications, public guidance, and incentives, they can help encourage ethical innovation in pricing technologies. Supporting interdisciplinary research spanning economics, law, computer science, and psychology will be important for understanding the long-term social and economic implications of AI-driven pricing. Finally, as digital markets are increasingly global, international cooperation will likely be required to promote consistent standards for pricing transparency, fairness, and accountability across jurisdictions. Of course, this is easier said than done.

Acknowledgments

I am deeply grateful to everyone who supported the work behind this book. Its content reflects the culmination of sixteen years of academic research, industry consulting, start-up advising, and countless conversations with colleagues and students. Special thanks go to Charles River Associates for the wonderful support in assisting and reviewing this book, and particularly to Sean Taylor, Neil Mathur, Daniel Garcia-Swartz, Mary Beth Savio, Jarrod Welch, and Margaret Sanderson. A special thank you to Nymisha Bandi for her precious help with chapter 4, to Eddy Hage-Youssef for his help with parts of chapter 7, to Neil Mathur and Sean Taylor for their support on chapter 9, and to Michael Benborhoum for his expert inputs on B2B pricing. I am also grateful to several companies and partners, including Aldo Group, Cherre, Couche Tard, ELNA Medical, Intelligems, IVADO Labs, Oracle Retail, Via, and Waze (and several others I can't disclose) for sharing valuable business knowledge and allowing me to develop and test new approaches using their data. I am deeply grateful to Georgia Perakis for having been the best doctoral supervisor I could have hoped for and for introducing me to the world of revenue management and pricing. I am also thankful to Anindya Ghose for inspiring me and for introducing me to the MIT Press. Finally, the support of the Bensadoun School at McGill University and several research grants (NSERC, Scale AI, SSHRC) are greatly acknowledged.

There are so many people I would like to thank for their support and inspiration in achieving the accomplishment of writing this book, so listing them will unavoidably incur the risk of forgetting some of them. Let me still take my best attempt to do so by extending my special thanks (in alphabetical order) to Jeremie Abbou, Marine Abbou, Gad Allon, Mor

Armony, Jonathan Assayag, Lennart Baardman, Nymisha Bandi, Michael Benborhoum, Alexandre Benchimol, Aldo Bensadoun, Aharon Ben-Tal, Carl Boutet, Michael Chemama, James Clark, Audren Cloitre, Tonton Samy Cohen, Alexandre Corbasson, Ruomeng Cui, Samuel Dahan, Tinglong Dai, Charles de Brabant, Helene Desmarais, Adam Elmachtoub, Harley Finkelstein, Michael-David Fiszer, Joshua Gans, Anindya Ghose, Daniel Guetta, Eddy Hage-Youssef, Pavithra Harsha, Marco Iansiti, Alexandre Jacquillat, Eli Katzman, Warut Khern-am-nuai, Adam Kitain, Jonathan Kluberg, Subodha Kumar, Xiao Lei, Retsef Levi, Alys Liang, Andrea Lodi, Erwan Makame, Drew Marconi, Sentao Miao, Vahab Mirrokni, Frank Neuman, Derek Nowrouzezahrai, Kiran Panchamgam, Georgia Perakis, Bob Pindyck, Mike Pinedo, Lisa Pinheiro, Edieal Pinker, Saibal Ray, Jimmy Royer, Olivier Rubel, L. D. Salmanson, Margaret Sanderson, Roy Sasson, Juan Camilo Serpa, Nahum Shimkin, Kalyan Singhal, Daniel Sokol, Haotian Song, Tim Spittle, Lisa Stockley, Tianshu Sun, Steve Tadelis, Chris Tang, Jitsama Tanlamai, Elie Toubiana, Alexis Turjman, Hal Varian, Yining Wang, Ovunc Yilmaz, Morty Yalovsky, David Zemmour, Dennis Zhang, and Renyu Zhang. Finally, I am deeply grateful to the team at the MIT Press, including Kathleen Caruso, Caroline Helms, and Catherine Woods, for believing in the vision of this book and for their outstanding support throughout the process.

Notes

Chapter 2

1. Tyler Lawson, "What You Need to Know About Amazon's Subscribe & Save Program," *GoAmify* (blog), August 22, 2024, https://goamify.com/blog-articles/what-you-need-to-know-about-amazons-subscribe-save-program.

2. Sarah Perez, "Target Launches Its First Subscription-Based E-Commerce Service, Focus for Now Is Baby Care Items," *TechCrunch*, September 25, 2013, https://techcrunch.com/2013/09/25/targets-launches-its-first-subscription-based-e-commerce-service-focus-for-now-is-baby-care-items.

3. Jess Weatherbed, "Delta Air Lines AI Ticket Price Rollout," *The Verge*, July 18, 2025, https://www.theverge.com/news/709556/delta-air-lines-ai-ticket-price-rollout.

Chapter 3

1. Olivia Solon, "How a Book About Flies Came to Be Priced $24 Million on Amazon," *Wired*, April 27, 2011, https://www.wired.com/2011/04/amazon-flies-24-million/.

2. Constance L. Hays, "Variable-Price Coke Machine Being Tested," *New York Times*, October 28, 1999, https://www.nytimes.com/1999/10/28/business/variable-price-coke-machine-being-tested.html.

3. Harry Low, "The London Pub Where Prices Jump £2 After 10pm," *BBC News*, November 11, 2024, https://www.bbc.com/news/articles/c4g2z6405zpo.

4. Hayley Berg, "2023 Travel Trends Report: Post-Pandemic State of Travel and Consumer Spending," Hopper, April 6, 2023, https://media.hopper.com/research/2023-travel-trends-report.

5. "A New Textiles Economy: Redesigning Fashion's Future," Ellen MacArthur Foundation, November 27, 2017, https://www.ellenmacarthurfoundation.org/a-new-textiles-economy.

6. Aayushi Nevatia, "Embrace the Future of Fashion: H&M's Conscious Collection Unveiled," *Medium*, August 27, 2023, https://medium.com/@aayushi.nevatia/embrace-the-future-of-fashion-h-ms-conscious-collection-unveiled-9bf602e6de14.

7. Zalando, *Sustainability Progress Report 2023* (Zalando, 2024), https://corporate.zalando.com/sites/default/files/media-download/Zalando_SE_Sustainability_Progress_Report_2023.pdf.

8. Michael V. Marn, Eric V. Roegner, and Craig C. Zawada, "The Power of Pricing," *McKinsey Quarterly*, February 1, 2003, https://www.mckinsey.com/capabilities/growth-marketing-and-sales/our-insights/the-power-of-pricing.

Chapter 4

1. Cora Lewis, "Why Are More Shoppers Struggling to Repay 'Buy Now, Pay Later' Loans?," *AP News*, May 21, 2025, https://apnews.com/article/buy-now-pay-later-missed-payments-regulation-f7fd30f2a0e900460919fad76a1e0dbf.

2. NYC Department of Consumer Affairs, *From Cradle to Cane: The Cost of Being a Female Consumer*, December 2015, https://www.nyc.gov/assets/dca/downloads/pdf/partners/Study-of-Gender-Pricing-in-NYC.pdf.

Chapter 5

1. Jenniver Velentino-DeVries, Jeremy Singer-Vine, and Ashkan Soltani, "Websites Vary Prices, Deals Based on Users' Information," *Wall Street Journal*, December 24, 2012, https://www.wsj.com/articles/SB10001424127887323777204578189391813881534.

2. Maya Kosoff, "You're More Likely to Accept Uber's Surge Pricing When Your Phone's About to Die," *Vanity Fair*, May 20, 2016, https://www.vanityfair.com/news/2016/05/uber-surge-pricing-low-phone-battery.

3. "Low Phone Battery, Higher Uber Fares? Delhi Entrepreneur's Shocking Discovery Sparks Debate over Fare Manipulation," *Economic Times*, October 2, 2023, https://economictimes.com/news/new-updates/low-phone-battery-higher-uber-fares-delhi-entrepreneurs-shocking-discovery-sparks-debate-over-fare-manipulation/articleshow/117387009.cms.

4. Dana Mattioli, "On Orbitz, Mac Users Steered to Pricier Hotels," *Wall Street Journal*, August 23, 2012, https://www.wsj.com/articles/SB10001424052702304458604577488822667325882.

5. Paulina Okunytė, "Top Travel Apps Harvesting Your Data Without Asking—Cybernews Exclusive," *Cybernews*, July 11, 2024, https://cybernews.com/privacy/top-travel-apps-privacy/.

6. Will Preston, "Uber Is Ripping Off Frequent Riders—and Here's How to Avoid It," The Rideshare Guy, last updated December 6, 2019, https://therideshareguy.com/uber-is-ripping-off-frequent-riders-and-heres-how-to-avoid-it/.

Chapter 6

1. "2026 World Cup Tickets: FIFA Confirms Use of Dynamic Pricing," ESPN, September 3, 2025, https://www.espn.com/soccer/story/_/id/46147005/2026-world-cup-tickets-fifa-dynamic-pricing-prices.

2. Clareese Packer, "'Not Fair': Uber Fare Prices Double as Trains Cancelled amid Rail Dispute and Wild Weather in NSW," news.com.au, January 16, 2025, https://www.news.com.au/travel/travel-updates/incidents/uber-fare-prices-double-as-trains-cancelled-amid-rail-dispute-and-wild-weather-in-nsw/news-story/081ebe1abd09f4fa48fe23fe27f268e7.

Chapter 7

1. "The RISEN Framework," Juuzt AI Knowledge Base, accessed October 3, 2025, https://juuzt.ai/knowledge-base/prompt-frameworks/the-risen-framework/.

2. All y-axes in this chapter are prices in USD.

3. Maxime Cohen, "Car Pricing Prompts," 2025, GitHub Repository, https://maxccohen.github.io/Car-Pricing-Prompts.pdf.

4. Maxime Cohen, "Prompt Example," 2025, GitHub Repository, https://maxccohen.github.io/Prompt-Example.pdf.

Chapter 8

1. Sumathi Reddy and Danny Gold, "City Nails Sex-Based Pricing," *Wall Street Journal*, May 23, 2012, https://www.wsj.com/articles/SB10001424052702304019404577420651136722954; Molly Triffin, "Meet the Woman Who's Calling Out Companies for Charging Women More," *TIME*, March 4, 2016, https://time.com/4245619/pink-tax-study; Bill de Blasio and Julie Menin, "From Cradle to Cane: The Cost of Being a Female Consumer," December 2015, https://www.nyc.gov/assets/dca/downloads/pdf/partners/Study-of-Gender-Pricing-in-NYC.pdf.

2. Olga Khazan, "Should Men Pay More at All-You-Can-Eat Buffets?," *Atlantic*, April 9, 2014, https://www.theatlantic.com/health/archive/2014/04/should-men-pay-more-at-all-you-can-eat-buffets/360393/.

3. "BBQ Chain's Half-Price Women-Only Deal," News on Japan, September 4, 2025, https://newsonjapan.com/article/143406.php.

4. Kerry Allen, "Chinese Restaurant Offers Bra Size Discounts," *BBC News from Elsewhere*, August 7, 2017, https://www.bbc.com/news/blogs-news-from-elsewhere-40851224.

5. "Samoa Air Charges Customers per Kilogram," *ABC News (Australia)*, April 1, 2013, https://www.abc.net.au/news/2013-04-02/an-samoa-air-charging-per-kilo/4604540.

6. Associated Press, "Southwest Airlines' New Policy Will Affect Plus-Size Travelers. Here's How," *CNN Travel*, August 26, 2025, https://www.cnn.com/2025/08/26/travel/southwest-airlines-plus-size-seating-rule-hnk.

7. Peter Burke, "Restaurant Offers Food Discount to 'Skinny' Customers Who Can Squeeze Through Bars," *Fox News*, April 10, 2025, https://www.foxnews.com/food-drink/restaurant-offers-food-discount-skinny-customers-who-can-squeeze-through-bars.

8. Tom Philips, "Korean Restaurant in China Offers Free Food to Attractive Diners," *Sydney Morning Herald*, January 14, 2015, https://www.smh.com.au/goodfood/eating-out/korean-restaurant-in-china-offers-free-food-to-attractive-diners-20150114-12nmsy.html.

9. Kim Bo-eun, "Cosmetic Surgery Ad Triggers Controversy," *Korea Times*, September 23, 2012, https://www.koreatimes.co.kr/southkorea/20120923/cosmetic-surgery-ad-triggers-controversy; "Plastic Surgery in Korea in 2025," Seoul Clinic, last updated January 30, 2025, https://seoul.clinic/plastic-surgery-korea/.

10. Kyle Potter and Jon Shallbetter, "After Blowback, Delta & United Dump Fares That Punish Solo Travelers," Thrifty Traveler, May 30, 2025, https://thriftytraveler.com/news/airlines/airlines-charging-solo-travelers-higher-fares/.

11. Susan Meyer, "Women Now Pay More Than Men for Car Insurance in Only 4 States," The Zebra, April 28, 2025, https://www.thezebra.com/resources/research/men-women-auto-insurance-differences-by-state.

12. "NAIC Announces Special Committee on Race and Insurance," NAIC, July 23, 2020, https://content.naic.org/article/news-release-naic-announces-special-committee-race-and-insurance.

13. Mallika Bender, Margaret Brinkmann, Eric Krafcheck, Craig Sloss, Gary Wang, and Mike Woods, "Practical Application of Bias Measurement and Mitigation Techniques in Insurance Pricing," CAS Research Paper Series on Race and Insurance Pricing, https://www.casact.org/sites/default/files/2025-01/Practical_Application_of_Bias_Measurement_Part_1.pdf.

14. "Top 10 Location Based Marketing Examples in Retail Sector," *Sekeltech*, December 8, 2022, https://sekel.tech/blog/top-10-location-based-marketing-examples-in-retail-sector.

15. Julia Angwin, Surya Mattu, and Jeff Larson, "The Tiger Mom Tax: Asians Are Nearly Twice as Likely to Get a Higher Price from Princeton Review," ProPublica, September 1, 2015, https://www.propublica.org/article/asians-nearly-twice-as-likely-to-get-higher-price-from-princeton-review.

16. Julia Angwin, Jeff Larson, Lauren Kirchner, and Surya Mattu, "Minority Neighborhoods Pay Higher Car Insurance Premiums Than White Areas with the Same Risk," ProPublica, April 5, 2017, https://www.propublica.org/article/minority-neighborhoods-higher-car-insurance-premiums-white-areas-same-risk.

Chapter 9

1. Maureen K. Ohlhausen, "Should We Fear the Things That Go BeepIn the Night? Some Initial Thoughts on the Intersection of Antitrust Law and Algorithmic Pricing," Federal Trade Commission, May 23, 2017, https://www.ftc.gov/system/files/documents/public_statements/1220893/ohlhausen_-_concurrences_5-23-17.pdf.

2. Maureen Ohlhausen, Taylor Owings, and Cora Allen. "What About Bob? Revisiting the Intersection of Antitrust Law and Algorithmic Pricing in 2024," in *Artificial Intelligence and Competition Policy*, ed. Alden Abbott and Thibault Schrepel (Concurrences, 2024), 187–200.

3. See, for example, Christopher R. Leslie, "Predatory Pricing Algorithms," *New York University Law Review* 98, no. 1 (2023): 49–112.

4. New York State Department of State, Division of Consumer Protection, "Consumer Alert: NYS Department of State Division of Consumer Protection Reminds Consumers That Gender-Based Pricing Is Illegal in New York State," August 26, 2022, https://dos.ny.gov/news/consumer-alert-nys-department-state-division-consumer-protection-reminds-consumers- .

5. Federal Trade Commission, "Surveillance Pricing," accessed January 17, 2025, https://www.ftc.gov/news-events/features/surveillance-pricing.

6. United Kingdom Financial Conduct Authority, "AI Update," April 22, 2024, https://www.fca.org.uk/publication/corporate/ai-update.pdf.

7. Amended complaint, *US and Plaintiff States v. RealPage, Inc. et al.*, January 7, 2025.

8. Brief in Support of Defendant RealPage Inc.'s Motion to Dismiss Under Federal Rule of Civil Procedure 12(b)(6), *US and Plaintiff States v. RealPage, Inc. et al.*, December 3, 2024.

9. Office of Public Affairs, US Department of Justice, "Justice Department Requires RealPage to End the Sharing of Competitively Sensitive Information and Alignment

of Pricing Among Competitors," press release, November 24, 2025, https://www.justice.gov/opa/pr/justice-department-requires-realpage-end-sharing-competitively-sensitive-information-and.

10. Judge Crenshaw, the judge overseeing the civil *RealPage* case, noted that the allegations in *Gibson* and *RealPage* differ in that the *RealPage* civil complaint "unequivocally alleges that RealPage's revenue management software inputs a melting point of confidential competitor information through its algorithm," while this was unclear in the *Gibson* case (which was dismissed). See memorandum opinion, *In re RealPage, Inc. Rental Software Antitrust Litigation (No. II)*, December 28, 2023.

11. Statement of Interest of the United States, *Cornish-Adebiyi et al. v. Caesars Entertainment, Inc. et al.*, March 28, 2024.

12. Complaint, *FTC and States v. Amazon.com, Inc.*, September 26, 2023.

13. Complaint, *FTC and States v. Amazon.com, Inc.*

14. New York State Office of the Attorney General, *Notice of Proposed Rulemaking: General Rule for Determining Pre-Disruption Price (OAGPG-2502-NPRM-600.5)*, January 5, 2025.

15. Richard Blumenthal, *The Sky's the Limit: The Rise of Junk Fees in American Travel*, Majority Report, Permanent Subcommittee on Investigations, November 26, 2024, https://www.hsgac.senate.gov/wp-content/uploads/2024.11.25-Majority-Staff-Report-The-Skys-the-Limit-The-Rise-of-Junk-Fees-in-American-Travel-1.pdf.

16. Jonathan Stempel, "Booking.com Parent in $9.5 Million 'Junk Fee' Settlement with Texas," August 19, 2025, https://www.reuters.com/legal/litigation/bookingcom-parent-95-million-junk-fee-settlement-with-texas-2025-08-19/.

17. Federal Trade Commission, 16 CFR Part 464 (Trade Regulation Rule on Unfair or Deceptive Fees).

18. Donald J. Trump, "Combating Unfair Practices in the Live Entertainment Market," The White House, March 31, 2025, https://www.whitehouse.gov/presidential-actions/2025/03/combating-unfair-practices-in-the-live-entertainment-market/.

19. In re WF Consolidated Complaint, March 24, 2023, https://bencrump.com/wp-content/uploads/2023/03/In-Re-WF-Consolidated-Complaint-3.24.23.pdf.

20. Jeffrey Dastin, "Insight—Amazon Scraps Secret AI Recruiting Tool That Showed Bias Against Women," *Reuters*, October 10, 2018, https://www.reuters.com/article/us-amazon-com-jobs-automation-insight/amazon-scraps-secret-ai-recruiting-tool-that-showed-bias-against-women-idUSKCN1MK08G/.

21. Plaintiffs' class action complaint, *Estate of Gene B. Lokken et al. v. UnitedHealth Group, Inc. et al.*, November 13, 2023.

References

Abada, Ibrahim, and Xavier Lambin. 2023. "Artificial Intelligence: Can Seemingly Collusive Outcomes Be Avoided?" *Management Science* 69 (9): 5042–5065.

Agrawal, Ajay, Joshua Gans, and Avi Goldfarb. 2022a. *Prediction Machines: The Simple Economics of Artificial Intelligence*. Updated and expanded ed. Harvard Business Review Press.

Agrawal, Ajay, Joshua Gans, and Avi Goldfarb. 2022b. *Power and Prediction: The Disruptive Economics of Artificial Intelligence*. Harvard Business Review Press.

Ariely, Dan. 2008. *Predictably Irrational: The Hidden Forces That Shape Our Decisions*. HarperCollins.

Baardman, Lennart, Maxime C. Cohen, Kiran Panchamgam, Georgia Perakis, and Danny Segev. 2019. "Scheduling Promotion Vehicles to Boost Profits." *Management Science* 65 (1): 50–70.

Bandi, Nymisha, Maxime C. Cohen, and Saibal Ray. 2024. "Behavioral Retail Operations: Tactics to Win Customers." *Foundations and Trends® in Technology, Information and Operations Management* 18 (3–4): 214–420.

Bandi, Nymisha, Maxime C. Cohen, and Saibal Ray. 2025. "Discounting or Add-On Bundling? Field Experiments for Healthy and Unhealthy Snacks." Working paper. McGill University, February 10.

Bapna, Ravi, and Anindya Ghose. 2024. *Thrive: Maximizing Well-Being in the Age of AI*. MIT Press.

Bergemann, Dirk, Benjamin Brooks, and Stephen Morris. 2015. "The Limits of Price Discrimination." *American Economic Review* 105 (3): 921–957.

Bertini, Marco, and Oded Koenigsberg. 2021. "The Pitfalls of Pricing Algorithms: Be Mindful of How They Can Hurt Your Brand." *Harvard Business Review* 99 (5): 74–83.

Bertrand, Joseph. 1889. *Calcul des probabilités*. Gauthier-Villars.

Besbes, Omar, Adam N. Elmachtoub, and Yunjie Sun. 2020. "Pricing Analytics for Rotable Spare Parts." *INFORMS Journal on Applied Analytics* 50 (5): 313–324.

Bijmolt, Tammo H., Harald J. Van Heerde, and Rik G. Pieters. 2005. "New Empirical Generalizations on the Determinants of Price Elasticity." *Journal of Marketing Research* 42 (2): 141–156.

Blattberg, Robert C., and Scott A. Neslin. 1990. *Sales Promotion: Concepts, Methods, and Strategies*. Prentice Hall.

Brand, James, Ayelet Israeli, and Donald Ngwe. 2023. "Using GPT for Market Research." Working Paper No. 23-062. Harvard Business School.

Brown, Zach Y., and Alexander MacKay. 2023. "Competition in Pricing Algorithms." *American Economic Journal: Microeconomics* 15 (2): 109–156.

Cachon, Gérard P., and Pnina Feldman. 2010. "Dynamic Versus Static Pricing in the Presence of Strategic Consumers." Working paper. University of Pennsylvania, December 21.

Calvano, Emilio, Giacomo Calzolari, Vicenzo Denicolo, and Sergio Pastorello. 2020. "Artificial Intelligence, Algorithmic Pricing, and Collusion." *American Economic Review* 110 (10): 3267–3297.

Campbell, Margaret C. 1999. "Perceptions of Price Unfairness: Antecedents and Consequences." *Journal of Marketing Research* 36 (2): 187–199.

Caro, Felipe, and Jérémie Gallien. 2012. "Clearance Pricing Optimization for a Fast-Fashion Retailer." *Operations Research* 60 (6): 1404–1422.

Chen, Zhisheng. 2023. "Ethics and Discrimination in Artificial Intelligence-Enabled Recruitment Practices." *Humanities and Social Sciences Communications* 10 (1): 1–12.

Chen, Ningyuan, and Guillermo Gallego. 2019. "Welfare Analysis of Dynamic Pricing." *Management Science* 65 (1): 139–151.

Chen, Hongqiao, Ming Hu, and Georgia Perakis. 2022. "Distribution-Free Pricing." *Manufacturing & Service Operations Management* 24 (4): 1939–1958.

Chen, Le, Alan Mislove, and Christo Wilson. 2016. "An Empirical Analysis of Algorithmic Pricing on Amazon Marketplace." In *Proceedings of the 25th International Conference on World Wide Web*, 1339–1349. International World Wide Web Conferences Steering Committee.

Chen, M. Keith, and Michael Sheldon. 2016. "Dynamic Pricing in a Labor Market: Surge Pricing and Flexible Work on the Uber Platform." In *Proceedings of the 2016 ACM Conference on Economics and Computation (EC '16)*, 455. Association for Computing Machinery.

Chen, Xi, David Simchi-Levi, and Yining Wang. 2022. "Privacy-Preserving Dynamic Personalized Pricing with Demand Learning." *Management Science* 68 (7): 4878–4898.

Chitla, Sandeep, Maxime C. Cohen, Srikanth Jagabathula, and Dmitry Mitrofanov. 2023. "Customers' Multihoming Behavior in Ride-Hailing: Empirical Evidence from Uber and Lyft." Working paper. New York University, McGill University, and Boston College.

Cialdini, Robert B. 2009. *Influence: Science and Practice*. 4th ed. Pearson Education.

Cohen, Maxime C. 2024. "AI: What Is It and Why Is It Good for Us and for Society?" White paper.

Cohen, Maxime C. 2026. "How AI Is Reshaping Pricing Litigation?" *ABA Antitrust Magazine* 40 (2).

Cohen, Maxime C., and Tinglong Dai. 2025. *AI in Supply Chains: Perspectives from Global Thought Leaders*. Springer.

Cohen, Maxime C., Adam N. Elmachtoub, and Xiao Lei. 2022. "Price Discrimination with Fairness Constraints." *Management Science* 68 (12): 8536–8552.

Cohen, Maxime C., Michael D. Fiszer, and Baek J. Kim. 2022. "Frustration-Based Promotions: Field Experiments in Ride-Hailing." *Management Science* 68 (4): 2432–2464.

Cohen, Maxime C., Paul-Emile Gras, Arthur Pentecoste, and Renyu Zhang. 2022. *Demand Prediction in Retail: A Practical Guide to Leverage Data and Predictive Analytics*. Springer.

Cohen, Maxime C., and Eddy Hage-Youssef. 2025. "Generative AI for Data Scraping." Working paper. McGill University.

Cohen, Maxime C., Eddy Hage-Youssef, and Warut Khern-am-nuai. 2025. "When AI Sets Wages: Biases and Labor Discrimination in Generative Pricing." Working paper. McGill University.

Cohen, Maxime C., Alexandre Jacquillat, Juan C. Serpa, and Michael Benborhoum. 2023. "Managing Airfares Under Competition: Insights from a Field Experiment." *Management Science* 69 (10): 6076–6108.

Cohen, Maxime C., Jeremy J. Kalas, and Georgia Perakis. 2021. "Promotion Optimization for Multiple Items in Supermarkets." *Management Science* 67 (4): 2340–2364.

Cohen, Maxime C., Adam Kitain, Drew Marconi, and Andrew Raftery. 2024. "Lessons from More than 1,000 E-Commerce Pricing Tests." *Harvard Business Review*. https://hbr.org/2024/03/lessons-from-more-than-1000-e-commerce-pricing-tests.

Cohen, Maxime C., Ngai-Hang Z. Leung, Kiran Panchamgam, Georgia Perakis, and Anthony Smith. 2017. "The Impact of Linear Optimization on Promotion Planning." *Operations Research* 65 (2): 446–468.

Cohen, Maxime C., Ilan Lobel, and Renato Paes Leme. 2020. "Feature-Based Dynamic Pricing." *Management Science* 66 (11): 4921–4943.

Cohen, Maxime C., Sentao Miao, and Yining Wang. 2025. "Dynamic Pricing with Fairness Constraints." *Operations Research* 73 (6): 2867–3452.

Cohen, Maxime C., Georgia Perakis, Robert S. Pindyck. 2021. "A Simple Rule for Pricing with Limited Knowledge of Demand." *Management Science* 67 (3): 1608–1621.

Cohen, Maxime C., Tim Spittle, and Jimmy Royer. 2024. "Assessing Algorithmic Versus Generative AI Pricing Tools." Law360. https://www.law360.com/articles/1879101/assessing-algorithmic-versus-generative-ai-pricing-tools.

Cui, Ruomeng, Dennis J. Zhang, and Achal Bassamboo. 2019. "Learning from Inventory Availability Information: Evidence from Field Experiments on Amazon." *Management Science* 65 (3): 1216–1235.

Dubé, Jean-Pierre, and Sanjog Misra. 2023. "Personalized Pricing and Consumer Welfare." *Journal of Political Economy* 131 (1): 131–189.

Elmachtoub, A. N., and P. Grigas. 2022. "Smart 'Predict, Then Optimize.'" *Management Science* 68 (1): 9–26.

Elmachtoub, Adam N., and Michael L. Hamilton. 2021. "The Power of Opaque Products in Pricing." *Management Science* 67 (8): 4686–4702.

Elmachtoub, Adam N., Vishal Gupta, and Michael L. Hamilton. 2021. "The Value of Personalized Pricing." *Management Science* 67 (10): 6055–6070.

Ferrara, Emilio 2023. "Fairness and Bias in Artificial Intelligence: A Brief Survey of Sources, Impacts, and Mitigation Strategies." *Sci* 6 (1): 3.

Ferreira, Kris J., Bin H. A. Lee, and David Simchi-Levi. 2016. "Analytics for an Online Retailer: Demand Forecasting and Price Optimization." *Manufacturing & Service Operations Management* 18 (1): 69–88.

Fish, Sara, Yannai A. Gonczarowski, and Ran I. Shorrer. 2024. "Algorithmic Collusion by Large Language Models." Working paper. Harvard University and Penn State University. arXiv:2404.00806.

Fisher, Marshall, Santiago Gallino, and Jun Li. 2018. "Competition-Based Dynamic Pricing in Online Retailing: A Methodology Validated with Field Experiments." *Management Science* 64 (6): 2496–2514.

Foroughifar, Mohsen, and Nitin Mehta. 2023. "The Challenges of Deploying an Algorithmic Pricing Tool: Evidence from Airbnb." Working paper. Carnegie Mellon University and University of Toronto.

Gallego, Guillermo, and Huseyin Topaloglu. 2019. *Revenue Management and Pricing Analytics*. Vol. 209 of *International Series in Operations Research & Management Science*. Springer.

Greenleaf, Eric A., Eric J. Johnson, Vicki G. Morwitz, and Edith Shalev. 2016. "The Price Doesn't Include Additional Taxes, Fees, and Surcharges: A Review of Research on Partitioned Pricing." *Journal of Consumer Psychology* 26 (1): 105–124.

Gümüş, Mehmet, Shanling Li, Wonseok Oh, and Saibal Ray. 2013. "Shipping Fees or Shipping Free? A Tale of Two Price Partitioning Strategies in Online Retailing." *Production and Operations Management* 22 (4): 758–776.

Guittar, Stephanie G., Liz Grauerholz, Erin N. Kidder, Shameika D. Daye, and Megan McLaughlin. 2022. "Beyond the Pink Tax: Gender-Based Pricing and Differentiation of Personal Care Products." *Gender Issues* 39 (1): 1–23.

Haws, Kelly L., and William O. Bearden. 2006. "Dynamic Pricing and Consumer Fairness Perceptions." *Journal of Consumer Research* 33 (3): 304–311.

He, Li, Liang Wang, Kaipeng Liu, Bo Wu, and Weinan Zhang. 2018. "Optimizing Sponsored Search Ranking Strategy by Deep Reinforcement Learning." Working paper. arXiv:1803.07347.

Hmurovic, Jillian, Cait Lamberton, and Kelly Goldsmith. 2023. "Examining the Efficacy of Time Scarcity Marketing Promotions in Online Retail." *Journal of Marketing Research* 60 (2): 299–328.

Iansiti, Marco, and Karim R. Lakhani. 2020. *Competing in the Age of AI: Strategy and Leadership When Algorithms and Networks Run the World.* Harvard Business Press.

Inman, J. Jeffrey, Anil C. Peter, and Priya Raghubir. 1997. "Framing the Deal: The Role of Restrictions in Accentuating Deal Value." *Journal of Consumer Research* 24 (1): 68–79.

Kalyanaram, Gurumurthy, and Russell S. Winer. 1995. "Empirical Generalizations from Reference Price Research." *Marketing Science* 14: 161–169.

Keppo, Jussi, Yuze Li, Gerry Tsoukalas, and Nuo Yuan. 2025. "AI Pricing, Agent Heterogeneity, and Collusion." Working paper. Boston University, National University of Singapore, and University of Pennsylvania.

Lei, Yanzhe, Sentao Miao, and Ruslan Momot. 2024. "Privacy-Preserving Personalized Revenue Management." *Management Science* 70 (7): 4875–4892.

Lichtenstein, Donald R., Nancy M. Ridgway, and Richard G. Netemeyer. 1993. "Price Perceptions and Consumer Shopping Behavior: A Field Study." *Journal of Marketing Research* 30 (2): 234–245.

Liu, Jiaxi, Yidong Zhang, Xiaoqing Wang, Yuming Deng, and Xingyu Wu. 2019. "Dynamic Pricing on E-Commerce Platform with Deep Reinforcement Learning: A Field Experiment." Working paper. arXiv:1912.02572.

Liu, Maggie W., and Dilip Soman. 2018. "Behavioral Pricing." In *Handbook of Consumer Psychology*, 656–678. Routledge.

Liu, Xiao. 2023. "Dynamic Coupon Targeting Using Batch Deep Reinforcement Learning: An Application to Livestream Shopping." *Marketing Science* 42 (4): 637–658.

Lopez Mateos, David, Maxime C. Cohen, and Nancy Pyron. 2022. "Field Experiments for Testing Revenue Strategies in the Hospitality Industry." *Cornell Hospitality Quarterly* 63 (2): 247–256.

McCartan, Cory, Robin Fisher, Jacob Goldin, Daniel E. Ho, and Kosuke Imai. 2025. "Estimating Racial Disparities When Race Is Not Observed." *Journal of the American Statistical Association* 120 (552): 2140–2153.

Morwitz, Vicki G., Eric A. Greenleaf, and Eric J., Johnson. 1998. "Divide and Prosper: Consumers' Reactions to Partitioned Prices." *Journal of Marketing Research* 35 (4): 453–463.

Moshary, Sarah, Anna Tuchman, and Natasha Vajravelu. 2023. "Gender-Based Pricing in Consumer-Packaged Goods: A Pink Tax?" *Marketing Science* 45 (1):1–14.

Mousavi, Nasim, Panagiotis Adamopoulos, and Jesse Bockstedt. 2023. "The Decoy Effect and Recommendation Systems." *Information Systems Research* 34 (4): 1533–1553.

Nasiry, Javad, and Ioana Popescu. 2011. "Dynamic Pricing with Loss-Averse Consumers and Peak-End Anchoring." *Operations Research* 59 (6): 1361–1368.

Qin, Zhiwei, Xiaocheng Tang, Qingyang Li, Hongtu Zhu, and Jieping Ye. 2025. *Reinforcement Learning in the Ride-Hailing Marketplace.* Springer.

Qin, Zhiwei T., Hongtu Zhu, and Jieping Ye. 2022. "Reinforcement Learning for Ridesharing: An Extended Survey." *Transportation Research Part C: Emerging Technologies* 144. arXiv:2105.01099.

Orme, Bryan. 2010. *Getting Started with Conjoint Analysis: Strategies for Product Design and Pricing Research.* 2nd ed. Research Publishers.

Phillips, Robert L. 2021. *Pricing and Revenue Optimization.* Stanford University Press.

Rao, Vithala R., ed. 2009. *Handbook of Pricing Research in Marketing.* Edward Elgar Publishing.

Santana, Shelle, Steven K. Dallas, and Vicki G. Morwitz. 2020. "Consumer Reactions to Drip Pricing." *Marketing Science* 39 (1): 188–210.

Schlereth, Christian, Bernd Skiera, and Fabian Schulz. 2018. "Why Do Consumers Prefer Static Instead of Dynamic Pricing Plans? An Empirical Study for a Better Understanding of the Low Preferences for Time-Variant Pricing Plans." *European Journal of Operational Research* 269 (3): 1165–1179.

Shah, Virag, Ramesh Johari, and Jose Blanchet. 2019. "Semi-Parametric Dynamic Contextual Pricing." In *Advances in Neural Information Processing Systems* 32.

Sutton, Richard S., and Andrew G. Barto. 1998. *Reinforcement Learning: An Introduction*. MIT Press.

Talluri, Kalyan, and Garrett van Ryzin. 2004. "Revenue Management Under a General Discrete Choice Model of Consumer Behavior." *Management Science* 50 (1): 15–33.

Tan, Soo-Jiuan, and Seow Hwang Chua. 2004. "'While Stocks Last!' Impact of Framing on Consumers' Perception of Sales Promotions." *Journal of Consumer Marketing* 21 (5): 343–355.

Tanlamai, Jitsamsa, Warut Khern-am-nuai, and Maxime C. Cohen. 2025. "Generative AI and Price Discrimination in the Housing Market." Working paper. McGill University.

Tellis, Gerard J. 1988. "The Price Elasticity of Selective Demand: A Meta-analysis of Econometric Models of Sales." *Journal of Marketing Research* 25 (4): 331–341.

Tran, Kevin D., Leonardo Madio, Michelangelo Rossi, and Mark J. Tremblay. 2024. "Transparency of Add-On Fees on Peer-to-Peer Platforms: Evidence from Airbnb." Working paper. University of Bristol, University of Padua, Télécom Paris, and University of Nevada, Las Vegas.

Varian, Hal R. 1985. "Price Discrimination and Social Welfare." *American Economic Review* 75 (4): 870–875.

Varian, Hal R. 1989. "Price Discrimination." *Handbook of Industrial Organization*, vol. 1, edited by Richard Schmalensee and Robert Willig. Elsevier.

Xia, Lan, Kent B. Monroe, and Jennifer L. Cox. 2004. "The Price Is Unfair! A Conceptual Framework of Price Fairness Perceptions." *Journal of Marketing* 68 (4): 1–15.

Index

Page numbers in italic refer to figures.

Publisher contact:
The MIT Press
Massachusetts Institute of Technology
77 Massachusetts Avenue, Cambridge, MA 02139
mitpress.mit.edu

EU Authorised Representative:
Easy Access System Europe, Mustamäe tee 50,
10621 Tallinn, Estonia
gpsr.requests@easproject.com

Printed by Integrated Books International,
United States of America